DANCING W

A WALK FROM SOURCE TO SEA OF THE RIVER SEVERN

To Enid, who inspires me
and tolerates my temporary absences.

DANCING WITH SABRINA

A WALK FROM SOURCE TO SEA OF THE RIVER SEVERN

Bob Bibby

TravellersEye

Published by
TravellersEye Limited
Colemore Farm
Colemore Green
Bridgnorth
Shropshire
WV16 4ST
United Kingdom

British Library Cataloguing in Publication Data
A catalogue record for this book is available from the British Library.

ISBN: 1 903070 24 4

Printed and bound in Great Britain by Creative Print and Design Wales, Ebbw Vale.

Contents

Acknowledgements *vii*

Prologue *ix*

1 Plynlimon to Llanidloes 1

2 Llanidloes 11

3 Llanidloes to Newtown 20

4 Newtown 31

5 Newtown to Welshpool 40

6 Welshpool 51

7 Welshpool to Shrewsbury 59

8 Shrewsbury 68

9 Shrewsbury to Ironbridge 80

10 Ironbridge 91

11 Ironbridge to Bridgnorth 99

12 Bridgnorth 108

13 Bridgnorth to Bewdley 117

14 Bewdley 126

15 Bewdley to Worcester 137

16 Worcester 147

17 Worcester to Tewkesbury 159

18 Tewkesbury 169

19 Tewkesbury to Gloucester 178

20 Gloucester 189

21 Gloucester to Slimbridge 200

22 Slimbridge 210

23 Slimbridge to Littleton-upon-Severn 218

24 Littleton-upon-Severn to Severn Beach 230

Useful Reading *236*

Acknowledgements

Special thanks to the following: Angela and Gareth Morgan, Angela Kaye, Peter and Mike Gibson, Helen and Ron Gracey, Steve Goodchild and Steve Clarke, who all happily allowed me to mention them in this narrative, to Hilary Hyde and Brian Basham, who provided me with helpful information, to Glynis Frater and Brenda Bakewell, who transported me when necessary, and to the nameless people I met on my journey, encounters with whom I have used shamelessly but, I hope, always affectionately.

Oh, 'tis jesting, dancing, drinking
Spins the heavy world around.

A.E. Housman, *The Shropshire Lad*

And I wish the reader also to take notice, that in writing of it I have made myself a *recreation* of a *recreation*; and that it might prove so to him, and not dull and tediously, I have in several places mixed, not any scurrility, but some innocent, harmless mirth, of which, if thou be a severe sour-complexioned man, then I disallow thee to be a competent judge.

Izaak Walton, *The Compleat Angler*

Prologue

Not many people know this, as Michael Caine is famous for saying, but the name that the Romans gave to the river we know in Britain as the Severn was Sabrina.

If you are over fifty, you will remember Sabrina as the impossibly shaped pin-up girl of the 1950s, who appeared with comedian Arthur Askey in a television show called *Before Your Very Eyes*, saying absolutely bog all but flaunting her mammoth assets. Sabrina's real name was plain Norma Sykes and she came, just like the river, from Wales. Her 41½–19–36 figure earned her the nickname of 'The Hunchfront of Lime Grove' and she was very big in Australia.

If you are between sixteen and thirty-four, you will know Sabrina as the eponymous heroine of the American television sit-com, *Sabrina the Teenage Witch*. This programme follows the rites of passage experiences of a sixteen-year-old girl with a black cat called Salem, who moves in with her aunts and discovers that they and she are all witches (a common experience in the USA apparently). It was first shown in 1996 and stars actress Melissa Joan Hurt in the central role. It is now in its fifth series with its canned laughter and array of B-list actors with good American teeth and little else to shout about.

On the other hand, if you are a male Internet porn-surfer, of whom there are millions so you don't need to be shy, you may know of Sabrina Ferilli whose lovely flesh is tastefully exposed in a variety of 'natural' poses – though I've never seen anyone shopping like *that* – on her Home Page.

But it is none of these latter I wish to celebrate.

The genius of my tale is Sabrina, the secret love child of the ancient British king, Locrine, whose wife gave orders for the child to be thrown into the river and for the river to be named after her, so that her husband's infidelity would be remembered for ever. It is the River Severn, as she came to be known after the Romans had left Britain to its own devices, that I decided to explore from her beginnings in the Welsh mountains.

At first, somewhat surprisingly, Sabrina heads north-east through Llanidloes, Newtown and Welshpool before crossing into England and turning south at Shrewsbury. Then she descends through the Shropshire towns of Ironbridge and Bridgnorth and the Worcestershire towns of Bewdley, Worcester and Upton-upon-Severn. Thence her route speeds her into Gloucestershire, passing Tewkesbury and Gloucester, Slimbridge and Oldbury-on-Severn, till she reaches her ending where the Bristol Channel becomes the sea.

Her distance from Plynlimon to the Severn Estuary is 220 miles. And, wonky knee or not, I was determined to follow her on a Dance with Sabrina.

I live beside the River Severn.

Twice in the autumn of the millennium year the Severn broke over its banks and flooded the road in front of my house. On both occasions the road was closed for several days and I was unable to get my car out of the garage. Others suffered more, their houses being flooded while they stood watching in their wellies. My neighbours Glynis and Graham, who moved into an older property with a sitting room below road level seven years ago, had to move out.

'They told us it only flooded once every hundred years,' Graham told me philosophically on the second occasion. 'It's bloody filled our sitting room twice in the last three years! You can still smell it!'

All I could do was sympathise and offer my best malt whisky, which he, of course, did not hesitate to gurgle keenly.

The brown river roared down the valley, spreading into empty fields like spilled blood, carrying all before her as she raced. Whole trees, dead sheep, useless rowing boats, plastic dustbins, all sped past my window as I watched, mesmerised by the Severn's power and ferocity. The river rose sixteen feet above its normal level – that's roughly the equivalent of three people standing on each other's shoulders. Can you imagine?

Thousands of people elsewhere along the Severn, and in other parts of the country, suffered more. They were evacuated from their homes, as floodwater seeped through their doors and over their Axminster carpets and up to their stacked G-plan furniture. Rowing boats and canoes replaced motor cars on the streets of some villages. As river levels became so much higher than normal, bridges were closed, forcing traffic to seek alternative routes and bringing the country almost to a standstill.

Because the last time the Severn flooded in such fashion was 1947 following a prolonged period when the Welsh hills were covered in deepest snow which suddenly thawed, we have started to think of flooding as unnatural. Not so, of course. Sabrina has a long recorded history of breaking her banks. The Romans built embankments around their fort at Caersws to keep the river out, for instance, and the flood known as 'The Duke of Buckingham's Water' in 1484 helped towards that noble's defeat and death. In 1606 hundreds of men, women and children died in the stretch between Gloucester and Bristol, when floodwater coming downstream met the upcoming Severn Bore south of Gloucester. Reputedly the worst of the lot was in February 1795, again due to severe frost and snow followed by a quick thaw. The resulting severe flooding swept away many Severn bridges, including sixteen in Shropshire alone. In 1847 the river rose 18 feet 6 inches in five hours. In 1862 a train which had left Worcester during the floods was greeted on arrival at Bridgnorth by the band of the Bridgnorth Rifles playing *See the Conquering Hero Comes*. In 1868 flooding at Caersws destroyed the railway embankment and a train from Newtown went off the rails, killing the driver and fireman.

And there have been others.

A wall just outside the cloisters by Worcester Cathedral has plaques that indicate each of these floods, each plaque carefully fastened at the exact height of that year's floodwater.

So, it seemed like a good time to examine this Sabrina, before she broke her banks again after a new record height.

First, though, indulge me a little longer, for I wish to introduce you to a few other travellers who visited some of the places along the Severn in previous times. The first of these – indeed, he might be called the first great travel writer – is John Leland, known as 'the king's antiquary'. He was appointed by Henry VIII to go hunting for all the records then extant in England in the monasteries, cathedrals, priories and so on that were being closed down by the king after his break with Rome and subsequent marriage to Anne Boleyn. Leland recorded details of his horseback journeys in the *Itinerary*, a book that gives us our first systematic description of the topography of England and Wales. Among many other places, he called at Shrewsbury, Bewdley, Worcester, Upton-upon-Severn, Tewkesbury, Gloucester and Berkeley, all on the Severn. Leland was travelling in the years between 1533 (the year of Anne Boleyn's coronation) and 1547 (the year of Henry VIII's death). It was in this latter year when sadly he suffered a mental breakdown to the extent that a contemporary described him as: 'mad, insane, lunatic, furious, frantic, enjoying drowsy or lucid intervals, so that he cannot manage his affairs'.

Other than that, he was fine.

Next there is that indefatigable horsewoman, Celia Fiennes, ancestor of the modern-day explorer Sir Ranulph Twisleton-Wykeham Fiennes. Celia set off on her travels, in 1685, some twenty years after the restoration of the monarchy following England's only flirtation with republicanism under Oliver Cromwell (warts and all). Her travels were conducted riding side saddle with only two servants as company and continued for the best part of the next twenty years, during which she visited every county in England. In some ways, Celia could be described as the first tourist, returning home with her detailed notes rather than her snapshots. The notes turned into *The Journeys of Celia Fiennes*, which, even with the lady's idiosyncratic spellings, give an invaluable insight into the social and domestic attitudes of seventeenth-century England.

Celia began her journeys 'to regain my health by variety and change of aire and exercise' at the age of twenty-three. She was merely succumbing to the rampant hypochondria of the day, which manifested itself in the sudden popularity and fashionableness of spas, or 'spaws' as Celia called them. She herself visited several of them, and not just once – Bath, Epsom, Hampstead, Tunbridge, Buxton, Dulwich. Being of good Puritan stock she naturally disapproved of skimpy bathing costumes, preferring ones where 'the water fills it up so that its borne off that your shape is not seen, it does not cling close as other linning' (so not likely to be worn by any of the Sabrinas). Either her journeys successfully repaired her health or she was robustly healthy anyway, for she lived to be seventy-six. Of interest to me is that she called in at Shrewsbury, Worcester, Gloucester and Bristol. Of interest to you is that the well-known nursery rhyme

> Ride a cockhorse to Banbury Cross,
> To see a fine (Fiennes) lady upon a white horse

may actually be based on Celia Fiennes and her travels, as Banbury is the home of the Fiennes seat, Broughton Castle.

And now you know how to pronounce Fiennes.

Daniel Foe, who Frenchified his name to Defoe for effect, was a contemporary of Celia Fiennes but his *A Tour through the Whole Island of Great Britain* is a book of a very different water. Whereas Celia was a very private figure whose journal of her travels was primarily for the entertainment of friends and family and was not published until 1888, Defoe was a notorious public figure of his era. We know him as the author of *Robinson Crusoe* but he had had a variety of careers before his most famous book appeared in print. He was a failed businessman, who was bunged into prison for debt; he was a journalist publishing his own newspaper and political pamphlets, for which he was again bunged into prison and pilloried; and he was a spy.

It is the latter occupation that I find most interesting because there is little doubt that *A Tour through the Whole Island of Great Britain* draws on his travels around the country on espionage purposes as well as the subsequent journeys he made in order to write the book. Indeed, Defoe is credited by many as being the unofficial founder of the Secret Service, because he recruited and trained an army of spies around the country to feed him with data about the gentry and their political sympathies. He also garnered information about magistrates and clergymen and their moral behaviour. Many suspect that much of this information fed into his travel writing which appeared initially in three volumes in the mid-1720s.

And I always thought it was James Bond's mysterious boss M who set up the Secret Service!

We shall meet Daniel Defoe, on horseback, probably masquerading as a merchant named either Alexander Goldsmith or Claude Guilot, in Bristol, Aust, Berkeley, Gloucester, Tewkesbury, Worcester, Shrewsbury and Welshpool. At least, we may meet Mr Foe/Goldsmith/Guilot, or we may not, for there is considerable doubt as to whether he himself visited all the places he writes about or whether he was relying on the knowledge of his local spies.

Another traveller under an assumed name was Peter Porcupine, better known under his real name of William Cobbett, whose *Rural Rides* was published in 1830, a century after Defoe's book. Cobbett too led a colourful life, serving as a sergeant major in the British army in Canada, then as a teacher in America, before settling into a career as a journalist. He also spent time in prison and later became a Member of Parliament. Nothing new there then, though it's usually the other way round nowadays. Journalism suited Cobbett, because he was an argumentative man, steeped in prejudices, and a stubborn if irrational thinker. His views were extremely reactionary and unrealistic, for he sought to bring back a pre-industrialised England where all classes would live in harmony on the land. He would have easily got a job on today's *Daily Mail*.

It is unsurprising, then, to find that Cobbett's journeys were not to the new industrial towns but to the great agricultural lands of England, particularly in the Home Counties. However, he did spend time in Gloucester and Worcester, and later visited Shrewsbury, so his choleric and iconoclastic view of those places is worthy of consideration. He travelled at a time when the Enclosure Acts had dramatically changed the face of the countryside, forcing agricultural labourers and their families into the towns to seek work in the new factories.

The last traveller from earlier times who needs to be introduced is another man of many parts, George Borrow, who was apparently (and coincidentally) inspired to learn to read by Defoe's *Robinson Crusoe*. He began life as a tinker, mixing with Gypsies and other gentleman of the nineteenth-century roads, but then miraculously became the Bible Society's agent in Russia and later in Spain, where, like so many of my other adventurous forerunners, he was imprisoned. Borrow was fifty-one when he set off on his trip around Wales, accompanied by his wife ('a perfect paragon of wives – can make puddings and sweets and treacle posset') and daughter, whom he was too stingy to take to take to the more fashionable Harrogate or Leamington. His book *Wild Wales* was published in 1862 and contains a highly idiosyncratic set of tales about the history, culture and people of the Principality. Borrow's aim, as his introductory section explains, is to show his readers: 'the genuine Welsh, and . . . what they have to say about Cumro and Saxon, buying and selling, fattening hogs and poultry, Methodism and baptism, and the poor, persecuted Church of England'.

Some idea of Borrow's approach to the truth can be gleaned from the description of his expedition to the source of the Severn, begun in his Devil's Bridge inn at ten o'clock on a November morning. Collecting a guide en route, our valiant traveller then climbs Plynlimon, pausing at the source of the River Rheidol, all the time holding conversation with his guide in the most syntactically correct English: '"This does not seem to be a country of much society," said I to my guide. "It is not, sir. The nearest house is the inn we came from, which is now three miles behind us."'

They reach the source of the Severn, where Borrow takes a drink, and then that of the Wye, also on Plynlimon, where he insists on taking off his hat to sing a Welsh song, before returning to Devil's Bridge by six o'clock. At a conservative estimate, that would mean that Borrow, in his top coat and hat and umbrella, covered a distance of some 35 miles, much of it uphill, in less than eight hours on a darkening November day.

And he still had time to form his perfectly worded sentences and to sing songs.

Economical with the truth or what?

Still, we mustn't mock old George, for it is his sampling of the Severn's source that started me on my journey.

The more perceptive of you will have noted by now that none of these aforementioned travellers went by foot, except for George Borrow, whose exploits I have suggested need to be taken with a pinch of salt. So what made me decide to venture on this journey down the Severn from Plynlimon to Bristol on foot?

There is something peculiarly Anglo-Saxon about long-distance walking. It's all originally down to Wordsworth and his hunt for the perfect daffodil. He inspired generations of town-dwellers to leave their urban roots and seek solace by walking in the countryside. This hobby of the middle classes eventually became a mass movement in the early twentieth century. The first long-distance path in Britain was the 250-mile Pennine Way, opened in 1965, largely as a result of the efforts of one man, Tom Stephenson. He was the first secretary of the Ramblers' Association, a body which arose in the 1930s in response to the growing number of people who were persuaded to get out of the industrialised towns and cities and breathe the fresh air of the countryside. This open-air movement flourished as the age of mass motoring began to loom, and as a resistance to it. The movement's most famous moment was the Mass Trespass on Kinder Scout in Derbyshire, when hundreds of ramblers asserted their right to walk over land that had been closed by its owners for shooting.

It is sometimes forgotten that this open-air movement was part of a much wider reaction to the perceived sloth of modern people of the time. As well as the Ramblers' Association, the 1930s also saw the birth of the Youth Hostels Association, of the Women's League of Health and Beauty, and of Laban's Modern Dance. These might at first sight seem odd partners but they all grew out of the same perception, namely that ordinary people in the towns and cities needed to be re-educated about the use of their bodies.

And that was where I got my idea for a Dance with Sabrina. If rambling and dancing stemmed from the same set of ideas, then why shouldn't I see my walk along the length of the River Severn as a sort of dance, one in which my mind and body would be at one with the universe?

Well, you have to dream, don't you?

The opening of the waymarked Severn Way long-distance footpath in 1999 together with the publication of the excellent *Severn Way Official Walkers' Guide* by the Environment Agency in the same year provided me with the necessary tools to accomplish my walk. I originally planned to do it in midsummer, in order to get the best of the weather and the longest of days.

My plans, however, were thwarted by the outbreak in February 2001 of foot-and-mouth disease in the north of England, beginning with sixteen infected sheep sent to market in Hexham. Within ten days, the disease had spread throughout Britain, leading to the government having to take draconian steps to cull huge numbers of animals. Nightly television news stories told of burning pyres in the fields and showed us vivid pictures of the slaughtered animals being taken to the pyres. Official figures showed that almost 4 million animals were slaughtered.

Inevitably, the countryside was virtually closed down to prevent the further spread of the infection. Farms were isolated, cattle and sheep markets ceased trading, footpaths were closed, while farmers and government ministers blamed each other for the bad handling of the crisis. At one time, as new outbreaks were reported daily, it began to seem as if it would never end. And yet, less than 2 per cent of the national herd was actually infected.

I deferred my plans from May to July and then again to September, hoping that the disease would have run its course by then and that the countryside would be returning to something like normality. And lo, it was so. By some miracle, things began to improve steadily through August and restrictions on the Severn Way in Wales and Shropshire were lifted just before I set off in the first week of September. My plan had always been to do the walk in three stages, as I didn't believe my feet would cope with a non-stop journey of over 200 miles. And how right I was, as I discovered very painfully.

So, finally, on the first Sunday of September 2001, on the day after England had beaten Germany 5–1 at football, thus adding a third unexpected event to the floods and the foot-and-mouth outbreak, I set off on my Dance with Sabrina.

1 Plynlimon to Llanidloes

> The source of the Severn is a little pool of water some twenty inches long, six wide, and about three deep. It is covered at the bottom with small stones, from between which the water gushes up.

This was how George Borrow described his sighting of Sabrina's beginning high up on Plynlimon. It was this vision, exactly how I in my sentimental naivety thought that rivers should commence, that had focused my attention for over a year. It was this that had finally brought me on a Sunday morning in early September to the small car park at the picnic site in the middle of the Hafren Forest known as Rhyd-y-benwch. It was, inevitably, raining so my wife, who was equally keen to see the source of the Severn, and I donned our cagoules and waterproof overtrousers in readiness for what the *Severn Way Official Walkers' Guide* describes as a steep climb.

The path through the forest (called after the Welsh name for the Severn) is steep in places but it is a genuinely pleasant walk. Even in the mizzle of that morning, we couldn't help but be impressed by the boardwalk that starts the route as it marches beside the gurgling waters of the infant Severn, surprisingly strong in its flow even at this early stage. A temporary diversion, caused by work on a scheme to create an 'exciting' (according to the *Powys County Times*) new access route to the Source of the Severn, slowed us briefly as we started to climb, but soon we were following white-topped posts through a narrow track covered with pine needles and smelling of fresh fir trees in the rain.

'What are you thinking about?' my wife asked me, after I

had been non-communicative for some minutes.

'I was thinking about racial prejudice,' I explained. 'I listened to the Chief Rabbi, Jonathan Sacks, on the radio the other day explaining why he felt unable to attend that conference in Capetown. You know, that UN thing about racism. He was arguing that Zionism wasn't racism but it wasn't so much what he said as the way he said it. He's got one of those really soft, gentle, reasonable voices that makes you just want to believe what he's saying.'

'So?' she asked.

'Well, that got me thinking about that Anne Robinson business. You know, when she said she found the Welsh "irritating" and asked what they were for.'

'And she was reported to the Equal Opps people, wasn't she?'

'Mm, that's right,' I said. 'I was just wondering how people would have reacted if someone like the Chief Rabbi, in his calm, reasoned, almost self-deprecating tone, had said something similar about the Welsh. Would it have been more acceptable?'

'I don't see where you're heading,' she said.

We were heading, as it happens, in the wrong direction. I'd got so carried away by my musings that, when we had reached the top end of the forest, I led us off in the direction of some white-topped posts, ignoring the sign that pointed a different way to the Source of the Severn. In fact, we got closer to the source of the River Wye, which also begins on Plynlimon, than to that of the Severn, so, after a quick study of my sodden map and the usual discussion about my map-reading skills, we retraced our steps. This subtle detour had added an extra uphill (and then downhill) mile or so and a good forty minutes to our trek but eventually we found the correct path and by midday we were standing on a patch of boggy ground in the mist staring at two large wooden posts stuck in the ground. These two posts proclaimed, in English and in Welsh, that this was the Source of the Severn.

I looked around. Where was Borrow's little pool? Where was the spring gushing between small stones? Where was my romantic image?

Alas, they were not there. Maybe Borrow went to a different spot on Plynlimon or maybe he never got there at all, but sat in the pub at Devil's Bridge getting sozzled on porter while he invented his story. Who knows?

This, however, was to be the start of my Dance with Sabrina, as I followed her course for over 200 miles down to the Bristol Channel. This was where Sabrina began to gather into her arms the waters from the heavens that eventually turned into that mighty stream that flowed past my window in Bridgnorth. The underground gurgles that I could hear around me could transform themselves rapidly into the floods that I had witnessed the previous November and that had brought the country almost to a standstill with their ferocity and expansion.

I could not follow Borrow's example as I had intended by taking a drink from the source, because there was no water there to be seen or drunk. So I made do with a glug from the bottle of Ty-Nant spring water (I always carry Welsh water in Wales) that I had brought with me for refreshment. Then we headed back down through the forest to the Rhyd-y-benwch car park, where my wife was to leave me in order to return home.

What I had been feebly trying to explain to my wife earlier was my feelings about the Welsh. It is very easy to fall into the Anne Robinson trap of mocking the Welsh. It's something the English do frequently. After all, we've had centuries of practice. Julius Caesar described them thus: 'All the Britons,' he wrote (meaning the Welsh), 'paint themselves with woad, which gives their skin a bluish colour and makes them look very dreadful in battle'. The Venerable Bede, no lover of the Celtic tribes, wrote: 'The Britons for the most part have a natural hatred for the English and uphold their own bad customs against the true Easter of the Catholic Church'. Celia Fiennes, who ventured across the border in 1698, wrote 'they speake Welsh, the inhabitants go barefoote and bare leg'd a nasty sort of people'. Even one of their own greatest poets, Dylan Thomas himself, referred to his country as 'a land entirely peopled by perverts'.

There is a curious blend of English chauvinism, demonstrated most commonly by those who have themselves come from underprivileged sections of English society, that tends to adopt a condescending attitude to the Welsh. It's an attitude that emerges in jokes about the Welsh, which are usually concerned with unnatural relationships between Welshmen and sheep. It also emerges in derogatory remarks about the Welsh language and its supposed impenetrability, especially when spoken by Welsh women to each other in the seaside guest house that you've paid a lot of money to stay in, which you believe gives you the right to demand they speak *your* language.

In truth, the poor old Welsh are of course the descendants of the original settlers of what we now call England. They themselves were settlers, being part of that huge Celtic migration that spread over much of northern Europe long before the Roman Empire came into its pomp. They were driven into Wales initially by the Romans. The fierce resistance of its tribes meant that two out of the three Roman legions in Britain were stationed on the Welsh borders. Deva (Chester) in the north-east, was the largest Roman fortress in Britain, covering some 60 acres on the banks of the River Dee and guarding the approaches to North Wales, while Viroconium (Wroxeter) was a huge camp lower down the river, guarding a fording place into mid-Wales.

The Welsh were kept there by the Anglo-Saxon tribes, most notably by Offa, king of Mercia, who built his dyke to keep them out. This was a lengthy extension of an earlier fortification that had more or less fixed the boundary between the Welsh and the Saxons from Chester to Shrewsbury. Crossing Offa's

Dyke for centuries was a highly risky business, often ending in blood and tears, even though many Welsh-speaking communities remained to the east of the boundary in England and English-speaking communities existed to the west in Wales. Behind this barrier, the people of Wales were able to think of themselves as a separate nation and they thought in their own language.

Then, in the great battles of early Norman times, the Welsh again tested themselves against the new lords of England, none more so than the legendary Owen Glendower who was responsible for creating in 1404 the first and last Welsh parliament. Glendower (or Glyndwr, as the Welsh would prefer it) came to prominence when he sacked the town of Ruthin in north Wales, largely to gain revenge over stolen land. Almost immediately Welsh scholars at Oxford downed their books and returned to Wales to support him, presumably in order to write his press releases. Soon the English king, Henry IV (Parts 1 and 2), was facing a major rebellion, as Glendower marshalled all the armies of Wales into one fighting force and summoned representatives from throughout the land to attend his parliament at Machynlleth. It couldn't last, of course, and it didn't. By 1408 the rebellion was over and Glendower took to the hills. Welsh independence was finally broken and its people became a subjugated nation.

According to local legend, Glendower rallied his troops here on the very slopes of Plynlimon that I was walking down as I made my way, musing thus, past the spectacular waterfall known as Severn-Break-its-Neck and on to the narrow road that was to take me towards Llanidloes. To tell the truth, there wasn't much else to think about. Once out of the Hafren Forest, the scenery is pleasant but unspectacular. The road passes above several farms whose lush green fields were full of cattle or sheep. The occasional dog bark was the only sound that disturbed my reveries as I walked past hedges smelling of sweet honeysuckle, yellow-flowered broom bushes, banks of purple heather and stray foxgloves. Grey squirrels bounced on the road ahead of me, pausing to sight my intrusion before leaping for the cover of trees.

Near a farm called Old Hall, the official route took me for the first time across the Severn and past an old Methodist chapel, and I found myself singing that stirring melancholic song that speaks forever of Welsh rugby and Welsh Methodism:

> Guide me, O thou great Redeemer,
> Pilgrim through this barren land;
> I am weak, but thou are mighty,
> Hold me with thy powerful hand;
> Bread of heaven, bread of heaven,
> Feed me till I want no more,
> Feed me till I want no more.

Suddenly I was back at that Methodist church whose scout group I had attended as a boy, dressed in long shorts, neckerchief fastened with a leather woggle, and an Australian bushwhacker's hat. It was church parade when we were expected to process behind our troop's flag down the aisle and on to the front row where we sang hymns from the *Methodist Hymnal* and listened to the preacher mouthing something or other. Then we went home.

Now what was all that about? I ask myself now. Why did we have to go to church parade once a month? Why did we have to wear such daft clothes? When in my adult life has it proved useful to know what a woggle is or what it's for? What likelihood was there of me or any of the rest of us Wolverhampton boys ever becoming bushwhackers?

Even more puzzling was why I actually enjoyed all this daftness. I think now that I loved the whole business of scouting because it introduced me to the Great Outdoors and the idea of hiking in it. I suppose that, if it hadn't been for that early introduction to the pleasures of walking in the countryside, I would never have chosen, of my own free will, to do this 200-mile Dance with Sabrina. Instead, I would have been back at home reading the Sunday papers, sipping a glass of cold Chardonnay, and growing old disgracefully.

Already, you see, towards the end of my first day's walking, I was having second thoughts about my mission. The main reason for this was that I had stupidly put only one pair of hiking socks on and I could feel my feet aching as they pounded over the tarmacked road that was leading me towards Llanidloes. So when, after re-crossing the Severn once more, I finally entered the little town, I was relieved. I had covered about 15 miles in the day and my feet were telling me that this was enough.

I was glad to find my accommodation for the night.

The Severn View is instantly identifiable on China Street in Llanidloes because its walls are painted in a bright yellow colour-wash. I was greeted by Gareth Morgan, who was not expecting me, and his wife Angela, who fortunately was. The welcome was truly wonderful. Angela ushered me into the sitting room, telling me not to bother about my boots because 'it all Hoovers up afterwards'. She asked if I wanted to watch television and insisted on making me a pot of tea. While she was making the latter, I eased my boots off and idly zapped channels on the television, settling eventually on the Welsh language channel S4C.

The programme I was watching was called *Pobol y Cwm* and it was clearly a Welsh soap opera. It seemed to be about two brothers, Llew and Drew, I think, who had fallen out with each other, and there was a woman called Sheryl with a Kevin Keegan perm apologising to another man and offering him a free ride in a taxi! In short, it was the usual badly acted rubbish about who did what to whom, when and where, but set in Wales. I hadn't worked out the connection between these people before Angela arrived with a tray on which were a teapot, a cup and saucer, and a plate of biscuits. Never has tea tasted so fine as it did that evening and it was a long time since I had devoured a plate of biscuits so quickly, as I listened to Angela's description of how Severn View had been transformed over the years into its present condition.

During our conversation, I learned that Angela Morgan was mayor of Llanidloes and I can't imagine a better advocate for this lovely little town. She spoke enthusiastically about the annual Patchwork Quilting Exhibition, which had been started a few years previously and now attracted local and international quilts and quilters. She talked honestly about the difficulties of integrating 'the hippies', as she called them, who had settled in the area and whose activities were centred on the Great Oak Café, although she recognised that they also brought benefits to the town. She waxed lyrical about the possibilities for Llani, if everyone would come to recognise that its future was in meeting the demands of the tourist trade by becoming a centre of specialist shops.

'It could be a really brilliant place,' she said.

Listening to Angela, I found it hard not to be convinced by what she was saying. And I have to say I think she is right. Llani is a lovely place now. Given a bit of luck and some shrewdness from its politicians and business leaders, it could become even better without losing any of its present charm.

Much as I had enjoyed conversing with Angela, I needed to see to my feet and it was not long before I was shown to my room, instructed in how to treat her two Burmese cats and recommended to the Mount Inn for my evening meal. When I examined my feet, I thought that I had got away with not wearing two pairs of socks. True, they were red and sore but they did not seem to have blistered. I showered, changed into dry clothes, handed my wet boots and socks to Angela for drying by the stove, and went to explore the town before making my way to the Mount Inn, stopping en route at the Spar shop to buy a newspaper and a bottle of Ty-Nant for the following day.

In the Mount Inn I ordered my meal and a pint of Bass, which I drank thirstily as I read the *Sunday Mirror*. It was full of jubilant accounts of the England football team's victory over Germany the day before, including reports of the behaviour of English soccer fans in Munich after the match. Matches between the two countries are, for the English anyway, opportunities for the most tasteless reliving of the great wars of the twentieth century, encouraged frequently by the jingoistic national press. This was no exception. The fans' chants had included 'There's only one Bomber Harris', 'Land of Hope and Glory' and the theme of *The Dambusters*, accompanied by outstretched arms mimicking aeroplanes in flight. There was also the weird 'Meat pie, sausage roll/ Come on England, give us a goal', whose origins neither the newspaper reporter nor I had any clue about.

I went back to my room later and, just before settling down to sleep, flicked through the advertising pages of the *Sunday Mirror*. Now I don't know how the *Sunday Mirror* calculates who its regular readers are or how it sells its advertising space, but there was one page full of advertisements designed to help people with their sexual needs. Fair enough, you might say, but I think you'd be surprised that three of these ads, and these were not small potatoes either, were for transsexuals.

'Confused about your gender?' asked one, before going on to indicate that it was quite normal to dress up in women's clothing every now and again, thus avoiding that confusion. Though I'd have thought that added to it.

This theme was even more explicit in another of these ads., which featured a picture of a man wearing a wig and a long flowing dress underneath the caption 'I'm a real man – Are you?'

Well, to be honest, no, I'm probably not, according to the apparent criteria of this advertisement.

But even more worrying to me was the thought that the

people who regularly purchase the *Sunday Mirror* include largish numbers of such transsexuals who double up as football hooligans in their spare time. Where do they hide their wigs and dresses at a football match?

I fell asleep, deeply troubled.

2 Llanidloes

When I was seventeen and possessed of more testosterone than I knew what do with (and before I knew what testosterone was, or what to do with it), I cycled from my home in Wolverhampton in the West Midlands to Barmouth on the Welsh coast. The distance is roughly 100 miles. I did the trip, with a pal of mine, in one day. We had a small tent with us, in which we slept that night, and then the next day we cycled home. Why? I ask myself now. What was I trying to prove? What on earth made me do such a stupid thing? Was I thinking of entering the Tour de France or something?

I don't remember now but, in our haste, we almost certainly cycled past Llanidloes. If you are travelling on the main road, it is entirely possible to miss Llanidloes, one of the little gems of mid-Wales. This is a big mistake which, fortunately, a walker along the Severn Way will not make, for the path leads over a bridge, known as the Short Bridge, directly into the town. Llanidloes is the first major settlement on the Severn, growing originally around a ford where old tracks met as the River Severn and the River Clywedog converge. Slap bang in the centre of Llanidloes sits the ancient half-timbered Market Hall which is at the crossroads of the four streets of the original medieval town. The upper part of the hall has also served as a Quaker meeting place, a Working Men's Institute, a library and a museum. The lower part of the building is arcaded and open to the street, and used to be the official home of market traders. But it has always been, and still is, the unofficial heart of Llani, as the locals refer to their home town.

Here it was that John Wesley preached several times in the 1740s, finding 'the wind so piercing that, whenever it came into my face, it almost took away my voice'. The stone on which he stood to preach has been preserved at the side of the building so that the Llani dogs can pay regular tribute to him. And here it was that the Chartist uprising, which is the occasion of Llani's only excursion onto the national stage, was plotted and begun. It has been called 'the lower chamber of Llanidloes politics' which I think is a very apposite description. It is the place where Llani people meet. During the day the elderly ease their old bones on the wooden bench next to the building's stone end. Here they gaze at the passing trade and traffic, swapping prejudices and ailments and words of wisdom, as is meet and proper for elders of the tribe to do. At night the young gather here, swapping tales of bravado and sexual conquest, while they stuff their faces with kebabs or pizzas from the Star Kebab House.

Let's return to that Chartist uprising. It happened like this. From about the fifteenth century, once the English kings and their Marcher Lords had got the feudal Welsh rulers under control, they began to turn Wales into one large sheep farm, employing the natives to tend those sheep. The mid-Wales towns became important centres for the buying and selling of sheep and, naturally enough, of wool. Now our ancestors fairly quickly (I mean over several aeons) worked out that wool straight off a sheep's back tended to fall to earth if they tried to put it on their own backs. So, having tried cow-muck to stick the strands of wool together and finding it a bit sniffy, they invented spinning and weaving. Inevitably these trades flourished in places like Llanidloes, which prospered in the seventeenth and eighteenth centuries.

However, the workers began to get restless when the economic downturn occurred because of competition from northern England mill towns. So, before you could say Llanfairpwllgwyngyllgogerychwyrndrobwyll-llantisiliogogogoch (once the longest name in the world of any railway station. It literally means 'the Church of Mary in a white hollow by a hazel tree near a rapid whirlpool by the church of St Tisilio by a red cave'. The railway ceased calling there in the 1960s but it remains a reason for visiting Wales. Truly!), they decided to become Chartists – a sort of early trade unionism that did not involve having to follow Arthur Scargill. The Llani magistrates, who were inevitably also the local landowners, became alarmed at the rumours of trouble at t'mill, especially since the only police force in the town consisted of an old nightwatchman and a few part-time, unpaid bobbies. So they sent for reinforcements from London.

What they got would be hilarious if the results hadn't been so sad. The reinforcements were three London constables, who proved to be utterly incompetent. They arrived in Llani on 30 April 1839 and promptly arrested three men, holding them in the town's largest hotel, the Trewythen Arms. This, of course, fired up the local boyos and they stormed the hotel, beating up one of the London bobbies and chasing the other two into hiding. For four days the Chartists controlled the town, much to the annoyance of the local landowners, who, of course, were not to be beaten. So, on 4 May the cavalry arrived – literally, a 200-strong force of Yeoman Cavalry with sabres drawn, supported by infantry troops. The Chartist ringleaders were arrested and three of their number were transported to Australia, while others were placed in Montgomery gaol.

What is really sad about all that is that five of the Chartists' six demands subsequently became enshrined in the laws of the United Kingdom. Universal suffrage for men (and now women, of course), the secret ballot, the removal of property qualifications for Members of Parliament, salaries for Members of Parliament and electoral districts representing equal numbers of people are now taken for granted. The only demand that has never been seriously contemplated was for annually elected parliaments, and heaven help us from having to watch the Conservative party repeating their death throes every year as they seek to elect a new leader.

Llanidloes has the unusual distinction of having produced a saint and a great sinner. The saint in question, canonised only in 1970 by Pope Paul VI, was Richard Gwyn who was born in the town in 1537, just a year after Henry VIII created the Protestant Church and ordered the dissolution of the monasteries. It was this religious ferment that was to determine Richard Gwyn's life. He was brought up as a Protestant and, after studying at Oxford and Cambridge, returned to Wales to open a school. At some point in his time at this school he converted to Catholicism, which was not a very smart move in the short term because Elizabeth I passed an Act in1580 that made it treasonable to be reconciled to the Catholic faith. That year Richard Gwyn was imprisoned and four years later, having been brought before eight different courts, tortured and fined several times, he was sentenced to death. And so, at Wrexham in 1584, he was hung, drawn and quartered, in the sensitive way they handled things in those days. Still, he's been made a saint now, so I expect he's quite chirpy about it all really.

The great sinner who owes his origins to Llani is Murray Humphries, otherwise known as Murray 'The Hump', Al Capone's chief lieutenant. 'The Hump's' parents came from Llanidloes and settled in Chicago, where the young boy moved rapidly from being a newspaper boy to membership of the feared Sicilian gang running crime in the windy city. One of his enterprises involved the use of Chicago laundries and he invented the jokes about 'taking people to the cleaners' and about 'laundering money'. When Capone was imprisoned in 1933, Murray was described as America's Public Enemy Number One. He was considered to be the 'brains' of the crime mob and was greatly admired by Capone, because of his entrepreneurism in buying into legitimate businesses and in buying off some of the leading politicians and lawmen in the Chicago area. He married a Native American princess who bore him a daughter, Luella, later to marry the Italian actor, Rosanno Brazzi. Warren 'The Hump' was imprisoned only once, in the early 1930s, for a minor tax evasion misdemeanour and died of natural causes at the age of sixty-six in 1965.

Another noted person with Llanidloes connections is Ian Beale, the owner of 'Beale's Plaice' chip shop in the BBC soap opera *EastEnders*. Adam Woodyatt, the actor who plays the insipid Beale, spent much of his early life in the town and I like to think that his fictional life has been influenced by it. He has certainly been on the side of the angels at times, notably when he was being cheated on and double-crossed by first wife, Cindy, so the Richard Gwyn influence is traceable there. And there is no doubt that he has also been involved in some dodgy business deals, so the links to Murray 'The Hump' are also recognisable. Even more crucially, the chief hangout for the Llani adolescents is the Star Kebab House – surely the model for the young Ian Beale's entrepreneurial activities in the chip shop business.

The Trewythen Arms, scene of the Chartist uprising, stands in Great Oak Street, a broad and attractive thoroughfare that runs from the old Market Hall up towards what was once the railway station. When you walk up this street, as I did that evening, you are struck by three notable premises. First, there's the Great Oak Bookshop which is much bigger than it looks from the outside, since it stretches downstairs to a bargain basement then out through a covered courtyard to a converted barn and boiler room. Among its second-hand stock is an ever-changing collection of Welsh interest titles, from which on a previous visit I purchased Brian Waters's *Severn Stream* – the first book I read in my research.

On the opposite side of the road is the National Milk Bar – a reminder of all the milk bars of my youth where we would gather in those pre-Starbucks, pre-MacDonald's, pre-health food days and guzzle gooey milk shakes. One of these, the Two I's in London, was the birthplace of British popular music, as it spawned the likes of Tommy Steele, Wee Willy Harris and Cliff Richard. Even in Wolverhampton, where I grew up, there was a steamy-windowed milk bar where the local skiffle groups used to play to their adoring fans. Strange that milk bars should still exist in Wales – maybe they're historical monuments with conservation orders on them.

Further up the street is the equally interesting Great Oak Café which is at the heart of the alternative lifestyle embraced by many of the New Agers who have settled in the Llani area. It was closed that Sunday night but on a previous visit I had bought a delicious cup of coffee and a slice of freshly made chestnut and mushroom pie, and found a table to sit at. There were a couple of women in those funny woolly hats that New Agers like to sport over their dreadlocks or shaved heads. They were smoking roll-ups which had that odd smell you don't want to ask about. A noticeboard announced a Belly Dancing Workshop ('Tone up, lose weight and a great aerobic workout'), a Homeopathic Children's Centre, an African Drumming Workshop, an Acupuncture Centre, Reflexology Classes and a Living for Change Group (winding-up meeting). And there was a photocopied letter promoting homeopathic borax as a preventative for foot-and-mouth disease.

You know the sort of place. It's easy to mock and I'm aware of a growing old fartism in me that makes me want to do just that, but there was another notice on the wall which gave me pause for thought. The Great Oak Café is owned by the Compton's Yard Trust which was set up by Nicholas Carr-Saunders, who wrote the first *Alternative London* guides, transformed Neal's Yard in Covent Garden into an oasis of greenery and alternative businesses, and became renowned in the media as the guru for the drug Ecstasy. The Trust sought to replicate the alternative agenda in rural Wales by creating centres of self-sufficiency that would lead a rethinking of lifestyles.

And that's exactly what the Great Oak Café does. As well as providing excellent home-made vegetarian food, it holds exhibitions of art by local artists, it provides a facility for the Llani Film Club, it is a venue for folk and rock music concerts and it organises a wide range of events for young and old. It is truly at the heart of its community and is living testimony to the vision of Nicholas Carr-Saunders who sought to promote the importance of a sustainable community and economy.

Next door to the café and complementary to it is the Llanidloes Resource Centre, one of a network of centres set up by an imaginative Powys County Council to provide access to information technology facilities for everyone. It's another strand in the rethinking of the way we live that is illustrated here. In the Resource Centre the Llani locals can have instant access to the knowledge of the world through the Internet in ways that were not even dreamed of just ten years ago.

If only those Chartists had had this potential, they could have galvanized every rebel in the country to come to their support. Their modern-day counterparts are part of a genuine revolution. Good luck to them! Llani deserves their success.

For a moment, I was even prepared to sign up to the Belly Dancing Class!

Back past the old Market Hall and at the edge of the Severn stands the church from which Llanidloes gets its name. It is literally the church of St Idloes, a seventh-century saint who, as far as anyone knows, did diddly squat apart from giving his name to this place. Now I'm no great shakes as far as visiting churches goes. I spent quite a bit of my childhood going to church and never really got much from it then, and I still find the whole thing a bit overpowering. I suppose it's meant to be, but I just find all that gloominess rather heavy and I get really irritated by all those vicars who sound like parodies of themselves with their unctuousness and their earnestness and their cheesiness. And why do they still insist on wearing those long white dresses and doing that oh-so-solemn slow march down the aisle at the start and end of a service? Mind you, I'm equally queasy about the happy-clappy types who wear jeans and tote guitars around to prove they're really with it.

Anyway, Llanidloes parish church is one of the few churches that I can bear to be in. This is because it is just so beautiful inside, mainly because of the magnificent hammer-beam roof that is above the nave of the church. This roof is made of richly aged dark oak rafters which rest on hammer beams, each of which is decorated with an angel on its end. Above these angels intricately carved circular ribs create a vaulted appearance to the roof. The whole thing is just breathtaking.

This hammer-beam roof, together with the arcade with its five arches, were not part of the original church. Both were brought here by cart over 10 miles of rough pathways from Abbey Cwmhir when the Cistercian monastery there was closed down in 1536 at the behest of Henry VIII. It's ironic really that Henry's break from Rome and his invention of the Protestant Church led to this kind of nifty work. This transplanting of bits of old monasteries occurred all over the country at the time and continued for quite a while afterwards. It was a bit like a medieval car-boot sale, where people traded on their unwanted angels or roofs or fonts. Whoever the Llani citizen responsible for this particular act was, he deserves a genuine vote of gratitude.

While I was in the church gazing at this wondrous roof, I was approached by a young Dutchman called Pieter who had entered after me.

'This is so unlike our churches,' he said. 'The people here are worshipping a wall.'

Now I don't know what Netherlander churches are like. In fact, I didn't know what he was talking about but, hell's teeth, I thought, this is my Britain, so I've got to pretend I know what's what. So I tried to distract his attention.

'Can you imagine them carrying all those beams 10 miles

on those old pathways?' I tried, for I had already read and absorbed the stuff about Abbey Cwmhir.

'It is a very old roof,' said Pieter, nodding sagely, though still with a querulous expression on his face. 'It is not like our Dutch churches. Even after the Reformation, even after Luther, our churches do not expect us to pray to a wall.'

This was getting nowhere. Either he was an expert on all things episcopal or he was a Lutheran priest in mufti or he had been sent by the thought police to check up on me for daring to enter a church.

I made some feeble apology and left, vowing never to get into conversation with anyone in a church ever again.

Some chance with Worcester Cathedral, Tewkesbury Abbey and Gloucester Cathedral awaiting me downstream!

3 Llanidloes to Newtown

I left Llanidloes the following morning in high spirits, buoyed by a full breakfast cooked by Angela Morgan with local produce. As I said goodbye outside Severn View, she explained to me the bright yellow colour scheme.

'If I can't always have sun, at least I'll always have sunny colours,' she said in her cheery and optimistic way.

She was right about no sun for it was a grey day as I crossed the Long Bridge just past the Severn's confluence with the River Clywedog. Two miles north-west of Llanidloes is the Llyn Clywedog Reservoir, built in 1966 to control the flow of water into the Severn, supposedly to prevent future flooding. The reservoir is 6 miles long and its deepest point is 66 metres from the surface, the equivalent of fifteen double-decker buses. When full, it holds 11 billion gallons. That's 11,000,000,000 gallons. That's enough for 550 million people each to have a good long soak in a bath. And you can bet that one of them would be careless enough to accidentally pull the plug out and leave the rest of them exposed!

You'd think that holding all that lot back would stop the Severn from flooding, wouldn't you? But it doesn't. As we all saw in November of millennium year.

Still, that was none of my concern that September day as I left Llanidloes via an agreeable forest path. I have to say that, pleasant as it was for much of the early part of my journey, I was a bit irritated that the official Severn Way footpath did not go close to the river for a good 10 miles. In fact, I barely saw Sabrina all morning as I valiantly sought to follow the route. Even when evident, it was much overgrown and in places it was downright impossible to find because farmers had removed or defaced the waymarking signs. At times, as I approached farm buildings, I actually became anxious that some ruddy-faced Welsh farmer would appear with a sawn-off shotgun to deny me access or swear terrible oaths at me for daring to expose his land to the terrors of foot-and-mouth disease.

'Gwlad, Gwlad, pleidiol wyf i'm gwlad,' he'd shout from behind his loaded gun.

Now in fact I wouldn't be frightened by this, because I know that it is the first line of the chorus of the Welsh national anthem and all it means is 'Country, country, I'm partial to my country'. And it's hard to be frightened by that sentiment, isn't it?

I presume it's people like this who have refused permission for the Severn Way to follow the river more closely on this stretch, so I'll make my protest here. The path between Llanidloes and Caersws is a lie. Though it appears to broadly follow the route of the river, it actually has no direct relationship with it. Much of the time, as is obvious to anyone who, unlike me, can understand contour lines on Ordnance Survey maps, it actually is high up in the hills and in places is quite demanding walking. I have to say that, even though the sun appeared briefly late that morning, I did not enjoy this part of the walk. I was constantly on the alert for absent or badly situated waymarking signs, for footpaths overgrown with nettles and brambles, for stiles that did not exist or gates that would not open.

I was particularly sorry that the path skirted the heights above the little village of Llandinam because I had seen the statue of its one famous son, David Davies, on its outskirts when driving through en route to the beginning of my walk. David Davies has a fascinating history. He was born in Llandinam in 1818 and started life as a sawyer with little or no formal education. Somehow or other he made his fortune in the construction and management of the burgeoning new Cambrian Railway in mid-Wales, before developing Ocean

Collieries, the biggest mining operation in south Wales. Then, with a number of fellow mineowners, he was responsible for the building of Barry Docks to ensure that his coal could be shipped easily to England and elsewhere. Davies was much reviled by the south Wales miners when he was alive, though he was doing no more than capitalism always requires of its servants.

I wonder what David Davies would have made of the sight which dominated the skyline all through my morning's walk – that of the Llandinam Wind Farm, the biggest in Europe when it commenced operations in 1993. Actually, he'd probably have bought shares in the 109 giant wind machines that appear to march across the tops of the hills above Llandinam, each generating 300 kilowatts of electricity. Every time I turned a corner or came to the brow of a slight rise, they were visible, eerie in the greyness of the day. Romantics, who love their hillsides to be covered with grey boulders and purple heather, hate them. Environmentalists, who are always lauding alternative and cleaner sources of energy, love them. Me? I don't know. I must say that at times, when I was having difficulty relating to instructions in the *Severn Way Official Walkers' Guide* to my Ordnance Survey map, I was glad of their presence, because they served as a sort of compass.

But no one could pretend that they're pretty. And I really would have preferred to have been walking closer to the Severn and contemplating *its* power rather than that of these Mitsubishi turbines.

Eventually, after fighting my way through some unpleasantly high bracken, the path I was following popped out of forestation and on to a road on the edge of Caersws. At the junction of path and road stands a cottage with a plaque to Ceiriog Hughes, a Welsh poet who won prizes at the eisteddfods in the mid-nineteenth century. Most people think that the Welsh eisteddfods are part of an ancient tradition and that's certainly how the Welsh would like you to view them. In fact, the modern eisteddfods were an invention of a certain Edward Williams, who called himself Iolo Morgannwg. He was a contemporary of the Romantic poets, Wordsworth and Coleridge, and prone to the same sort of daftness that affected them. However, instead of picking daffodils or snorting opium, Edward Williams opted for dressing up in a white sheet and calling himself a Druid. This was in 1792, not in Wales at all, but at a private do on Primrose Hill in London.

For some reason the idea caught on, and by the early nineteenth century a tradition of the eisteddfod had been established. At each eisteddfod, men and women did, and still do, process on stage looking like members of the Ku Klux Klan in their white robes in order to listen to a load of poems in Welsh. Prizes are then awarded to the poems they deem the best and a new bard is crowned. It's all a bit like a Welsh-speaking pop music festival really, but without the pop music – or the fun.

Anyway, Ceiriog Hughes was one of these bardic Druids. He actually wrote the words to *Men of Harlech*, or at least one of the sets of words for there have been several. The reason why the plaque is on this cottage on the edge of Caersws is that Hughes in his real life (that is, when he wasn't scaring little children in his white sheet) was a railwayman in charge of the station at Caersws.

Half a mile past his cottage is the station itself, which I approached humming *Men of Harlech* to myself. I quite liked this notion of a railwayman who composed poetry and wondered whether anyone now working at the station knew of him.

Ceiriog Hughes's modern incarnation was pushing the road crossing gates back after allowing the Pwllheli train through. He nodded to me as I came up to him.

'F***in' farmers,' he said. 'See them? In their f***in' new Landrovers?'

I could see that Ceiriog Hughes's poetic strain had left its mark.

'Sorry,' I said. 'What d'you mean?'

'That one,' he replied, pointing at a Landrover that had pulled over the railway crossing and parked some 20 yards down the road. 'We're payin' for that, y'know. They couldn't care f***in' less. F***in' farmers.'

'What d'you mean?' I repeated, still mystified at the reasons for this angry diatribe.

'Foot-and-mouth,' he explained. 'I've seen them coming through here with their filthy f***in' lorries. They never clean them out. They carry f***in' infection. F***in' farmers.'

'So you think it's the farmers who caused the foot-and-mouth outbreak?' I asked, showing him that I might look bedraggled but I was quick on the uptake.

'And the f***in' lorry drivers,' he continued. 'Why do they have to drive hundreds of f***in' miles to get sheep slaughtered? It's f***in' mad. They used to travel by train and that was much cleaner. Nowadays it's everything has to go by f***in' lorry. Does it make any sense to you?'

I hadn't expected to be quizzed on the government's transportation policy, so I was a bit weak on this one. I muttered something which I thought sounded suitably sympathetic but actually said nothing, then told him I had to be on my way.

'Watch out for them f***in' lorries,' he called as I strode off in search of refreshment, past the field which once was a Roman fort.

Mindful of his advice, I looked three times before crossing the road to reach the Red Lion pub in the centre of Caersws, which has a sign above its front door stating that it is 39½ miles from the sea. Now why would anyone want to know this? I asked myself as I entered. And, to tell the truth, I do not know. Nor, I suspect, does anyone in Caersws, for the sign is clearly an aged one. What if everyone did this? I mean, I could put up a sign outside my house saying '89¾ miles to the sea' or 'X million miles to the moon'. You could wear a sign around your neck saying 'Two hundred pages to the end of this book'. The possibilities are endless.

There were the usual old caps inside, four of them to be precise.

'Good morning,' I called out, as cheerily as I could, for I had not enjoyed my morning's exertions and my feet were beginning to hurt really badly.

'Has your watch stopped?' asked one of the old-timers, who was stood at the bar.

'No,' I answered innocently and glanced at it. 'Why?'

'What time is it?' he asked.

'It's a quarter to two.'

'So why are you saying 'Good morning'?' he asked with a twinkle and all his pals chortled.

I lifted him up by the collar till his face was centimetres from mine. 'Listen, you little Welsh git!' I began. 'One more squeak out of you and you're dead meat. Got it?'

Actually I didn't do anything like that. I'm far too nice a person. Instead I grinned weakly at his joke, ordered a pint and a sandwich and sat down away from them to ease my aching feet. To pass the time I looked at my Ordnance Survey map and was disappointed to find that my afternoon route was to take me even further away from the River Severn. As I took my lunch, I listened to the desultory chatter of the old-timers, much of it about foot-and-mouth, and looked at them. Is this what I could become? I asked myself. The Lunchtime O'Booze of Bridgnorth? Sitting in the snug of some local hostelry every day, mouthing off my opinions on anything and everything and taking the micky out of a stranger for a bit of sport?

Actually, it didn't look too bad an option to be honest. I was having doubts again about the wisdom of this jaunt I had undertaken. I was sure that my feet were blistering badly. I was fed up with the non-existent footpath and even more with the fact that it went nowhere near the river. For a minute or two I actually considered going back to the station and catching a train to my next port of call, Newtown. Who would know?

But something stopped me. I don't know what it was – dogged determination? Bulldog spirit? Sheer cussedness?

Or was it that I just couldn't take another lecture on the f***in' farmers!

I'm not going to bore you with an account of my afternoon's walk to Newtown. What I will say is that it required a lot of close attention to the guidebook as it led through fields, over stiles, past dead trees, up stony tracks and down minor roads. What I will also say is that at one point I did not pay close enough attention and found myself at the wrong point on one of these minor roads. When I consulted the map, I saw that I was only about half a mile off the official route but I also saw that this was going further and further away from the river. Telling myself (this is one of the stupid things you do in this sort of situation) that I was owed 2 miles because of the mistake I'd made on the first day in heading for the source of the River Wye, I decided I would take an alternative route.

This involved me in quite a lot of road walking, probably not such a good idea given the state of my feet, and took me for about a mile along a much busier road through the village of Aberhafesp. From there I planned to follow farm tracks to rejoin the Severn Way footpath for its final stretch into Newtown itself.

What I hadn't reckoned on, however, was the fact that, although restrictions on the official footpath had been lifted, they might not have been on other tracks. Certainly I got the feeling, as I climbed a long slow gradient towards a farm and saw two dogs come bounding ferociously and noisily towards its main entrance, that no one had informed this particular farmer of the change in policy. So I decided to take a detour around the farm. Niftily, I leapt over a gate into a field, hoping to pass the farm, which was shielded by a tall hedge, without being noticed.

This was probably the daftest decision I had made all day. For, as I leapt daintily off the gate and looked behind me, I saw I was in a field of cattle. And the cattle did not have udders, they had protuberances of a different order. Yes, I was in a field full of bullocks. And, because it had been drizzling lightly for the past half an hour, I was dressed in my bright red cagoule. Meanwhile the farm dogs had sensed where I was and were straining their lungs on the other side of the hedge. For a fleeting second I told myself that the business about bulls being driven mad by the colour red was an old myth but then, as one of their number took a threatening pace in my direction, I fled, heart thumping and rucksack bouncing against my shoulders, till I reached a gate at the other end of the field and clambered over.

I didn't pause to regain my breath for the dogs were still yelping and any minute I expected to feel shotgun pellets in my backside. I sprinted away from that farm as fast as I could, forgetting my blisters, forgetting my aching bones and focusing solely on finding the Severn Way footpath again to escape from all my quite unfounded fears. When, miraculously, the footpath marker with its small blue circle stating Llwybr Hafren appeared in the hedge, I was mighty relieved and glad to rejoin it for the final mile into Newtown.

I was absolutely knackered by the time I reached Newtown, so I sat on a bench in Broad Street and read the *Guardian* while eating an ice cream. I tried ringing the Cross Guns, where I had booked in for the night, but got no reply. So, after a quick tour of the town, I went to find the place, with some half-baked notion that the landlady might be there but refusing to pick up the phone. On the way I passed the Liberal Democrat office and thought I saw the local Member of

Parliament, Lembit Opik, inside through a window. I even thought of going in to pass time of day with him.

'Hello, I'm Bob Bibby and I'm walking the Severn Way,' I would begin.

'I'm Lembit Opik, MP for Montgomeryshire,' he'd reply.

But then what would we say? He, being a politician, would certainly have no difficulty in talking nineteen to the dozen about the government's failure to recognise the needs of long-distance walkers or about the need to ensure that farmers' livelihoods were not threatened by wayward walkers marching across their crops and disturbing their cattle. But I, in truth, had nothing to say to him, other than hello.

So I went to visit some of the sites in the town instead and, when the Cross Guns still didn't reply to further phone calls, sat in the park and read an obituary of Christian Barnard in the *Guardian* and wished he'd pioneered foot transplants as well as heart transplants.

At the centre of this park stood the council offices and I became aware of a youngish male and female chatting in the car park. Obviously from their dark suits and name-badges dangling on chains around their necks (why does everyone have to wear these nowadays?) they were from the county council offices. Just as obviously, they were chatting each other up, under the pretence of consulting each other's diaries. First one, then the other, would move towards his or her car, then slowly return to resume the smiling conversation. Then they would pretend to consult their diaries. Then there would be another half-hearted attempt to get to the car. Then the dance would begin again. Finally, each got into their separate cars and immediately spoke into their mobile phones. I just *knew* that they were making excuses to their regular partners for their lateness.

Eventually I was let into the Cross Guns to find that the licensee was not present and wouldn't be back till the next day, that I wasn't expected and that no breakfast was possible the following morning. Charlie the barman, however, was happy to let me have a bed for the night at a reduced rate and, even when I saw the sparse and spartan bedroom and felt every spring in the mattress digging into my back, I was too weary to protest or to find anywhere else.

I was told by Charlie that the only other lodger was a sixteen-year-old girl and, knowing now that no one else was apparently staying at the Cross Guns that night, instantly I had a fear of being mistaken for Nabokov's Humbert Humbert. In the bathroom there was a hair extension with little coloured ribbons in it, a pair of black knickers, a hairbrush and various other potions that adolescent girls use to prettify themselves. I tiptoed around to make sure 'Lolita' and I didn't meet in an embarrassing state of semi-nakedness in the corridor outside the bathroom, then quickly locked the door of my room while I changed clothes. My feet now were very blistered so I decided to swathe them in plasters so as not to see the damage caused but that wasn't going to stop me from hitting the high spots of Newtown, oh no!

I was soon on my way back into town for my evening meal. Outside the Robert Owen Museum I saw a gang of teenage boys Sellotaping a teenage girl into a phone box with great glee. Was this 'Lolita'? I wondered. And how soon would she escape?

I went into a pub called the Black Boy which had a sign indicating vacant rooms and where I wished now I had stayed. Thinking to ingratiate myself with the locals I ordered something on the menu called Tan-y-Ddraig, which I attempted to say as if I spoke fluent Welsh.

'What's that?' the middle-aged barmaid asked me.

'Sorry, didn't I pronounce it right?' I said and I pointed to it on the menu.

'I can't speak Welsh,' she replied, implying that it was a bit daft of me to think that anyone in Wales could. 'It doesn't always sound the way it looks when it's written down. But, if that's what you say it is, I'm sure that's right.'

You just can't please everybody, can you?

A while later I was ushered into the restaurant, which was in reality just an extension to the bar with tables laid, for my meal. Tan-y-Ddraig turned out to be a hot chicken curry with leeks (that was the Welsh bit) in a sauce with chips, chutney, naan bread, peas and carrots. It was an interesting combination, to say the least, and not obviously from the Delia Smith recipe book but I was hungry, so I guzzled it and washed it down with a couple of pints of Worthington bitter.

Later while I was replacing lost liquid with a further pint of Worthington, three twenty-something lads arrived looking for rooms, which they were lucky enough to find because I was stuck at the Cross Guns with Lolita. Within minutes of being shown their rooms, they were down at the bar, ordering pints of lager and eyeing up two local eighteen-year-olds with low-cut blouses and cleavages thrust forward, who were sat in a corner of the bar. These girls had in front of them half-drunk bottles of Smirnoff Ice and were more interested in the mobile phones in their hands, where they were reading and sending txt msgs. I guess it was one of these that finally took them off, because they suddenly upped and went, to be shortly afterwards pursued by the lads.

The only other occupant was a morose old bloke sitting on a stool at the bar, smoking and drinking, saying nothing. Maybe he was, like me, reflecting on all that sexual chemistry that seemed to hang in the Newtown air.

Maybe he had himself recently partaken of some of it.

Or maybe he was just dead drunk.

Or just dead.

4 Newtown

Everything has its price, so it is said, and nowhere is this more true than in Newtown. Its anonymous Anglicized name notwithstanding, Newtown has been at the heart of the way we clothe ourselves for the past 200 years and one of the people most responsible for that was named Pryce. Pryce Pryce-Jones, as in fact his name was, founded the world's first mail-order firm for woollen goods in the town, even managing to persuade Queen Victoria to fill in her coupon from his catalogue in order to purchase some flannel knickers. For this he was knighted and allowed to call his factory the Royal Welsh Warehouse. The building is still there and still the most prominent building in Newtown, though it now is a sort of downmarket car boot sale and not somewhere that you'd really want to buy your best-quality knickers from, whether you're a queen or a commoner. But I am getting ahead of myself, for there is another Pryce whose story is central to Newtown's history.

This Pryce was the descendant of the town's most important family, originally known as the ap Rhys family – proper Welsh, see? The family seat was Newtown Hall, which is now used as council offices, and there was the usual tribe of baronets who fought in various campaigns and entered Parliament and all those kind of things that historians of various times have thought important enough to record for our benefit. So we can't tell much about the distant generations of Pryces as regards their capacity for drinking, thinking or bedwetting from the Wendy-house of their mausoleum in the abandoned St Mary's churchyard on the riverside – abandoned because of, yes that's right, flooding. However, we do know quite a lot about Sir

John Pryce, the fifth baronet, who can justifiably lay claim to the title of 'eccentric toff', such as P.G. Wodehouse would have placed as a natural inhabitant of the Drones Club.

This Sir John married three times. His first two wives died young and, after the death of the second, he took to visiting the family vault where both these good ladies had been entombed. What was he doing there? Was he overcome with grief at their loss? Was he maybe feeling guilty that he had brought about their sad demise through excessive snoring? We do not know. What we do know is that he got a bit brassed off with visiting them regularly in the vault and decided he wanted them closer to him. So he had his two former wives embalmed and moved into Newtown Hall, where they were placed either side of his four-poster bed.

Bliss, eh?

Now, if you think that's a bit weird, imagine what the third Lady P. thought! Of course, he hadn't wed her when he arranged for this bit of closet necrophilia but, as soon as she saw them there, she ordered him to shift them, so he had to have them returned to the vault. And that's where they all are now, their hot-blooded lives reduced to this stone memento that has become little more than a place in which gardeners keep their grass-cutting tools.

Now, back to Pryce Pryce-Jones. As I've already pointed out, once the English Marcher Lords had conquered Wales, they turned the whole country into a vast sheep farm. Newtown, because of its central position, inevitably became one of the places at the heart of the wool trade and its citizens soon learned that they could spin and weave this stuff into flannel for clothing as well as anyone. The invention of the carding engine and the spinning jenny, together with the town's proximity to the fast-flowing Severn, made the town into somewhere that became known as 'the busy Leeds of Wales' (that was supposed to be a compliment!). Factories grew on the river's banks and the flannel industry was soon in full swing, bringing great prosperity to Newtown. Pryce Pryce-Jones's genius was in spotting the opportunities presented by the coming of the railway line in the middle of the nineteenth century. This, he quite sagely foresaw, opened up more distant markets for the flannel trade and he set about exploiting these, sending out his biannual catalogues which offered the latest fashionable items – grey flannel blankets, particularly good on the battlefield, and grey flannel knickers, as approved by Her Maj.

The wool trade declined, as is the way of old trades, in the wake of technological advance and Pryce Pryce-Jones is now only a thumbprint in our history, but an important one. For, without him, we would not have those ill-fitting fawn cardigans for the elderly or those imitation-leather blousons for the young that seem to be the staple product of catalogue shopping. Without him, many of us would be £1.76 a week better off – and we wouldn't have to wear those dreadful bri-nylon dressing gowns!

A curious side-story to this is that there is now a successful textile manufacturer in Newtown and that is Laura Ashley, which is one of the town's biggest employers. This was all Audrey Hepburn's doing. The patterned headscarf she wore in the 1953 film *Roman Holiday* set a worldwide trend at exactly the time that Laura Ashley was producing her first designs for the same fashion accessory on her kitchen table in Pimlico. Lucky, eh? Her scarves were amazingly successful and that was the start of what became an international operation of a brand name known by everyone. The long Laura Ashley patterned maxi-dress of the 1960s helped establish that brand, which went on to produce aprons, oven gloves, gardening smocks, baby clothes and so on. Oh, but I don't think Laura went into knickers, if you know what I mean. Much of what the company now produces is made right here in Newtown.

The textile industry, therefore, still matters in Newtown.

Newtown's most famous son is the proto-socialist, Robert Owen, who is commemorated by a bust over his grave outside the derelict St Mary's church by the riverside. Beneath the bust are inscribed these words of Owen: 'It is the one great and universal interest of the human race to be cordially united and to aid each other to the full extent of their capacities.' Around the grave are attractive art nouveau railings erected by the Co-operative Union, which are decorated with the motto 'Each for All'.

Like just about everyone of my age, I flirted with left-wing politics in my younger days and I'm still more inclined to the notion of a just society than those who espoused the Thatcherite policy of the 1980s, with its deliberate use of mass unemployment as a tool for managing the economy. I was interested to learn more of the man widely regarded as one of the originators of socialist thinking, so I went into the Robert Owen museum in the middle of the town and read about him.

Robert Owen, born in Newtown in 1771, was a precocious child, so quick to learn that, at the age of seven, he became a pupil-teacher in his school. I won't bother with all of the growing up stuff but, coming from a town known for its textile trade, it was natural Owen should make his career in the cotton industry. However, the thing he did that was different was to actually notice the human beings who were working for him. He did this at his factory in New Lanark, south of Glasgow. Disturbed by the dreadful living conditions of his workers, most of whom had been forced into factory work by the impoverishment of agricultural work, and appalled particularly at the poor quality of the education offered to the workers' children, Owen set about conducting a series of reforms. He believed that people's characters were formed by their environment and so invested in improving the housing and sanitation of New Lanark and in creating free schools for children who previously had been set to work in the mill from as young as six years of age.

Soon New Lanark attracted interest from all over the world,

as manufacturers and politicians sought to grapple with the tensions in society created by the rapid advances of the Industrial Revolution. Owen was not satisfied to be a model employer, however. He wanted to change society, as he himself made clear:

> I had done all I could to enlighten the evils of those whom I employed; yet with all I could do under our most irrational system for creating wealth, forming character, and conducting all human affairs, I could only to a limited extent alleviate the wretchedness of their conditions, while I knew society possessed the ample means to educate, employ, place and govern the population.

The remainder of his life was devoted to creating such change, against the self-serving wishes of those who were getting rich on the backs of what amounted to slavery. He petitioned Parliaments, he wrote and published argumentative tracts, he was involved in the early trade union movement, he tried to re-create New Lanark in America and he opened the first Labour Exchange.

In the end the boss class beat him, as it always does. He died in Newtown in 1858, an old man who had returned to his place of birth for the last days of his life. Many of his ventures eventually proved to be failures, but Robert Owen pioneered better schools, cleaner towns, better working conditions in factories, trade unions and co-operative societies. He therefore has an honourable place in the development of the just society – an idea which seems to have left the mindset of many politicians today.

The small museum in the centre of the town is free to enter and Owen's statue stands on a nearby street corner. Whatever you do, if you visit the museum, *don't* ask to see the video about Owen. It is the most boring pap you can imagine. Even the curator who was on duty the day I called agreed with me.

'It's a bit long now, isn't it?' she sang in her mid-Welsh lilt. 'I don't know why they don't do a shorter one.'

She's right, of course, but she should be grateful for her working conditions to this pioneer of social welfare whose memory she guards. He was a remarkable man.

I visited another museum in Newtown, the WH Smith museum which occupies two rooms above the shop of the same name – the retailer which claims that, in its 500-plus High Street stores, it sells 'enough pens to circle the earth; enough books to fill a library shelf from London to Edinburgh; and enough paper to write a letter to everyone in the world'. Now why would anyone want to do any of those three things? I ask myself. I can come up with no answer.

This small museum tells the history of WH Smith from the days of its founder Henry Walton Smith in 1792, his wife Anna who kept the business going after H.W. died prematurely, and his son William Henry, after whom the whole caboodle is named. It's as much a social history as a family history, because the development of newspaper distribution, of railway book stalls, of circulating libraries and of transport itself are all graphically explored in the displays.

To get into the free museum, I had to ask one of the sales assistants.

'Oh, it's alright,' she answered my query about whether it was open, since the stairs were blocked off by a rope. 'We only do that to keep the children out. You can go up whenever you want really.'

'Is there a curator?' I asked. 'Or someone who can tell me about it all?'

'There is,' replied the sales assistant, lifting the rope barrier from its hook. 'Only she's not here today. Mind, it's not very big. You can go round it by yourself. It's self-explanatory really.'

So I did and saw all the exhibits I've just referred to and

many others too boring to list here. But I was puzzled about one particular thing and that was the rationale for this museum being here, in Newtown, in the first place. There did not seem to be any reason for this, at least none that was advanced to me by the exhibition in the museum. Indeed, Henry Walton Smith had begun his business in London. So why put a museum to the WH Smith name in Newtown of all places? What was the special connection?

When I asked downstairs, no one knew. They said I should write to the curator, so that's exactly what I did. Her reply was fascinating. Allow me to quote you some of her words:

> You are correct in thinking that there is no particular link between the town and Smiths. Newtown was not, as many people assume, the birthplace of W.H. Smith, as it was of the philanthropist, Robert Owen. Nor was it the site of the very first of our retail branches. That honour (*sic*!) goes to Clacton.
>
> No, our branch was chosen to be restored to its original 1927 condition and to contain the company museum for purely economic reasons, as with many retail decisions.

The curator's letter went on to explain how the chairman of WH Smith in 1975 wanted one of his shops to make a contribution to European Architectural Heritage Year and how this had to be achieved within a limited budget. The Newtown shop was chosen because, like many of its mid-Wales counterparts, it had not been modernised and still had several authentic features. The town's geographical position in the middle of Wales and close to the English border made it even more attractive and so, in 1978, it came to be.

I thought then and I think now that this is a bit of a con trick, or, as the curator wrote in her letter, it is 'disappointingly rather prosaic'. I know it's free and I don't suppose that many people are especially interested in the history of a newsagent, so they probably don't get many visitors. Even so, I spent a good 30 minutes of my life in there. I could have saved that time by starting to write my letters to everyone in the world!

I have forsaken any attempt at a physical description of Newtown, as Defoe or one of his ilk might have written, because it is fairly nondescript. The original town, built to a grid pattern, was situated on a bend in the River Severn and that is where the heart of it still is, though industrial and housing estates have spread across the river and out both ways along its banks. Leland described it as 'meately well buldyd after the Welche fashion', which is damning with faint prose. The tourist information leaflets guide you to the two museums I have mentioned and to a third, the Textile Museum, housed in the flannel-weaving floors of old cottages, and to the Pryce-Jones building. But that's about it.

I was left contemplating what I felt about Newtown when I remembered the following:

> There is no present in Wales,
> And no future;
> There is only the past.

Those words were written by poet R.S. Thomas, when he was rector of Manafon, some few miles north of Newtown. This strange, bardic, private man wrote widely about Wales, not always to the pleasure and satisfaction of the Welsh themselves. Born in Holyhead and brought up in an English-speaking household, Thomas only began to learn Welsh when he was in his thirties and settled at Manafon. His poems are equally critical of the Welsh ('men of Wales/With your sheep and your pigs and your ponies, your sweaty females/How I have hated you . . .') as of the English incomers who bought up Welsh cottages as holiday homes ('an Elsan culture/ Threatens us'). But his criticisms of the Welsh were because he was an extreme nationalist who believed his countrymen had yielded to an alien culture and were merely clinging to the relics of their history ('Wind-bitten towers and castles/ With sham ghosts;/Mouldering quarries and mines').

Thomas must have come to Newtown frequently, though as far as I'm aware he has never written about it. His poetry deals largely with the hill farmers who were his pastoral flock, not with the town-dwellers, though the clinging to the past is as true for both. I wonder if he would have recognised the town from the comments of some of its current young people:

> It's so far from anywhere, people can be a bit narrow minded

or,

> All the bloody small-minded men that prefer sheep to women

or,

> If you're into countryside views or beer then go. If you want to entertain your teenagers then stick to Butlins!

Maybe not. Or maybe not phrased exactly like that, though the sentiments Thomas might well have shared. The trouble is it's hard to pin Newtown down. As you approach, it seems a pretty enough place, set below the green Kerry Hills, its grey-slated roofs glistening in the sunshine. But it's hard to find its *raison d'être*. Its history is of interest but it will take the Welsh Development Agency a lot of time, and money I suspect, to return Newtown to its historical position of prosperity.

Everything has its price, as they say. And I'm not sure that the United Kingdom really knows what price (or Pryce) it will have to pay to make small Welsh towns like Newtown worth living in again.

5 Newtown to Welshpool

Next morning I rose early on purpose, wishing to escape from the Cross Guns before 'Lolita' had any opportunity to slouch provocatively along the corridor, chewing gum and giving me that coquettish look I feared. Furtively I sneaked into the bathroom where the hair extension and the black underwear lay undisturbed, quickly and quietly as possible showered, then silently packed my rucksack and joyfully left.

In my weariness of the previous evening, I had not felt like taking any photographs so now I rectified this, quickly visiting the WH Smith shop, the Robert Owen Museum and the statue to the founder of the Co-operative Movement. Charlie had told me there would be plenty of early morning cafés open but the only one I could find was the ubiquitous yellow arches of McDonald's. I swallowed my pride and, soon after, a bacon roll and two cups of coffee, while studying my route for the day in globalisation's champion.

I had two more photographs to take I realised as I broke my fast – Owen's grave and the Pryce memorial in the grounds of the abandoned St Mary's church by the riverside. So that's where I headed.

Three ten-year-old boys were sitting just inside the church walls.

'We're just studying Robert Owen,' one called out as I lined up Owen's gravestone for my photograph.

'Okay, would you mind just ducking down for a second?' I asked, still more intent on composing my photograph than on them.

'What are you taking photos for?' asked one of the boys, whose close-shaved head I could see peeping around the rim of the window of the derelict church.

'They're for a book I'm doing,' I answered, my faith in the innate curiosity of young people undiminished by many years of teaching the little buggers.

'We're studying Robert Owen,' repeated the second of the trio, a round-faced boy with spiky yellow hair and a twinkly grin.

By this time I had moved my position to take a photograph of the Pryce memorial and could see all three of the boys clearly, sat astride the window ledge of the old church, their eyes focused on something that rested on the stone surface between them.

'D'you want a picture of Mrs Owen?' the third boy suddenly ventured, holding up in his skinny hands the subject of their study for my inspection.

It was the centrefold of a girlie mag. – the sort of thing that ten-year-old boys have based their understanding of the human female anatomy on for aeons. 'Mrs Owen', for so I must call her since the magazine was just as quickly whipped out of my sight with many accompanying boyish giggles, was naturally *au naturelle*, posed provocatively on a fluffy white rug, and did not give the appearance of holding profound views on the just society.

'That doesn't look like Mrs Owen to me,' I said, smilingly declining the boys' offer as I packed my camera away and turned from the church in the direction of the Ha'penny footbridge that was to take me across the Severn and back on my journey.

I left them giggling and goggling at their chosen subject of study.

The attractive riverside walk below the floodbank was filled with early morning dog-walkers, enjoying the sunshine and catching up on the latest gossip. I 'good-morninged' each and every one for, though I was feeling my blisters, they were not as severely discomfiting me as they had at the end of the previous day. Besides, the sky was an azure blue, the sun's warmth was already tingling my forehead, and my day's route promised to be much flatter, much closer to the riverside, and much shorter than that of the day before.

As I left the riverside walk and Newtown behind me, I could not help but reflect on the sexual potency of much of what I had witnessed there – the county council workers in their courting dance, the invisible presence of 'Lolita', the teenage girl being Sellotaped into a phone box by her male admirers, the Smirnoff Ice girls with their txt msgs, and finally those pre-adolescent boys with their glossy picture of Mrs Owen. Never mind Sir John Pryce and his necrophilia, or Pryce Pryce-Jones and his linen knickers! What would Robert Owen have made of it all? Was this what he meant by 'co-operative union'?

Somehow I doubt it.

At the end of the floodbank, the Severn Way footpath joins the Montgomery Canal Walkway constructed by Severn Trent Water Board above the bed of what was once the canal that linked Newtown with the main canal system of the United Kingdom. An information sign at the beginning of this walkway tells of the building of the canal 'between 1982 and 1997, halted temporarily by the Napoleonic Wars, but then completed in 1821'. I read this sentence several times, trying to make sense of it, before I realised that there had been a mistake in the dates. They should have read 1782 and 1797. Has no one else in Newtown ever noticed this? I asked myself. Are they all too busy pursuing their sexual proclivities? Doesn't anybody care?

The canal bed itself is used as the main sewage pipe from Newtown to the sewage processing plant a short distance away, so the footpath I was following actually followed the same route as the Tan-y-Ddraig that had processed through my bodily system overnight.

Shit happens, as they say.

Still, the walkway was pleasant enough, the sun was dappling through the trees and to my right I could see the broad swathe of the River Severn gliding purposefully on its journey. This stretch of the Severn Way, I knew, had only just been opened, so I was not surprised that much of it appeared untrodden, nor that I met no one else for quite some time after leaving the dog-walkers.

In fact, the next person I was to see was a bulky middle-aged man, with a round and ruddy face, in the middle of which was the short end of a hand-rolled cigarette. He looked like Dylan Thomas might have done had he lived to be fifty. He wore stained green dungarees – some kind of county council or water board uniform – and brandished a powerful strimmer in front of him, with which he was clearing the undergrowth from the path I was following. Seeing me approach, he switched off his buzzing machine.

'Morning,' I said as I drew nearer. 'Fine day.'

He said nothing. Should I have tried addressing him in Welsh? I wondered. Was he about to turn his strimmer on me and wreak bloody revenge for centuries of abusive treatment of his countrymen by mine?

'That's a good job you're doing there,' I tried again, seeking to disarm him with my charm and obvious friendliness.

Dylan glowered again, then spoke.

'You walking then?' he growled between clenched lips, without removing the cigarette butt.

'No, I'm building an igloo,' I countered. What kind of fool question was this? I thought. And besides, I was now alongside of him and could see he would have difficulty in raising his strimmer at me from there.

'Nice walk along here, isn't it?' he continued.

'I told you I'm building an igloo. Pass me that three-by-three block of ice, would you?'

'It's not far to Welshpool like,' he concluded rather tamely, I thought.

Why did I behave like this? Well, the truth is, of course, that

I didn't, though I might just as well have done. Neither of us really wanted to talk to each other. He was busy strimming and I was busy walking. Our chance encounter was a hindrance, not an opportunity for acquaintance. And Dylan's initial reluctance to speak was perfectly understandable which I should have recognised and respected. But, naturally, being the sort of courteous gentleman that I am, I couldn't resist the politeness of greeting him and the consequent filling of space with meaningless rot.

When will I ever learn?

Despite the blisters, I made good time that morning and reached my planned lunch spot, Berriew, by one o'clock. Berriew is a picture postcard village, filled with black and white cottages, an attractive medieval church (restored, of course, in Victorian times) and a river with waterfalls and grey rocks that invite paddling youngsters. This isn't the Severn, however; this is the River Rhiw, which passes under an aqueduct carrying the canal on its way to flow into the Severn just beyond the village.

Berriew's most famous citizen is actually non-resident. He is Andrew Carnegie and it was his Museum of Sculpture that had drawn me from my route, although I was disappointed to find it closed. So, instead, ever a glutton for punishment, I went into the nearby Talbot Hotel bar to seek sustenance and information.

The permatanned barman was youngish, with bleach-blond hair and an earring in his left ear. He wore a T-shirt that announced INDUSTRY – a curious choice in this chocolate-box village surrounded by fields and farms. At the bar, on the stools that they no doubt sat on every lunch time, were three old caps, slurping their pints of beer – Dai One, Dai Two and Dai Three.

'What's the best beer here?' I asked Permatan.

'Banks's,' growled Dai One, winking at me as he raised his creamy pint in the air, demonstrating his choice.

'Really,' I said. 'Funny that. They make that in Wolverhampton. I come from near there.'

'Went there once,' said Dai One. 'Domino match or something like that. Went to see the football. Bloody rubbish! The boys from Welshpool could have done better 'n that lot. They're overpaid, that's the trouble. They don't know what real life is like.'

I could see that I was being accepted quite quickly here – it's not often that coming from Wolverhampton does you any favours, so I was determined to make the most of it. I moved to sit down, taking my pint of Banks's with me.

'Did you watch the match on Saturday?' I asked innocently, for I was curious as to whom these Welsh border men felt allegiance.

'What match?' Dai One asked, raising a shaggy eyebrow up to the peak of his stained cap.

Dai Two and Dai Three laughed, as they were meant to. They were clearly well trained in responding to Dai One's vaguely humorous remarks. Even so, Dai Two explained about the England against Germany match, as he was meant to.

'I seen the goals on the news,' Dai One said, 'but I didn't watch the match. Bloody Germans! They ought to bomb them again. Never liked them.'

Dai Two and Dai three seemed to agree with this piece of deeply thought-out political philosophy, for they nodded into their beer glasses.

There was then a pause as they turned back to their own private conversation, begun before my entrance. I heard mutters about 'suicides on farms' and 'Ieuan still driving his tractor' and 'never get over it' and 'Northumberland' and I knew this was private grief about foot-and-mouth again.

When Permatan brought my tuna baguette to my table, I asked him about the museum.

'How come that museum was built here?'

'Lottery money,' he answered.

I could detect a slight chill in his answer but pressed on regardless.

'Is this Andrew Logan local then?' I asked. 'From round here?'

'Ooh no! He's from London,' he said, with a slight sneer as he made his way back to the bar.

London might just as well have been New York or Beijing from the tone of his voice. Clearly metropolitan ways were seen as dangerously bold for Berriew's citizens.

'Not very popular then?' I quizzed.

Permatan's face squeezed into that sort of grimace you might make when you stand in a cow pat.

'I'll say!' he said, exiting the bar area.

'That used to be the squash courts,' said Dai Three, who previously had not addressed me at all, so I had assumed that he only communicated in Welsh. He was wearing a Yankee Dodgers baseball cap and over his corduroy trousers a money belt, slung as if he were a Wild West cowboy.

'I think they should have made them into swimming baths,' said Permatan, now safely ensconced behind the bar and pouring another pint of Banks's bitter for Dai One, whose attention was thus focused away from me and my enquiries.

'It's a bloody eyesore, if you ask me,' said Dai Two, who I hadn't asked at all. 'Should never have been allowed.'

'I had my first drugs in there,' announced Permatan suddenly out of the blue. 'I was only about twelve. We were invited to the opening and everyone was smoking stuff, you know. So I tried some.'

'Bloody drugs,' said Dai One, who now had taken the creamy head off his beer and deposited it on his rough-shaven face. 'They all need locking up. If I had my way, I'd kick them all out of the country. Bloody scroungers! What do we need them for? It's drugs what are ruining the country.'

And so saying, he took a deep draught of *his* drug of choice and lit a hand-rolled cigarette.

Andrew Logan is an internationally famous sculptor, who claims his reason for living is 'to give enjoyment and pleasure to others through his quirky and humorous mementoes of his life'. His works have been exhibited all over the globe and he is renowned for founding the Alternative Miss World contest, where men and women compete to see who can wear the most outrageous costumes. His museum in Berriew is the only museum dedicated to a living sculptor but I cannot tell you what's inside it because it was closed when I arrived and when I left.

Nor can I tell you why he chose to site his museum in this tiny picturesque village on the Welsh borders, with which, as far as I can tell, he had no previous connection. For all I know, the collective wisdom of the three Dais might have been correct. I suspect that they were not the only citizens of Berriew who would cheerfully have chased him and his museum back to the wickedness of London.

The remainder of my journey along the towpath of the Montgomery Canal into Welshpool was pretty uneventful. I kept hearing the two-tone call of buzzards from the wooded hills – a call like the breaking voice of a teenage boy. Or of Ann Widdecombe. A grey heron that seemed to have been breaking trail for me all the way from Newtown finally took off on his majestic wing-beat just as I came past the gates to Powis Castle on the outskirts of the town. And the Montgomery Canal Cruiser hove into sight on its short journey from its base in Welshpool as the town came into view.

My bed and breakfast accommodation for the night was at Montgomery House close to the centre of town. And it had a bath! Never was the chance to stretch out and soak so welcome as it was in Angela Kaye's big bath that late afternoon. I even used some of Mrs K's sweet-scented bath oil to lubricate the water and my aching joints before setting out on my tour of the town, which I knew I had to accomplish quickly because there was a meeting of SARPA in the Royal Oak Hotel that I desperately wanted to attend.

SARPA? I'd seen it advertised in the *Powys County Times* the day before. It was due to start at quarter to seven so I went on the hunt for somewhere to eat before then. Unfortunately, by the time I came to start hunting, the cafés had closed for the day, the restaurants weren't serving meals until seven o'clock, and, according to Dilys behind the bar in the Royal Oak, there were no pubs in Welshpool serving food all day.

Finally the chef at the Royal Oak was persuaded to get something ready for me for half past six and I was duly ushered into the dining room at said time. The Royal Oak is the oldest hotel in town and it's the place where all proper functions are held – Rotary Club, Round Table, that sort of thing. And I guess it's the only posh place in town for persons of a certain station in life to stay in – it was certainly way beyond my price bracket. And, of course, in order to maintain its status, the Royal Oak has to employ a considerable staff and my impression from eavesdropping on them while I ate was that they were not altogether happy bunnies. In fact, there were certain resemblances to *Fawlty Towers*, even down to having a Spanish waiter. It was his conversation with the barman which alerted me to the fact that the chef was temperamental, because they were both clearly worried about entering the kitchen to ask for anything. Then there was Dilys, with her black eye, who had been moved from the bar to the dining room, much against her will, and was sulking therein. The manager trying to control all this was no Basil Fawlty, however. He was young and keen and, while Dilys and the Spaniard squabbled, served me himself with a very tasty salmon and mackerel terrine.

Shortly afterwards I went upstairs to the function room where SARPA was meeting. SARPA? Oh yes, I forgot. The Shrewsbury and Aberystwyth Rail Passenger Association, whose Annual General Meeting I was now attending.

The first thing that struck me as I entered the room was that the audience was almost exclusively male, with bad haircuts, loud voices and ill-fitting clothes. They looked and sounded like extras from some long ago film set in the Welsh valleys. Any moment I expected to see Richard Burton or Huw Griffiths or some other star of the 1950s come through the door. Instead I heard a number of angry voices:

'When I was Chairman of the Blah Blah, we voted £5000 (or was it £5 million?) for a feasibility study into blah blah . . .' said the very loud-voiced former Chairman of Blah Blah in his Welsh lilt.

'What about the Duffie Loop?' someone else with tufts of ginger hair rising above his ears called out.

What on earth was the Duffie Loop? I wondered. It sounded like some part of a jacket but what had it got to with trains? Maybe all these people were trying to get away from the image of being railway-anoraks and planning to become railway-duffel coats instead?

'And don't forget Karno!' someone else called out.

As if they could. Fred Karno and his circus had to be around somewhere in mid-Wales, didn't they? Did they wear duffel coats too? Or were they stuck with the Duffy Loop?

Just then someone introduced the guest speaker, Lembit Opik, the Liberal Democrat Member of Parliament for Montgomery. I'd nearly spoken to him the previous evening in Newtown and now I was going to hear the great man speak.

'I love trains,' he began. 'They're low stress, fast and comfortable. At least, they are in Europe so why can't they be in this country? The government has got the safety issue out of all perspective. I know Hatfield was terrible but it's still safer travelling by train than by car. We need to bring back the glamour of the railways. If you don't know what I mean, go and see those two wonderful films, *Brief Encounter* and *Night Mail*.'

'J.B. Priestley,' called out the Chairman of Blah Blah.

'Auden,' I said quietly, surprising myself at daring to speak in such an august company.

'Yes, J.B. Priestley. That was him,' repeated the Chairman of Blah Blah in his loud Welsh lilt, nodding confidently to himself as if he had just answered the final question on *Who Wants to be a Millionaire?* and any moment now he'd be getting the huge cheque waved at him by Chris Tarrant.

I cleared my throat.

'W.H. Auden,' I said, more loudly this time, though clearly not loudly enough.

'J.B. Priestley,' he said again. 'I'm sure it was.'

It wasn't, of course, but it was enough for me. I made my feeble excuses and left rather shamefacedly. I don't know what I had expected from the meeting. It had been advertised as being open to the public and I suppose I'd half-hoped for some lively debate on transportation policies. What I got was rather like attending the initiation rites of some remote tribe half way up the Amazon.

Mind you, I was nearly a third of the way up the Severn. Or down, if you see what I mean.

I had a final pint of bitter at the bar then headed back for the comfort of my bed in Mrs K's bordello.

As if!

6 Welshpool

To English tourists from the Midlands, hell-bent on getting to their seaside holidays on the Welsh coast, Welshpool is little more than a stopping-off point mid-journey, a place to stretch their legs, urinate and buy a bag of chips. It can't help that. It's roughly halfway between Birmingham and Aberystwyth, so it's only natural that those family excursions in the Datsun Sunny should stop off here. The curious thing is that it's always served this function, even when road transport and roads themselves were slower and less straight. Generations of Midlanders have taken their comfort breaks in Welshpool.

The town was originally known as Pola, which later got transmuted to Pool, after a large pool at its centre. The pool still exists, apparently, though it's not especially obvious nor as big as it once was. The 'Welsh' bit was added in the nineteenth century because the townsfolk, allegedly, were brassed off with their mail going to Poole in Dorset instead of coming to them. There is an independent cinema in the town which calls itself Pola but otherwise I could find no reference to its original name.

In truth, the town arose because of the castle that abuts it – Powis Castle, which is probably the fourth castle to be built in the area and probably on or near its present situation. It's obviously a prime site on the borders of Wales and England and the early castles were Welsh ones, built to keep the English out. Now I'm not going to bore you with any more of those stories about the border wars between the two nations. If I tell you that most of them involved people with the names Llewellyn or Gruffud, then that's probably all you need to know. In the end another Welshman, named Gwenwynwyn, was given the castle in 1277 by Edward I because he had supported the English against the Welsh. The town owes its origins to this England supporter with the impossible Welsh name.

The town grew in prosperity in the late eighteenth and early nineteenth centuries thanks to that good old standby of mid-Wales, the flannel trade. Many of the pleasantest buildings in its main thoroughfare, Broad Street, stem from this period and it is actually worth a stroll up this street to see the variety of frontages and styles still evident. It is normally quite a busy town centre, never more so than on Mondays when the biggest sheep market in Europe is held in the livestock market area. Sadly, this had been cancelled for several months prior to my visit because of the foot-and-mouth restrictions. But if you want to see where your woolly jumper comes from, then you should make a beeline for Welshpool Sheep Market.

Just off Broad Street is the Cockpit, an unusual octagonal building, which has been recently restored and opened by the town council. This is said to be the only surviving example of such buildings, which were commonplace throughout Wales in the days when cockfighting was legal and popular. It was in use for such activities until 1849 when the sport was declared illegal. It is worth standing inside this building and imagining the noise, the excitement, the gambling, the cruelty, the ways of a different and more bloodthirsty time. Or do I mean a time when people admitted there was beastliness in themselves and found ways of releasing it thus?

Powis Castle with its red gritstone walls sits on top of a rocky ridge just outside Welshpool. Nowadays it is better known for its world-famous (or so it claims) gardens, but the castle itself has an interesting history. The present structure probably dates originally from 1277, though the historical sources are a bit vague about all of this, because there are remains of the other three previous castles evident in the area and no one knows which is being referred to in the documents of the time that have survived. We do know that it was attacked by Owen Glendower in 1401, but then what wasn't?

From the late sixteenth century till the beginning of the nineteenth century Powis Castle became the family seat of the Herberts. During this period a grand staircase and a state ballroom were added to the existing structure, and servants' quarters were developed in the outer courtyard. Considerable redecoration in the then fashionable classical style was carried out during this time too. In 1801 the Clive family took over occupancy when one of the Herberts, by then deeply in debt, married Clive of India's son. That was a clever move, because this son inherited all the untold wealth that Clive acquired, some would say illegally, in his time in India.

Clive of India, or Robert Clive as he then was, went to India as a clerk in the East India Company and ended up as Governor of Bengal province. His route to fame and fortune began when he got a commission in the British East India Company and led a couple of foolhardy but successful military campaigns against French troops, thus securing British power in southern India. He was then appointed lieutenant-colonel and led the army that defeated the Nawab of Bengal who had imprisoned British captives in the notorious Black Hole of Calcutta. For this he was personally given £250,000 by the man who was to become the new Nawab. Clive saw nothing wrong with this but, when he finally returned to England, he was accused of corruption and tried. Although he got away with this, he was censured and one year later he committed suicide. The historian Macaulay called him 'A savage old Nabob, with an immense fortune, a tawny complexion, a bad liver and a worse heart', though I prefer E.C. Bentley's short rhyme about him:

What I like about Clive
Is that he is no longer alive.
There's a great deal to be said
For being dead.

There's a collection of mementoes from his time in India on display in Powis Castle but it was his fortune that allowed it to be maintained and later extensively refurbished. It was bequeathed to the National Trust in 1952 but it was still lived in by the Clive family until 1988.

This is where I have to confess that I did not visit Powis Castle. I have no objection to the principle of rubbernecking at the evidence of the lives of old soldiers or old monarchs or old anybody really. In fact, I would consider myself to be quite a model citizen in my interest and enthusiasm for all things historical. Nor do I have a problem with the notion that bodies like the National Trust should act as guardians of so many of our historical buildings and sites. That seems to me infinitely preferable to some cowboy setting up stall outside a stately pile and flogging guided tours to unsuspecting tourists in order to line his own pockets.

But I do object to having to pay £7.50 to go and see Powis Castle and gardens. I don't care how attractive it all is, how captivating the view or how stunning the floral displays. I just think it's a rip-off, particularly as its advertising bumf makes clear that they don't want anybody in a wheelchair or anyone with a pushchair or anyone with a dog. And, even though there are no Clives living there now, I am opposed to the idea that the National Trust, which is a charitable body, should for over thirty years have been sponsoring these descendants of someone whose wealth came from dodgy activities in Bengal.

Besides, there are more interesting things to do in Welshpool.

The most fascinating place to visit in Welshpool is a former warehouse beside the canal. Here is housed the Powysland Museum which has an equally remarkable history. The present museum only opened in 1990 but its collection goes back to 1867 when the Powysland Club was founded by local worthies interested in the history and archaeology of mid-Wales. These intrepid Victorians pooled their individual collections of artefacts in order to form the basis of a museum and purchased land on which to build. On Victoria's 1877 jubilee these public-spirited souls transferred the museum to the ownership of the town, from which it passed into Powys County Council control almost 100 years later.

The Powysland Club still exists. It organises a number of lectures throughout the year on topics as quirky as 'The Windmills and Watermills of Montgomeryshire' and 'The Development of Welsh Furniture, 1500–1800, with Examples from Powys'. It also has a library which houses a collection of rare and valuable books, a treasure trove of local history in the collected editions of its house journal, *The Montgomeryshire Collections*, and a collection of maps, some of which are very ancient.

You only have to visit the Powysland Museum, however, to appreciate what the members of the Powysland Club have been responsible for collecting over the years. The initial display on the ground floor of agricultural tools and farming equipment is, I suppose, what might be expected of an area where farming is still the dominant observable occupation. But this is as nothing compared with the wealth of materials on display on the first floor, where the collections of the Powysland Club members together with those from later archaeological work in the area take you on a chronological trip. This begins with prehistoric times with locally discovered polished stone axe-heads, flint blades and arrowheads of the early neolithic farmers. The Bronze Age finds focus particularly on the remains of a Timber Circle, believed to be a burial site from approximately 2000 BC, found when the Welshpool bypass was being created in the 1980s. The remarkably well-preserved fragments of an Iron Age shield take the journey on and remind you of how humankind developed.

Later in the museum there is evidence of Viking attacks and the growth of Christianity, and the displays come bang up to date with items from the early and mid-twentieth century, such as a washing machine and a Sacha Distel record! It is a fascinating collection, beautifully and clearly displayed, and helpfully labelled in English and in Welsh. And it only costs £1 to enter.

For me, however, the most interesting exhibits were those from excavations in the area of the now extinct Roman fort at Caersws, reminding me of the advanced civilisation that once existed in these lands. It's the little things that do it – the bits of highly decorated Samian pottery, the hair-combs, the glass-bottle fragments, the amber beads, the clay cooking pot, the pieces of mosaic flooring and the brooches. They all speak of a society which had time to indulge itself beyond the daily grind and which had an aesthetic sense as well as a utilitarian one.

As I looked at these artefacts, I thought of those Roman soldiers who presumably had to spend large parts of their lives marching through England, and I thought of my poor blistered feet. Those Romans did not have the benefit of super-duper Gortex-enhanced, Italian leather boots, together with two pairs of specially designed hiking socks. They marched in sandals, at exactly 100 paces a minute for between 10 and 20 miles a day, along those straight Roman roads, carrying their military equipment, several days' food supplies (mostly spaghetti bolognese, I guess), their own tents and their Latin-English dictionaries.

And why did the Romans build straight roads?

To stop their soldiers going round the bend!

Just the thought of that old chestnut suddenly made me forget my feet.

Curiously, for a town so small, Welshpool has two railway stations, though neither is what you might at first expect. The first is a rather fine brick building, reminiscent more of a French chateau than of a railway station, built in 1860 at the time when the railways were confidently opening up speedier and safer travel to people and Welshpool fulfilled its traditional purpose as being a midway point between the English Midlands and the Welsh coastline. The station was originally intended to be the headquarters of the Cambrian Railway but it only fulfilled this function for a couple of years. Nevertheless train services have come through this majestic station on their way to Machynlleth and then Aberystwyth since Owen Glendower was a lad.

Over time the splendid station buildings began to be used for purposes other than just railway business, until the Welshpool bypass was built in the 1980s. Originally the plans for this bypass were for it to follow the line of the Montgomeryshire Canal but there was such a hoo-ha locally about this that the planners went back to the drawing board and came back with a different proposal. The new road would follow the line of the railway track instead. And that's what it does, going right past the old station, which unsurprisingly gave up all pretence and became a shopping outlet, selling woolly jumpers, golfing clothes, and a lot of Welsh tourist rubbish probably imported from Taiwan. The mid-Wales railway still calls at Welshpool, though it does not stop at what is now known as The Old Station; it stops about 50 yards away on the opposite side of the new bypass at a modern concrete platform reached by a windy footbridge.

It is shameful.

I've a good mind to write to SARPA about it!

Mind you, Welshpool's other station is a bustling hive of activity, for it has become a major base for entertaining the children. The Welshpool & Llanfair Light Railway is a narrow-gauge line travelling some 8 miles through attractive countryside from Welshpool to Llanfair Caereinion. Its steam trains carry thousands of passengers on this picturesque journey every year, thus allowing dads and granddads to reminisce about the nostalgia of steam and their children and grandchildren to get sooty particles in their eyes.

The line was originally built as a passenger service in the early 1900s but was never profitable and was closed to passengers in 1931, continuing for a further twenty or so years as a goods-carrying service only before finally closing in the mid-1950s. And that was just at the time when people started jumping up and down at the loss of our industrial heritage, so a preservation society was formed and hey presto! the line was saved, and children still not born could look forward to days out in the steam (and soot).

The Welshpool & Llanfair, like many such enterprises, would not exist without volunteers to do the bulk of the renovation and maintenance work. It has three paid employees but everything else is done by volunteers, who turn up at weekends and on summer evenings to refurbish derelict old carriages or to buff up some old Romanian engine or to fire up an ancient Lithuanian tender. They must be mad. Don't they have homes to redecorate? Or gardens to dig? Or wives to take shopping? I really don't understand all this nostalgic 'Romance of Steam' business. It wasn't romantic when I used to have to travel on those filthy trains to university in the early 1960s. It only became romantic when steam trains became obsolete. Do these people really want to return us to the polluted days of pea-souper smogs? Don't they appreciate how much better life on the railways is now that 'Sir Richard Virgin' is in charge?

I really don't understand it at all.

Mind you, I wouldn't mind signing up for one of their train driver courses!

7 Welshpool to Shrewsbury

There was some early morning sun to greet me as I headed next day along the canal towpath out of Welshpool, mingling with the mini-skirted teenage girls and the basin-haircut boys who were slouching towards the local high school with uncompleted homework in the bags over their shoulders and cigarettes in their hands. My blistered feet were not too displeased because they knew, as did the rest of my weary body, that this was the last day of walking for a while. That evening, come hell or high water, I would reach Shrewsbury and thus terminate the first stage of my Dance with Sabrina. Next day my feet would have nothing more strenuous to do than operate the pedals on my car. It was bliss to look forward to!

The Severn Way continues to follow the Montgomery Canal for approximately 3 uneventful miles out of Welshpool, passing various signs of past industry such as the virtually invisible remains of a lime-burning centre at Buttington Wharf and a swing bridge once necessary for larger craft to traverse the waterway. Where the towpath marches alongside the main A483 road it is joined by the Offa's Dyke Path and the two paths merge almost up to the border between England and Wales.

The Offa's Dyke Path is the only long-distance walk in the United Kingdom that follows a man-made feature of the land. Offa was the king of Mercia from AD 757 to 796 and in many ways the greatest of the Anglo-Saxon rulers who shaped our country. Little is known about him but what is known suggests that he was a formidable warrior and leader who unified the warring tribes of the eighth century from the borders of

Northumbria down to the South coast into one nation. He also invented the penny as the standard monetary unit and, in order to cause as much trouble as possible for future British schoolchildren, decreed that 240 of these pennies should equal £1. Not until 1974 was this daftness corrected by decimalisation.

Like every ruler before and after him, Offa had trouble with the Welsh and so had his great earth wall built as a defensive rampart and boundary. It originally consisted of a ditch on the Welsh side, so the boyos would fall in if they tried to attack, and an 8-metre high earthwork which was about 27 metres wide on top, so that his troops had room to play tennis on quiet days. It stretched 182 miles from Prestatyn in the north (where Offa went for his summer holidays) to Chepstow in the south (where he went for a spot of salmon fishing).

The first part of the coinciding footpaths leads to a place called Pool Quay which was once the head of the navigable River Severn, though only in winter when the water levels were high enough. It has not been used by river craft since the nineteenth century but it is the place where the Severn Way and the Offa's Dyke Path leave the canal and follow the floodbanks above the river for several miles of pleasant grassy walking. All along this stretch I was aware of the brooding Breidden Hills which follow the river on its eastern side and, certainly for the first part, of the huge masts of the Criggin Radio Station. Believe it or not, this is part of the telecommunications system that controls Trident submarines.

Maybe it was the unexpected sunshine that was getting to me, maybe it was just four days' exposure to the elements or maybe my brain was finally going pear-shaped, but, as I remembered all this about the Trident missiles, I had an overwhelming desire to shout out 'Ban the bomb!'. In milliseconds I was in marching mode, wearing my duffel coat (fastened with a Duffy Loop, of course!), waving my banner proclaiming 'Bob Bibby is a nuclear-free zone' and generally behaving as if I was going to make a real difference in the world.

It didn't last, of course. This riverside stretch of the walk is bedevilled by stiles every few hundred yards and it's hard to retain your marching dignity when you're having to negotiate stiles like these. In fact, after the fifth of them I was beginning to feel more like Sally Gunnell than Bruce Kent, so I glanced beyond the radio pylons to the top of the quarry-scarred Breidden Hill to see the other prominent local landmark, Rodney's Pillar.

Admiral Sir George Brydges Rodney was another of those great heroes of the past with local associations who had money troubles, like Clive of India. Rodney was born in 1718 and had a distinguished career in the Royal Navy at the time that would subsequently be immortalised by C.S. Forester in his Hornblower novels. His best match result was when he beat the French at the Battle of Les Saintes off Martinique, thus establishing Britain's control over the West Indies and enabling us all to have cheap bananas for ever after. In a way, I suppose, Rodney was responsible for the enriching of British culture in the latter half of the twentieth century by the West Indian families who left their homeland to fill the post-war labour market in our country and to introduce us to sweet potatoes and ganja.

Rodney's Pillar is a stone monument that reaches up to the sky from the top of Breidden Hill. It's there because, allegedly, it was timber from these hills that Admiral Rodney sent for in order to build his ships. All morning I could see it, as I walked atop the floodbank until at last I reached the road again at the village of Llandrinio, where I crossed the bridge and then shortly afterwards was back on the floodbank footpath which was to lead me across the border and into England.

At precisely one o'clock, I did just that, crossing the old iron bridge at Crewgreen and hearing my footsteps echoing as I crossed. Suddenly, the waymarking signs were no longer blue but white and the Welsh Llwybr Hafren had been replaced by the English Severn Way.

Less than a mile further on I was sitting in the Tontine Inn in Melverley, sipping a very welcome pint of shandy and munching on a tuna sandwich. It was lunchtime, it was sunny and it was England. I picked up a copy of the *Daily Mail* from the bar counter and was greeted with the news that Prince Charles, the Prince of Wales, was cancelling his planned holiday abroad with his very good friend, Camilla Parker-Bowles, because he was anxious about the health of the Queen Mum.

Where else could I be but England?

The back pages of the *Daily Mail* were full of articles and pictures about the upcoming football match between England and Albania, including a very useful (and typically *Daily Mail*) 'Ten Things You Need to Know About Albania'. The most important of these Ten Things seemed to be that ancient English comedian Norman Wisdom was the most popular entertainer in Albania. Wisdom, in his trademark too-short jacket and flat cap, had been seen by the country's communist rulers to epitomise the struggle of the working class against the wicked capitalists. His awful films were widely and frequently shown and nowadays Wisdom, pronounced as 'Pitkin' in Albania, attracts bigger crowds in Tirana than David Beckham does.

I was thinking of this because no sooner had I left the Tontine Inn than I was aware of the buzzing of a helicopter in the clear skies above me. For some strange reason, possibly to do with the two pints of shandy or maybe it was me just becoming demob happy as I saw the end of my journey approaching, I connected Norman Wisdom and this helicopter in my mind. I convinced myself that this helicopter was actually an advance party of Albanian football scouts, looking for evidence of the physical fitness of the average English person to weigh up in their calculations as they prepared their team for the vital World Cup qualifier. And they had spotted me crossing into England a little while earlier and decided to focus their attentions on me as a typical Englander.

Was 'Pitkin' piloting the helicopter? Or was he responsible for getting them to target me? Did they have a video camera trained on me? I could feel myself pulling my shoulders back and putting an extra zing in my stride as I headed across a field towards a non-existent stile, only to have to foolishly retrace my steps to the opposite corner where the stile had cunningly concealed itself. That must have filled the Albanians with confidence about the state of English abilities!

Maybe it was the tuna. After all, I'd had tuna every lunch time for the past four days and, although fish is supposed to be good for the brain (according to the *Readers Digest* anyway, and that's always right, isn't it?), maybe you can overdose on it. Maybe I had.

Or maybe my 'Ban the Bomb' march under the Criggion Radio Station masts had been spotted and secret microwaves had been beamed at my brain to upset my normally balanced perspective on life.

By the time I'd reached the entrance to Nesscliff Training Camp a couple of miles further on, with the helicopter still buzzing overhead as if it was following me and only me, I was in a state of complete paranoia. Any moment I expected to be stopped by armed military vehicles roaring in their camouflage through the camp gates. I had read that Nesscliff has been since the Second World War one of the major arms depots of the British army and, until the end of the Cold War, one of the Russians' number one targets. What if 'Pitkin' and his Albanians were spying on it and not on me? What if the military at Nesscliff thought that we were in league and that I was sending secret signals to the helicopter?

Enough! It was time to leave this fantasy and return to the walk.

The Severn Way is forced to branch well away from the river beyond Melverley because there is a substantive military training area on its northern bank just about here, which is unfortunate because it deprived me of the opportunity to see

Alberbury on the opposite bank. It was in the church of this little village that Thomas Parr, reputedly the oldest man who ever lived, is said to have done his penance.

Thomas Parr lived for a 152 years and 9 months through the reigns of ten monarchs and was buried in Westminster Abbey by order of King Charles I. The inscription on his small gravestone in the centre of the South Transept reads:

> THO: PARR OF YE COUNTY OF SALLOP. BORNE
> IN AD: 1483. HE LIVED IN YE REIGNES OF TEN
> PRINCES VIZ: K.EDW.4. K.ED.5. K.RICH.3.
> K.HEN.7. K.HEN.8. K.EDW.6. Q.MA. Q.ELIZ.
> K.JA. & K.CHARLES. AGED 152 YEARES.
> & WAS BURYED HERE NOVEMB. 15. 1635.

But that's not all. Parr married his first wife when he was eighty years old. Twenty years later, at the ripe old age of 100, he did penance in Alberbury church because he had been unfaithful to his wife! In 1635 Old Parr was discovered in his home village by one of Charles I's earls, who took him to London to present him to the king. When asked the secret of his long life, Parr replied: 'Sire, I did penance when I was a hundred years old.' Sadly, he died a few weeks later, a victim of the diet of rich food and wine at the court and of the London pollution.

So there you have it. If you want a long life, save up your fornication sins till you're a hundred and then do penance for them.

And don't go to live in London.

The historian Eric Hobsbawn once developed a theory about what he called 'social banditry' to describe the activities of certain criminals who stole from, kidnapped or murdered the rich and divided the spoils out among their kin and friends. Robin Hood is the best known English example; in America, there was Billy the Kid, Jesse James, Pretty Boy Floyd and John Wesley Harding; in Australia there was Ned Kelly. All were popular in their day with the underprivileged and suppressed peoples of their areas, and they continue to hold a fascination for people nowadays. So, although all of these clearly lived outside the law, we seem to grant them a special status and regard them with a fascination that borders on affection.

Shropshire had its own social bandit, known as Humphrey Kynaston, and his activities in the late fifteenth and early sixteenth centuries occurred in the area around Montford Bridge which was my next stopping-off point.

But before I tell you about Humphrey, I need to tell you how we know so much about him. His exploits are recorded in a remarkable book that appeared in the early eighteenth century, entitled *The History of Myddle* and written by Richard Gough. Myddle is a tiny unremarkable village a few miles north of Montford Bridge and Richard Gough was churchwarden in the village church. For some reason known only to him he recorded the life of the village and its parishioners in such a way that we have a complete picture of village life in the seventeenth century. And what a picture it is! Our picture postcard view of the English village is shown to be a total sham. In this one tiny and otherwise insignificant village of 600 people in the middle of the county of Shropshire, hardly known for being a hotbed of criminality, Gough records ten murders, regular violence (often alcohol related), marriages and relationships forming and breaking up, many illegitimate children (including some of clergymen), and rampant venereal disease.

Some idyll!

Humphrey Kynaston, according to Gough, was the owner of Myddle Castle but 'for his dissolute and riotous living was called the Wild Humphrey'. He was found guilty of murder in 1491, whereupon he fled from his castle and holed up in a cave in Nesscliffe Rock, called to this day Kynaston's Cave. The same year Henry VII declared him an outlaw.

Kynaston's Cave is divided into two rooms by a strong pillar of the rock, on which is carved 'H K 1564'. One of these apartments was the stall of Humphrey's celebrated horse, which some to this day believe to have been the devil. This horse would climb up to the cave at its master's whistle, though it can't have been too happy with the way its horseshoes were put on in reverse in order to fool pursuers. Though he was a notorious robber and thief, Kynaston did appear to have some elementary sense of justice for he gave freely to the poor and was in return kept supplied with hay, corn and other necessities.

His most famous exploit, recorded by Gough, occurred at Montford Bridge, which then was made of wooden planks supported by stone pillars. The local Under Sheriff or PC Plod, learning that Kynaston was on the Shrewsbury side of the river and therefore had to cross the bridge to return to his Nesscliff cave, laid an ambush. The middle planks of the bridge were removed and Plod's men hid by the riverside, jumping out to arrest the robber on his return. Kynaston, on spotting the danger, 'put spurs to his horse, and riding full speed, leaped clearly over the breadth'. So popular was Wild Humphrey and so impressive this feat that the length of this leap was marked out by two stones on a nearby heath and Gough claims the stones were still there in his time, over 100 years later.

Montford Bridge is 4½ miles from Shrewsbury by road but about 14 miles by the River Severn, which takes a huge loop north from Montford Bridge. The Severn Way footpath avoids this loop and so did I, but, whereas the waymarked route goes through fields and by-roads to reach Shropshire's county town, I had decided to give this short stretch a miss and travelled into Shrewsbury in the comfort of my wife's car.

I don't know if Old Parr or Thomas Kynaston would have approved, but there it is. My feet were now too badly blistered by the 18 miles I had completed that day, my energy had sapped and I was looking forward to sleeping in my own bed.

It was time to call a halt to the first stage of my Dance with Sabrina after I had spent a little time in Shrewsbury.

8 Shrewsbury

If you enter Shrewsbury by road, you will see that it announces itself as 'The Town of Flowers' and you may well wonder why, so I'd better tell you.

You may think, if you're a television or radio gardening show addict, that it's something to do with the fact that Percy Thrower comes from Shrewsbury. After all, Percy was the first great superstar of gardening, the pre-cursor of Alan Titchmarch and Charlie Dimmock and their ilk. When television bosses decided that they could do a little better than show still photographs of blooming flowers, they hit upon the notion of having a real-life man-in-the-potting-shed to stand in front of said vegetation. So they invented a show with the catchy title *Gardening Club* and they chose none other than Shrewsbury's long-serving parks superintendent, Percy, to front it. That was in 1956 and it lasted for thirteen years, before being transformed, also with the great Percy at the helm, into the equally snazzy *Gardeners World* in 1969.

Percy Thrower is, to many people, the epitome of gardeners, fondly remembered in his cloth cap, with his weather-worn face and his soft borderland burr. He has a sweet pea named after him and a garden centre on the outskirts of Shrewsbury, which he founded but which is now run by his three daughters. Among his noteworthy achievements was the creation of the *Blue Peter* garden for the children's television programme – a garden subsequently vandalised by some drunken professional footballers. Poor old Percy got the sack from the BBC, however, because in 1976 he did the unthinkable and appeared in a television commercial for Garden Plus fertiliser, which meant, in those innocent days, that we might see him endorsing a product on ITV and then switch over to see him mulching on BBC.

Bad man, eh?

The main reason why Shrewsbury is known as 'The Town of Flowers' is because it hosts one of the longest-established flower shows in the country, which has been in operation for well over 100 years. For many of those years Percy Thrower was the horticultural adviser to Shrewsbury Flower Show which takes place every August in the remarkable sunken gardens known as The Dingle, laid out originally by our Percy, in the middle of the 29-acre Quarry Park. Here over 3 million flowers, nurtured and cherished by professional and amateur gardeners worldwide, are featured in glorious floral displays and are entered for various competitions to win cash awards and trophies, such as the Best Rose By Any Other Name Cup, the Greensleeves 'n' Greenfingers Trophy, the Home Compost-Maker of the Year Certificate (with free supply of soap), etc.

And it's not just about flowers and gardens. Oh no! Every year there is lots of fun for all the family too. So there's riders from the Household Cavalry conducting complicated drills whilst nodding their white-plumed helmets and playing musical instruments. And there's a high-wire act (this year featuring a gentleman with the stage name of Sponge Plunge – I can only guess at what he does), and show jumping and the Agile Dog of the Year competition and male voice choirs, and on and on. In fact, there's so much that you wonder what many of these acts have to do with a flower show.

Personally, although I care little for gardening, gardeners or Charlie Dimmock, I think it's time that Shrewsbury Flower Show went back to some of its old-fashioned intentions. What about a bit more advice on forcing rhubarb – a lost art nowadays – or digging runner-bean trenches or the most economical way of sowing parsnips? Those were the sort of skills Percy was good at and, mark my words, there'll come a time when we'll need his advice again.

Mind you, Percy would have been gobsmacked to learn that the Royal Shrewsbury Hospital recently tried to discourage visitors from bringing flowers, because the water in the vases was developing bacteria that posed dangers to patients' health.

And all this time we thought that people were already ill *before* they went to hospital!

Picture this, if you will.

Opposite Shrewsbury Castle and outside the public library stands a very curious statue. Its head is of your archetypal Victorian gentleman, heavily bearded and serious visaged, but the body is that of a great ape, its limbs bent as its hairy body crouches ready to leap into the nearest tree.

The statue is, of course, of Charles Darwin, Shrewsbury's most famous son, and I'm sorry to say that the statue looks nothing at all like the cartoon-like image I have just described.

It is in fact no better than your typical common-or-garden statue of a worthy gentleman. What an opportunity was missed by the city fathers when they commissioned Darwin's memorial! Instead of going for the tried and trusted, as they did, they could have set a world trend by getting something that represented the controversies that its subject was responsible for creating. For, make no mistake about it, Darwin's theory about the evolution of species and, in particular, the notion that great apes and human beings shared a common ancestor was as world-shaking an idea as Copernicus's revelation that the earth wasn't flat.

In fact, evolutionary theory is still controversial. In the past three years the legislatures of the American states of Kansas and Arkansas have attempted to ban the teaching of evolution from the school curriculum. According to these people, Darwin's theory is unproven and, worst of all, makes a mockery of the biblical explanation of God's creation of the universe. America seems to have become the home of every nutter in the world and these nutters seem to congregate in certain parts of the States to promulgate their daft ideas. One of the favourite ways of doing that is to start a cult and then to get all their followers to settle with them wherever the cult is sited, preferably building in a sub-clause that gives the cult founder shagging rights with all of the women. I don't wish to be insensitive to the feelings of those who died, but, if you were going to found a cult, wouldn't you find a home for it somewhere that didn't have a name like Waco?

And then there's the Moonies, the Branch Dravidians, the Garbage Eaters, Heaven's Gate and the Natural Law Party. And every town in America seems to have its own UFO-spotters club, on the look out for little green men who visit in the night and borrow tractors from the local farmer to make corn circles! What is it with these people? Maybe it's all Darwin's fault after all. Maybe, if he hadn't gone and seen those giant turtles in the Galapagos Islands, we'd all be living very happily with our beliefs in God and the Creation perfectly sound and untroubled, so we wouldn't need to have Americans inventing new cults every five minutes.

Poor old Charlie D., what would he make of it all now, over a hundred years later, and at the same time as the Genome Project is seemingly validating so much of what he meant?

The oddity is that Charlie sort of stumbled into a career as a scientist. His father, the good Doctor Darwin of Shrewsbury, wanted his son to follow in his footsteps so whisked him away to Edinburgh to study medicine. One look at blood pouring out of some patient's body was enough to put him off that career, so then he was enrolled at Cambridge to study theology in preparation for getting a nice little vicarage somewhere safe and secure in the Home Counties perhaps. There he took his preparation for the priesthood very seriously, spending most of his time boozing and playing cards – useful skills for vicaring! He also formed a Beetle Brigade with some of his friends and started collecting insects, which led him into friendship with the Professor of Botany – these sorts of relationships happened in Cambridge in those times. This, amazingly, led to his invitation to be the official naturalist on HMS *Beagle*'s South American survey, which set off in 1831. And the rest, as they say, is history!

One of the more unremarked features of Darwin's seminal book, *The Origin of Species*, is that it begins with remarks about pigeons. Not the sort that now squat and crap all over his statue but the racing variety – tumblers, pouters, turbits, Jacobins and so forth. It was the way that pigeon-fanciers chose particular characteristics in birds which they then bred selectively that Darwin was interested in. His evolutionary theory was developed from his explorations on the isolated islands of Galapagos but it was reinforced by his observations of more common-or-garden species. In fact, those fat birds sitting on his bronze head might be very interested to learn that they were near relations not only of the tumblers, pouters, etc. but also of the extinct pterodactyls. But would they care?

I think not. They're much more interested in the chip fragments in the corner of a sad MacDonald's box lying on the pavement.

Anyway, the rest of *The Origin of Species* is taken up with Darwin's theorising about evolution, based largely on his explorations and observations on that original voyage in the *Beagle*. And it's that theorising which has convinced everyone, apart from a few nutty Americans, that the world didn't suddenly spring into existence in 4004 BC but rather that it evolved over millions of years by the process of natural selection.

Shame about the statue though!

Shrewsbury is one of my favourite towns. Its heart nestles in a loop of the River Severn and, as Leland put it in his sixteenth-century journal, 'the River Severn encircles it to such an extent that were it not for a little neck of land it would be an island'. William Cobbett declared it 'one of the most interesting spots that man ever beheld', while Defoe found it 'a town of mirth and gallantry', noting also that its people 'speak all English in the town, but on a market-day you would think you were in Wales'. Its border position is pointed up by the names of its two main road bridges – Welsh Bridge on its western side, built to kick the boyos out, and English Bridge on its eastern side, built to facilitate the movements of the squirearchy.

It was wool that made Shrewsbury what it is, for its real development occurred between the fourteenth and sixteenth centuries when many of its citizens became extremely wealthy on the back of the wool and other allied trades. This was the period when the Merchant Guilds became most powerful, creating and controlling local markets, and it is in the home of one such merchant that the town museum is to be found in the middle of Shrewsbury. Thomas Rowley was a master draper and his black and white timbered home was typical of its period. There are still many old properties in the centre of town and, despite the new shopping malls that have been developed in recent years, there are still many byways and alleyways that remind you of the medieval shape of the town.

The Rowley House Museum tells the story of Shropshire's development over the aeons in a particularly attractive way. Prehistoric findings, such as iron axe heads and flint shavings, are shown in the context of the growing technological capability of our earliest ancestors. Another room houses large numbers of artefacts from Roman times, all from archaeological work at Viriconium a few miles down the river. These include remnants of iron tools and weapons, bead counters used in games, pieces of Samian pottery made in France and transported by boat up the Severn from Bristol, coins, bone and antler goods, and so much more. Finally, there is a display about the Merchant Guilds and the prosperity that built Shrewsbury.

One thing not on display in the museum, but one that future curators might consider ways of demonstrating, is the story of 'Cadman's Last Flight'. Robert Cadman was another of the madmen, like Humphrey Kynaston and Jack Mytton, of which

Shropshire seems to have an abundance. He was the daredevil Evil Knievel of his day, a steeplejack who performed a balancing act on ropes attached to high steeples. While working on the weathercock of St Mary's church in Shrewsbury in 1739, he arranged to run a rope from the church's bell-tower some 800 feet across the Severn to its opposite bank. His plan was to attach himself at the top of the bell-tower to a wooden breastplate with a groove in it which fitted over the rope and then slide down with his arms outstretched, thus giving the illusion of being in flight. He'd done this sort of thing before, of course, though not always successfully. On one occasion the church spire crumbled and Cadman fell into a tree. Undaunted, on 2 February 1739, he launched himself from St Mary's but, unfortunately, the rope snagged on the stonework and broke, and poor Cadman met his maker a bit earlier than he'd planned.

There must have been easier ways to earn a living, even then.

Another of Shrewsbury's noted citizens was Ellis Peters, the pen name of writer Edith Pargeter. Peters's most famous creation is the twelfth-century herbalist, Brother Cadfael, who is a kind of medieval Sherlock Holmes, solving the complex crimes of his time with the usual supernormal deductive powers that we expect of fictional private eyes. Cadfael operated out of Shrewsbury Abbey, which stands just beyond the riverbank and is still used for worship. The Cadfael mysteries captured the imagination of British television viewers a few years back when the eponymous hero was cleverly and amusingly portrayed by actor Derek Jacobi. Personally, I can't stand the stuff and that has nothing to do with the fact that I also write detective fiction and my Tallyforth Mysteries have been nowhere near as successful, despite being far better written and full of moving, suspenseful moments, of fascinating and larger than life characters, of real close to the bone contexts, and of remarkably subtle plots. Honest!

Anyway, believe me or not, it is Edith Pargeter who leads me into the next part of the story of Shrewsbury.

Every decent town on the Severn has to have a battle and Shrewsbury had one of the best. It was so good, in fact, that Shakespeare actually built one of his plays around it, making it the climax of his *Henry IV Part 1* (*Part 2* taking place somewhere else, of course). It was called, with startling originality, the Battle of Shrewsbury and it was fought on 21 July 1403. And it is Edith Pargeter who has given us a fictionalised account of it in her book *A Bloody Field by Shrewsbury*.

To take part in the Battle of Shrewsbury, you really had to be called Percy or Henry. Not Percy Thrower, mind you – just Percy. And Henry could be abbreviated to Harry or Hal.

Who was the fight between? Well, it was between Percy and Henry, of course. Northumbrian big shot Sir Henry Percy (this is where it starts to get tricky, so pay attention at the back) got a bit miffed over some land in Cumbria that he thought should be his, so he decided to head south and challenge the king, who was Henry IV (Part 1). Percy had hoped to get Owen Glendower (yes, him again) to join up with him but that didn't materialise because Owen was too busy practising to say Llanfairpwllgwyngyllgogerychwyrndrobwyll-llantisiliogogogoch, so he had to face the king on his own (well, with maybe 20,000 soldiers).

Enter, at this point, Hotspur. No, not the boys' comic I used to read under the blankets, and not some Fancy Dan footballer from Tottenham. This was the son of Sir Henry Percy who was also called Sir Henry Percy but, to avoid confusion, was better known as Harry Hotspur. He was the undisputed champion of the Percys and it was he who led his troops into battle against the much more numerous royalist forces of the king. The battle only lasted a few hours but in that time many thousands of men were killed – it was reputed to be one of the worst slaughters known. Hotspur's death inspired the collapse and defeat of the Percys and their army. His body was subsequently quartered, the quarters being displayed in Newcastle, London, Chester and York, just to prove he was dead.

Shakespeare, ever the storyteller, had his Hotspur killed in battle by the Prince of Wales, who also happened to be called Henry, though he was better known as Prince Hal. So in most people's memory, this has become the truth, although there is nothing in the historical sources that Shakespeare drew on that confirms or even suggests this. Poetic licence, it seems, was the Bard's excuse. Mind you, Shakespeare also made up a remarkably unbelievable companion for Prince Hal – Falstaff,who was later to claim (that is, in *Henry IV Part 2*) that he had personally dispatched Hotspur at the Battle of Shrewsbury.

To tell the truth, we really don't know much of the detail of this infamous battle. The accounts we do have are often contradictory and get supplemented by later chroniclers who claim to know more than the contemporary sources. The only indication now that the battle took place is on the sign outside the church of St Mary Magdalene in an area to the north of Shrewsbury known, curiously enough, as Battlefield. The church was built five years after the battle as a place of prayer for those killed in the battle and has been worshipped in for 600 years since then, though it is now redundant. A statue of Henry IV (minus some of his Parts because of erosion) is mounted on its wall.

So, there you have it. A gang of Percys and Henrys having a punch-up in the traditional way, forever immortalised because of the overactive mind of the millennium's greatest writer and commemorated in this tiny church.

It's enough to make you weep.

Shrewsbury School did not come about until some time later but it has had its fair share of luminaries passing through its gates. It is one of the older and more prestigious of Britain's public schools and still clings to some of those vestiges of antiquity. Its calendar, for instance, for some godforsaken reason known as Fasti, is dominated by those three pillars of the establishment – sport (rowing, fencing, football, cricket), church (communion, choir, New Boys' Service) and the military (Combined Cadet Corps, RAF careers visits). One of its most renowned headmasters was named Kennedy, whose Latin Primer was *the* book to have when I were a mere lad at school. Its most distinguished scholar was Charles Darwin, though he was pretty ordinary at school as we've already seen. But the scholars it should be most proud of are those who have been responsible for giving me a laugh every Friday morning throughout those dreadful Thatcher years when all the news seemed gloomy.

I'm talking, of course, about Richard Ingrams, Willie Rushton and Paul Foot – the founders of *Private Eye* magazine which has punctured the pompous and slagged off the sleazy since its birth at Oxford in 1960. Ingrams and Rushton were fellow pupils at Shrewsbury School and their satirical work began there when Ingrams had some funny verses published in the school magazine, accompanied by a drawing executed by Rushton. At Oxford, they were joined by another former pupil of the school, Paul Foot, in writing for a privately financed humorous pamphlet called *Parson's Pleasure* which they gradually came to run. This eventually turned into *Private Eye* which has continued to print stories that many other newspapers are afraid to print, together with cartoons, topical columns and other humorous material for over forty years. Regularly, *Private Eye* has been sued for libel and, just as regularly, it has lost these cases, its fines being paid by public subscriptions raised by appeal from its pages.

Some of the phrases coined in *Private Eye* have passed into common parlance over the years. The term 'pseud', for instance, for some writing of gross pretentiousness was invented originally by Ingrams while at Shrewsbury and then continued into the regular feature 'Pseuds' Corner' in the magazine. Two illustrations from an issue to hand make the point well:

> News of the World: Are you lonely now?
> Michael Jackson: Of course. It's part of what I have to go through to be the artist that I am. I have to paint with a palette of different emotions.

And:

> CREWE-READ. – On October 21st, in London, to EMMA (nee Garton) and DAVID, a son. Sacha John-Randulph Offley, a brother for Honey-Bee and half brother for Caspian, Daniel and Gabriella. Direct descendant of Henry de Criwa c.1150 and Lord Crewe of Crewe.

Then there is the equally famous 'Colemanballs', named after the *faux pas* sometimes deliciously delivered by BBC sports reporter David Coleman. Here's a couple of those, again from a recent edition:

> And he (Zidane) . . . will have a private pool, with a gardener thrown in.
>
> (Des Cahill, presenter on Irish Radio RTE 1)

> Arsenal could have got away with a nil-nil if it wasn't for the two goals.
>
> (Des Lynam, football commentator on ITV)

There is also the long-running joke which consists of two portrait photographs with some apparent likeness placed side by side on the page and an accompanying reader's letter which asks 'are the two related? I think we should be told'. For example, the two contra-posed portraits in a recent issue were of John Knox, a Scottish Presbyterian, and Osama Bin Laden, the Muslim terrorist.

Private Eye is accused by some of being too male and too public school in its humour. Well, I am male but I didn't go to a public school and it still makes me laugh. I love the way it punctures the famous – some of its strongest editions were when it satirised some of the silliness that was being spouted when Princess Di was killed in that Paris underpass. I love the way it gets to the heart of some of the gret and good -- exposing the unctuousness of Tony Blair, for instance, in its St Albion column or making the financier Sir James Goldsmith look even sillier after he had won a libel action against the magazine by calling the public appeal for money to pay the huge fine 'Goldenballs'.

I don't suppose Shrewsbury School will thank me for saying so but, out of all the bankers, city dealers, industrial magnates, civil service mandarins, colonial governors and clerics that it has produced, none has added so much to the joys of being alive as those reprobates who began their joking lives within its portals and went on to found and foster *Private Eye*.

And if that doesn't get me into 'Pseuds' Corner', I don't know what will!

9 Shrewsbury to Ironbridge

The second stage of my Dance with Sabrina began on a cloudy Monday morning at the English Bridge in Shrewsbury. Just opposite is Shrewsbury Town's Gay Meadow football ground – no, they're not the Football League's only homosexual club – and I thought of the late great Fred Davies. For much of history, the main means of transport on the River Severn was the coracle, a round-shaped construction consisting of a wooden framework over which was stretched an animal hide. Coracles were used by our Celtic ancestors for hundreds of years before the Romans arrived and, as they were driven back into Wales, their craft remained the most viable mechanism for navigating the river that became the boundary between the Roman settlers in England and their Celtic rivals in Wales. Fred Davies was left behind too, but found useful employment in his coracle by fetching footballs that had been kicked over the stand at Gay Meadow. He was a legend in his lifetime but, when he died in 1994, his coracle died with him. Nowadays two men with nets have to retrieve errant footballs.

As I followed the riverside towpath opposite and underneath the railway bridge on to the northern loop out of the town, I was trying to envisage this stretch of the Severn when it was in full spate as it had been the previous winter. There was a period of two or three days when, according to news reports, Shrewsbury itself was cut off as the brown river roared over its banks and over the flood defences. But it was impossible to envisage now, as the river glided gently on its way beside me.

My companion for the day was a poet named Steve Clarke, who is a friend and was keen to stretch his legs for a day's activity. My journey hitherto had been accomplished alone, apart from the first day's climb to the source, so the addition of another person changed the shape of what I was doing. Inevitably, Steve wanted to know about the first week of my trip through Wales and, just as inevitably, I wanted to tell him the tales that are at the heart of my book so far. So the first part of our journey was spent in such chit-chat, to the extent that I noticed very little after passing under the railway until we came opposite the small hamlet of Uffington.

Here I paused our conversation to point out to Steve that another poet had lived here in the early years of the twentieth century – Wilfred Owen, who was born a few miles north of here in Oswestry but spent his adolescent years in nearby Monkmoor, now a suburb of Shrewsbury. With his family, Owen would use the now defunct ferry to cross the Severn just here in order to attend the village church in Uffington and would frequently stroll along the banks of the Severn.

'Do you remember that poem about "bugles calling for them from sad shires"?' I asked.

'No, sorry,' Steve answered.

'I think it was *Anthem for Doomed Youth*,' I continued, searching in my memory. 'I think it goes something like this:

> What passing-bells for those who die as cattle?
> Only the monstrous anger of the guns.
> Only the stuttering rifles' rapid rattle
> Can patter out their hasty orisons.
> No mockeries for them from prayers or bells,
> Nor any voice of mourning save the choirs, –
> The shrill demented choirs of wailing shells;
> And bugles calling for them from sad shires.'

Of course, I didn't remember all of this at all, never mind declaim it on the riverbank! But one of the pleasures of being a writer is that you can look things up later and incorporate them into the dialogue you write. In reality, all I remembered was the line I recalled initially, about the 'sad shires'.

'He must have been thinking about all this,' I said, waving my arm in an expansive gesture. 'Before motorways and trunk roads and all the noise they bring, this would have been countryside. This would have been part of a "sad shire". This is where he would have imagined those bugles blowing.'

Steve nodded. What else could he do?

So we pressed on, past a sign that said 'BULL IN FIELD' and into said field where six placid-looking cows sat chewing the cud, as they're supposed to do.

'I was chased by bulls last week,' I told Steve, filling out the story of my lucky escape. 'But those aren't bulls, are they?'

'You're supposed to make yourself big,' Steve told me, stretching out his arms to demonstrate. 'Cows don't take any notice.'

As if to disprove his theory, one of the cows started getting to its feet at this gesture of Steve's and our pace quickened until we were within a few feet of the next stile, beyond which were several fields of pigs.

'OK, which one's Napoleon?' Steve quipped merrily, his spirits lifted by our escape from the cows/bull.

That also wasn't a very clever thing to say because suddenly, as if at a signal, several of the largest pigs started sprinting in our direction. When I say sprinting, I mean wobbling quickly, like large lumps of animated pastry. But they were definitely heading in our direction.

'Is it us that's disturbed them?' Steve asked incredulously. 'What did I do?'

I wanted to tell him he shouldn't have mentioned Napoleon but I wanted rather more to get beyond the possible reach of these lardy monsters, so I saved my breath to run for the next stile, leaving him talking to a non-existent companion.

And that was really the main adventure of our morning. Soon we were away from the river-bank footpath and on the road into Atcham, crossing the twentieth-century bridge which runs parallel to the lovely arched bridge built in 1770 by John Gwynne, the Shrewsbury architect who also designed the well-known Magdalen Bridge in Oxford. Here we paused for a beer at the Mermaid Hotel. This was once known as the Mytton and Mermaid after the notorious Jack Mytton, who lived a rip-roaring life in the early years of the nineteenth century. Mytton was a rich man's son who was expelled from Westminster and Harrow, was kicked out of the army for obsessive gambling, drove a two-horse carriage at night full tilt across fields for a bet, picked fights at the drop of a hat, stole from dinner guests by posing as a highwayman when they returned home, regularly drank six bottles of port a day and died in prison, mistaking a container of boot polish for alcoholic drink.

You can see why the owners of the Mermaid did not wish to continue the hotel's association with Mad Jack.

Though I do have to say that the beer we had there did not taste of boot polish at all. Quite the opposite, in fact. It satisfied our thirst very nicely and sent us on our way to nearby Wroxeter even more garrulous.

If you reach Wroxeter on a hot day, you can look forward to cooling off in the Roman baths there. Or, at least, you could have done several centuries ago when the city, then known as Viroconium, was the fourth largest in the land after London, Cirencester and St Albans. Why build a large city in the middle of rural Shropshire? Because the Romans, like every other bunch that invaded Britain and set about colonising it, had trouble with the Welsh and so they had to keep troops at the western edge of their empire to keep the boyos back within their Celtic fringes. The site of Viroconium was conveniently close to a ford in the Severn and even closer to the A5, which of course in those days was known as Watling Street, after Julius Augustus Watling its builder (not really).

The site also gives a commanding view of the surrounding

territory, lying as it does in the middle of the floodplain with the surrounding hills jutting suddenly upwards. Several of these hills had Iron Age hill forts, the closest being that huge lump now known as The Wrekin, which is believed to share its progenitor with Viroconium. Both, supposedly, stem from the overlord known as Virico, leader of the Celtic tribe of the Cornovii.

The town was developed by the Romans in the first century and became the base for the Twentieth Legion (or Legio XX, as they preferred to be known). The Twentieth Legion was one of the Roman army's crack outfits when it came to a punch-up. They helped to put down Boadicea and they finished off Caractacus, or so it's said. Believe it or not, there's a modern gang in Washington, DC, who call themselves Legio XX. They dress up in fancy togas and helmets and all that sort of Roman stuff, and they have gatherings where they spout Latin at each other and admire each other's nifty togs (and togas). They even produce a *Handbook for Legionnaries*, just to make sure everyone stays in line!

Anyway, by the following century Viroconium had become an established town, ready to welcome the Emperor Hadrian who popped in, like royalty still do today, on his way to do a spot of wall-building in the north. The local Roman worthies organised a huge inscribed stone to mark Hadrian's visit but you can't see that at Wroxeter – it's kept in the Shrewsbury Museum.

Once the Welsh were hammered back, Wroxeter became a retirement home for ex-legionaries. One of these, called Mansuetus, left a fragment of his discharge certificate buried in the ground, awarding him with Roman citizenship after twenty-five years' service in the Roman army. One of the errors we sometimes make in thinking about the amazingly effective Roman army is to assume that it derived its sense of purpose from being Roman. Of course, when you think about it, the birth rate in Rome would have had to be remarkably high to service that kind of exponential growth over the centuries. No, what happened was that many soldiers were taken on from conquered territories and trained in the disciplines of Rome. This particular soldier, Mansuetus, was originally a Dalmatian – not one of the Hundred and One doggie type, but a man from that strip along the Adriatic coast which was known to the Romans as Dalmatia. He had served on Hadrian's Wall before retiring to Wroxeter where, presumably, he settled with a local woman and added his Dalmatian seed to the genetic pool. It's ironic that today he would probably have been regarded as a bogus asylum seeker and a social security scrounger, for Dalmatia is what we now call Croatia and many of its modern people have been forced to flee their homeland because of the internecine strife there.

Anyway back to the bathhouse, which is now, of course, nowt but a ruin. The site of the public baths is the only bit left of what once would have been a 2-mile wide town but don't let that disappoint you if you want to visit. For the bathhouse was central to the social life of the Romans. People went to the baths, not just to get clean but also to meet their mates, to take exercise and to play games. And, just like their modern golfing counterparts, they were not averse to using this social occasion as an excuse to do a little bit of, you know, 'I can offer you 10 per cent off this new Samian pottery – it's the next big thing'.

So, once we'd paid our money to the nice lady from English Heritage and collected our handset with its tape to guide us around the site, we followed this excellent guide. Pretty soon we were standing in front of that huge piece of masonry – one of the largest free-standing remnants of Roman Britain – that is known as The Old Work. Through it we could see displayed in front of us the remains of all the appurtenances of the Roman bathhouse – the changing rooms, the underfloor heating system, the sauna room, the cold plunge bath room and so forth.

I thought about Mansuetus, our poor old Dalmatian, going about his business therein. What would he have made of it all? Okay, so he might have had to do a lot of marching along Roman roads, he might have had to fight off a few Picts suffering from woad rage on Hadrian's Wall and he might be a long way from the Adriatic, but, what the hell! He was clean and well fed. He'd got his Roman citizenship now. And he could look forward to sitting down with a glass of Chianti and watching that new *Gladiator* video that he'd bought earlier from the market.

Mind you, I hope he hadn't read the scathing review in the Legio XX newsletter!

From Wroxeter the Severn Way leads by a country road to Eyton on Severn and then across fields where once a year there is a point-to-point horse racing meet. Two hurdles leaning into the hedge were the only evidence of this, for of course there had been no meet this year due to the foot-and-mouth problem. Steve had left me at Wroxeter so I was on my own again as I marched on through the village of Cressage, where St Augustine supposedly preached to the Welsh bishops in 584, and, with the towers of Ironbridge Power Station looming in the near distance, on to a muddy footpath through a coppice and out on to a main road to cross Buildwas Bridge.

Just up from the Severn here are the remains of the Cistercian Buildwas Abbey, which shares its structures between English Heritage, who manage the tourist bit in the roofless abbey, and TXU Europe, who manage the nearby power station from the connecting former infirmary and abbot's lodging. And there is another curious connection, which will be revealed shortly.

First, though, the abbey, which nestles in its serene woodland setting probably pretty much as it has since its foundation in 1135. The Cistercians were White Monks who broke away from their Benedictine brothers because they'd had enough of that God-awful sticky Benedictine and fancied a quiet life in the woods. They certainly found that here at Buildwas, and the abbey had a virtually uneventful existence until Henry VIII's dissolution of the monasteries in 1536. The only really interesting moment in its life was when one of its abbots was murdered, allegedly by a rebel monk called Thomas Tonge. This led to a spot of bother because they could not agree on a successor to the murdered abbot, so they had to manage without for a few years.

Tough life, eh!

During this period, a new monk arrived at the abbey who was assigned to help the other monks in copying the old texts by hand. He noticed, however, that they were copying from copies, not the original manuscripts. So he went to the oldest monk and pointed out that, if there were an error in the first copy, that error would be continued in all of the other copies.

'We have been copying from the copies for centuries, but you make a good point, my son,' the oldest monk said and he went down into the cellar with one of the copies to check it against the original.

Hours passed and nobody saw him. Then one of the other monks went to look for him. He heard sobbing coming from the back of the cellar, and found the old monk leaning over one of the original books crying. He asked the old monk what was wrong, and in a choked voice came the reply:

'The word is celebrate.'

Now that's an appropriate moment to point out that the Abbey's founder was one Roger de Clinton. Yes, that name rings a bell, doesn't it? For Roger Clinton is the brother of ex-President of the US of A., Slick Willy Clinton, who also mistook the word 'celibate' for 'celebrate' – many times over. And good old Roger is still under investigation by the FBI or the CIA, or one of those gangs in raincoats and trilbies, for allegedly selling pardons, which his brother granted in the final days of his presidency. You see? The selling of pardons was not restricted to medieval monks.

And that brings me on to the curious connection between Buildwas Abbey and its neighbour, Ironbridge Power Station.

TXU Europe, which in these days of globalisation owns the power station, is a branch of TXU, one of the world's top ten energy producers. TXU started life as Dallas Power and Light but under the entrepreneurial leadership of its chief executive, Erle Nye, has grown and grown. TXU's growth has been helped enormously by the deregulatory legislation enacted in Texas under the governorship of guess who? Yep, good ole George 'Dubya' Bush himself. So you won't be shocked to discover that one of Dubya's main financial backers on his way to the Presidency was none other than Erle Nye himself. And now you won't be too surprised to know why Dubya is not specially interested in cleaning up the environment and reducing global warming.

So I was reminded of the dodginess of humans as I gazed in wonder at the glorious shell of Buildwas Abbey with its beautiful curving arches and over my shoulder I could see the smoke belching out of the coal-fired Ironbridge Power Station.

Who would have believed that two dodgy American presidents would be the presiding geniuses of this hallowed spot?

It was only another mile or so from Buildwas to Ironbridge, which was to be the end of my journey for that day. By now I had rejoined the river bank, passing through mature woodland with the cooling towers looming ever closer on the opposite side of the Severn. A riverside park, filled with gorgeous blooming flower beds, took me finally into the town of Ironbridge itself, where Abraham Darby's cast-iron bridge dominates the scene. On a previous visit I had noted a public house that I thought looked interesting, known as the Tontine Hotel, so I passed several others which promised real ale and real food, and various other enticements, in order to get to the pub of my choice, which is situated right opposite the iron bridge itself.

This was one of my biggest mistakes. Not because of the interior decor of the Tontine, which is an appropriate reconstruction of what some pub designer thought inns of that era looked like. No, I'm used to all this and on this occasion, at least, I had no quarrel with it. The source of my complaint was the service, which the hotel's advertising bumf misleadingly called 'warm and friendly'.

I should have been warned when the youngish woman with a tattoo who served me my pint of Banks's bitter had difficulty opening the till.

'He'll be back in a minute,' she told me. 'Only he's just had to nip out to fetch something. I'll bring you your change then. It'll be all right. I won't forget.'

Fair enough, I thought, though I did wonder momentarily why she had been left in charge when she clearly didn't have a clue as to how the till worked.

'Can I order a sandwich then?' I asked, taking a welcome draught of beer.

'Yes, of course,' she answered. 'Can you come through to the other counter?'

Now the 'other counter' was actually the opposite end of the same counter she had served my beer from. I suppose it's quite possible, indeed likely, that at one time there were two different rooms here, each with its own separate bar. But, even if that were true once, it certainly was not true now and this tattooed lady was far too young to have known the Tontine Hotel in those days.

Still, never one to knowingly cause trouble, I carried my rucksack, my glass of beer and my weary body to the other end of the bar and ordered a prawn sandwich. For this second week of my Dance with Sabrina I was returning home each evening because of its proximity and on this Monday I had arranged for a friend to collect me and drive me home, where I planned to have something more substantial to eat later.

Forty-five minutes later, as my second pint was nearly finished, my sandwich had still not arrived. Four elderly tourists from Hampshire (I heard them say as much, in case you're wondering) who had arrived after me had meanwhile been served with plaice and chips. Two middle-aged local men in suits discussing business, who had also arrived after me, had been served with steak and kidney pie and chips. I had been served with nothing.

'Excuse me,' I called out to the tattooed lady as she placed the pie and chip dishes in front of the businessmen. 'Have you forgotten my sandwich?'

'No,' she assured me, trying to win me round with a cheesy grin. 'I've been rushed off my feet.'

'Rushed off your feet? Rushed off your feet? You mean to tell me it takes longer to make a bloody prawn sandwich than it does to make cooked meals? You've served six people before me and they all got here after me. What's going on? I demand to see the manager. I've a good mind to report you to the Ironbridge Tourist Police. It's bloody disgraceful, that's what it is.'

Of course, I didn't actually say any of that. I merely said, 'Oh', and then thanked her effusively when she arrived two minutes later with my delicious and long-awaited sandwich.

But I won't be going to the Tontine Hotel again, believe me. And, if you're ever in the area, think twice about going there yourself. Unless, of course, you want the plaice and chips.

10 Ironbridge

There's not many who would make a connection between the birth of industry and an attack of delirium tremens but, believe me, in Ironbridge that connection is alive and kicking. Everybody knows that Abraham Darby was the first person in the world to discover how to smelt iron with coke instead of the traditionally used charcoal, and that he did this in 1709 in his Coalbrookdale Works, thus setting off the growth of modern industry and the way our world is now. What you may not know is that there is a school named after the famed iron-founder in Ironbridge and this school is known colloquially as AbDabs. Now, from extensive research, I am able to inform you that the phrase 'screaming abdabs' arose in the 1930s as a slang expression for someone having a fit of delirium tremens.

See the link?

Anyway, Abraham Darby, or AbDab 1 as I prefer to call him, came to Coalbrookdale, as the area was then known, after serving his apprenticeship in Birmingham and then becoming a partner in a brassworks in Bristol. His father was a locksmith in the Black Country town of Dudley, so young AbDab 1 had knowledge of working with iron from a very early age. He would have become aware that the old method of using charcoal for the fires that smelted the iron out of the ironstone was destroying the natural woodlands of the country. As there became greater and greater demand for ironware products, he would not have been the only person scratching around for a solution. Quite where he got his brainwave from we'll never know, but he did it.

You can see the furnace where AbDab 1 first succeeded in smelting iron in this way at the Museum of Iron, a short distance uphill from the Severn. The museum, housed in what was once a company warehouse, tells the story of the discovery and of the later developments of the Coalbrookdale Works, but the remains of the furnace itself were re-excavated in the middle of the twentieth century and are now protected inside a spectacularly lit glass-fronted structure at the opposite end of the museum car park. When you stand inside, gazing at those bricks, think how so much of what we take for granted in our lives today arose because of what AbDab 1 discovered all those years ago.

I tried very hard to understand the process of iron-smelting while I was there. I read all the signage, double-checked in my guidebook, peered at the brick construction, and practised saying 'pig iron' and 'tuyère pipe' and 'slag' and 'tap hole' but somehow they just refused to make any real sense to me. I had to make do with my awe and wonder. And, trust me, they were genuine.

The reason why I have been referring to the great iron-founder as AbDab 1 is because, as you have almost certainly guessed, there were several other AbDabs, as was the way in those days. His son, AbDab 2, took over the Coalbrookdale Works in 1745 and expanded it further by opening new foundries in the valley and linking the mines where the iron ore was extracted to the factories with a network of wooden and later iron railways.

But it is *his* son, AbDab 3, that I really want to focus on here because it was he that was responsible for the iron bridge from which the modern town takes its name. This construction was one of the wonders of its age and it is still a highly impressive piece of engineering.

So why was it built in the first place? Well, as I've mentioned elsewhere, the River Severn is mighty unreliable because of its fluctuating heights – in summer it was often too shallow for deep-draughted boats to sail on it, in winter it was too fast and too high. As the growth of industrial activity in the

Coalbrookdale area hastened, there was a need for a more reliable way of carrying raw materials and finished goods across the river. AbDab 3 was the man chosen to solve the problem. The bridge was the first in the world made of cast iron. No one knows exactly where it was cast but the likelihood is that it was in that Old Furnace in Darby's Coalbrookdale Works whose remnants still stand. It consisted of 378 tons of iron and it opened on New Year's Day 1781.

People came, and still do come, from all over the world to marvel at the construction – among these were French and Swedish spies (Inspector Clouseau and Sven-Goran Eriksson), German engineers (Werner von Braun, VW Beetle), an American paper-maker (Rupert Murdoch), a Venetian count (Iago) and a Polish princess (Cherry Blossomov). The bridge became an essential stopping point on the grand tour undertaken by the rich and seriously idle. Artists flocked to paint it.

Mind you, there were doubters who thought it wouldn't withstand severe weather but they were proved wrong when the Severn flooded in 1795 to the greatest height that has ever been recorded of 29 feet and 3 inches above normal. Virtually all other bridges in Shropshire were swept away or badly damaged but the Iron Bridge survived. It has had to be strengthened several times since then and was closed to vehicular traffic in 1934 but you can still walk across it to this day, pausing midway to gaze in wonder before taking in the fascinating story of its construction in the old toll house on the bridge's far side.

It is still a wondrous construction to behold – a perfect semi-circle with a spider's web of struts and girders whose other half is reflected in Sabrina's water to make a full globe. At its mid-point the bridge is 40 feet above the normal water level which meant that sailing barges could pass easily beneath it. And this mattered because, of the 400 barges trading on the Severn between Gloucester and Welshpool, a third of them were owned by men of the Ironbridge Gorge. This was serious industry. It has been reckoned that in the eighteenth century in the 1½-mile radius from the bridge there was more industry than in any other part of the world. A panorama of the district displayed in the Museum of the Gorge at the riverside just a short way down from the bridge shows lime kilns, limestone quarries, ironworks, brickworks, ironstone mines, furnaces, potteries, inclined planes, boatyards, lead smelters and any other manner of industry you care to think of.

And now?

Well, of course, the industry has all gone and the whole gorge area has been named a World Heritage Site, deservedly so, for it contains so much evidence of our industrial beginnings. There are nine museums within the 6 square miles and an imaginative scheme allows you to buy a passport ticket for £10 which allows you to visit all of these museums any time you want to. So you don't have to try to do them all in one day.

You can pause to have a nice cup of coffee in one of the museum cafés and count your AbDabs, then come back another day!

In one of those museums, the Museum of the Gorge, there is a small display devoted to Captain Matthew Webb who I first came across when, as a boy, I used to collect matchboxes. I remember well that image printed on the matchbox of a handsome man with a large moustache. I can even remember why he was so famous, so presumably there must have been a legend printed beneath his image, because the exploit for which he will always be remembered occurred long before I was born.

Captain Webb was the first man to swim the English Channel. He learned to swim as a boy in the River Severn at Ironbridge, and no doubt people might have watched him from the bridge in his early efforts. Born in 1848, Webb enlisted in the navy at a young age and rose through the ranks, though it's not absolutely clear whether he actually reached the rank of captain or whether this was the title he gave himself when he left the navy to pursue a new career as a professional endurance swimmer. After successfully completing several shorter passages, Webb announced to the world that he was going for the big one – the English Channel. On 24 August 1875, smeared in porpoise oil for insulation and wearing a pair of scarlet silk knickers, he dived off the pier at Dover. Twenty-one hours and forty-five minutes later he waded ashore at Calais, accompanied by the singing of *Rule Britannia* from passengers on an outgoing mail-ship. He had swum 39 sea miles and, so legend has it, sustained himself with coffee, beer and steaks provided by his support boat.

When he returned to Dover by boat the next day, he was greeted as a hero by an adoring crowd and by the Mayor of Dover. The *Daily Telegraph* proclaimed him 'probably the best-known and most popular man in the world' while the *New York Times* reported that 'London baths are crowded, each village pond and running stream contains youthful worshippers at the shrine of Webb'. A testimonial fund raised £2500, which would have set him up for life if he hadn't been such a spendthrift.

After that, Webb turned himself into a travelling freak show. He won large sums of money in America by completing long-distance swims and by remaining afloat in a tank of water for extraordinarily long periods of time. This was an age of freak shows and, when the circus star Blondin completed a tightrope walk across the Niagara Falls, Webb decided to go for one last money-making wheeze. He announced that he would swim under and across Niagara Falls, straight through the fearsome whirlpool in its centre.

So, in July 1883, wearing the same scarlet silk knickers and surrounded by a crowd of thousands who had paid to watch, he dived into the swirling water. Sadly, he was instantly caught in the current and within minutes was dragged under and drowned. His body was washed up 4 miles downstream.

Matthew Webb is still a hero in Ironbridge and Coalbrookdale, where a memorial was built to him in the early 1900s. Its simple inscription says, 'Nothing great is easy'.

People still do daft things to get noticed. The *Guinness Book of Records* is full of them. There's a man in Germany who has cycled over 40 miles backwards while playing a violin. There's an Englishman who has balanced 95 milk crates on his head. There's an American woman who has spun 82 hula hoops simultaneously for three complete revolutions. There's an Austrian who has done 101 press-ups with his hands placed on raw eggs. And there are two Israelis who have the record for the world's longest kiss, of 30¾ hours.

Nothing great is easy indeed!

What is the matter with these people?

In the Museum of Iron (which I keep wanting to rename the Museum of Irony so that I can store some witticisms for future adoration), there is a display entitled 'The Great Exhibition'. This tells of the 1851 London exhibition of that name at which the original Crystal Palace was built and for which the Coalbrookdale Works made, amongst many other pieces of ironwork, the Coalbrookdale Gate that still stands near the Albert Memorial in Kensington Gardens. By this time the Coalbrookdale Company was a huge enterprise, producing masses of staircases, garden furniture, statues, balconies, balustrades and so on, but it is important to remember that the original products for which it initially was known were articles for the kitchen.

So it is appropriate that on the same floor as the displays about the Great Exhibition is another display, wittily entitled 'The Grate Exhibition' and showing a number of cast-iron black fire-grates designed by the Coalbrookdale Company. Everyone of a certain age will recognise these, as they were the standard fitting for generations of houses in the late nineteenth and early twentieth centuries. What is not so well known is that the link with fire-grates has continued to this day. The company, which is still operating in the Coalbrookdale Works area, is nowadays responsible for producing the Aga stove, which is now available in a choice of nine beautiful vitreous enamel colours including cream, British racing green, dark blue, royal blue, claret, pewter, golden yellow and sable.

The Aga Saga began in Sweden, curiously enough. Its inventor was Gustav Dalen, who won the Nobel Physics Prize for his work on lighthouse technology, before turning to the creation of a new, user-friendly cooking range on which his wife could cook his favourite meatballs and Ryvita. It was introduced into Britain in 1929 and became an instant hit with middle-aged, middle-class novelists, who have continued ever since to use it as the centrepiece for their novels of the lives and loves of their middle-aged, middle-class readers. Initially it was powered by solid fuel but by the 1960s gas Agas were available, followed in the 1980s by electric models.

There is an irony (Exhibit A in my new museum) about the Aga, in that this most quintessentially English of cookers should have been invented by a Swede. And there is another irony (Exhibit B) in that the Aga is regarded as a major status symbol in America. So much so, that a woman called Bonnie Fleming organises an annual Aga Expedition. She brings a party of fellow-American Aga-nuts (it sounds as if she ought to be married to someone called Jason, doesn't it?) to Britain for cooking demonstrations and to see the cookers being made at Coalbrookdale.

Does this sound like a dream holiday to you?

Me neither.

The AbDabs were well-known Quakers, so they didn't have much truck with organised religion. I bet they'd be amused to learn that there is a business in modern Ironbridge which sells cassocks for priests. One of their latest designs contains a special secret pocket in which priests can stash their mobile phones, so they can always be in touch with their Maker even when they are preaching.

The other major retail opportunity in Ironbridge is for Teddy Bear selling. There is a shop opposite the iron bridge itself, called Bears on the Square, and further away near the riverside there is a factory called Merrythought, which manufactures Teddy Bears and claims to be one of England's oldest toymakers, having been founded as long ago as 1930. If you're really interested (which I'm not) the company will tell you about its history, how it moved from hand-stuffing each toy to machine-stuffing, how every Teddy Bear is unique and uniquely made, and how its chief designer gets her inspiration.

Can you tell me of anywhere else that can (and does) boast of two independent Teddy Bear shops? It's just not right, is it? To my mind it's all part of that dumbing down of Ironbridge that has occurred as it has been turned into a centre for tourism. As I've already pointed out, the museums are splendid and access to them is reasonably priced. The bridge itself is magnificent and worth the visit on its own. But Ironbridge, which once used to be ablaze with manufacture and industry is now just like something off the front of a chocolate box. It's almost like a theme park in some ways. Apart from the Teddy Bear shops, there are loads of others selling tourist tat, such as cheap plastic models of the bridge, keyrings, pencils, penknives, calendars, jars of honey etc. Then there are the catering establishments that promise you cream teas, which has never been a Shropshire delicacy.

In short, I was rather disappointed with the modern Ironbridge. It's not somewhere you'd choose to go for a night out or for a day's shopping. The character that it must have once had has disappeared. What's left is a sham really. It's a pity, because its place in history is central to our understanding of life nowadays.

I think they should open that Museum of Irony after all.

11 Ironbridge to Bridgnorth

Next day my wife dropped me off in Ironbridge and I rejoined the Severn Way across the bridge where the path leads out on the western bank of the Severn past the old railway station. My route for the day was to take me alongside the river all the way to my home town of Bridgnorth but en route I was to have time in two more of the Ironbridge museums.

The Ironbridge Gorge was created after the last ice age some 15,000 years ago when a huge lake overflowed east of the Welsh mountains and carved a deep chasm through layers of coal, iron ore, clay and limestone. It was these extensive raw materials that led to the area becoming the birthplace of modern industry. If iron ore had been the theme of my time in Ironbridge, it was clay that was to dominate this day. The first stop on my day's journey was to be at a factory where clay had been the main source of wealth creation.

The Jackfield Tile Museum tells the story of how this tiny hamlet was for a brief period in Victorian times the centre of the world's greatest decorative tile industry. Wow, I can hear you saying already, so this is where the action really starts! Now you would be correct in assuming that I had never previously discovered an uncontrollable urge in myself to explore the wonderful world of tiles. In fact, I was more likely to adopt a glazed expression – pardon the pun, I was thinking of the Museum of Irony again – than to rush hotfoot into the Jackfield Tile Museum. But I had my Ironbridge Museums Tourist Pass, I knew I could use it whenever I fancied and, so, I thought I would.

Last of the great adventurers, eh?

I have to say that this museum, housed in what used to be

one of two great tile manufacturers' factories of the Gorge, is absolutely fascinating. There's no special route around the museum, no all-singing, all-dancing, interactive displays, no computer simulations to demonstrate urine splashing against porcelain tiles. There are just miles and miles of tiles.

First, there's the restored Trade Showroom, as it looked when the Craven Dunnill factory in which the Tile Museum is now housed was at its prime. Here, on the walls and in old-fashioned display cases, are hundreds of those tiles manufactured here at the time of the great Victorian tile boom. It's impossible to give you more than a small flavour of these but one of the things that the tile designers discovered to be particularly attractive on tiles was the curved line. So the overwhelming impression is of graceful curves and flowing twirls in every colour of the rainbow.

Just beyond the restored Director's office there is a lavishly tiled washroom and toilet, presumably for the exclusive use of that same Director (where some trendy museum curator might well have placed a computer simulation). And then there are more fascinating examples of the tiler's art from Craven Dunnill and from its neighbour, Maws, whose factory was just a short distance down the valley. Until you see all these, you forget the uses to which tiles have been put – shop and pub frontages, Turkish baths, the side panels of fire-grates, desktops, walls and floors, for instance. Popular designs in Victorian times included birds and flowers, portraits, landscapes, and motifs from classical literature.

My favourites, though, were the large tile mosaics made for the children's wards of hospitals, featuring nursery rhyme characters such as a beaming Humpty Dumpty, a wizened Old King Cole with his three dancing fiddlers, a plump Queen of Hearts baking her tarts while the Knave eyes them greedily through a window. I also loved the Rochdale Pigs – three distinctly piggy heads in green made in the 1920s for a Rochdale butcher's shop. But the pièce de résistance has to be the wonderful North Eastern Railway map, commissioned in the late nineteenth century for display in the fourteen major stations of that railway company. You need to go to York railway station to see a complete version of this, but the incomplete one here gives you a fine impression of how it looks.

Fashions come and go, as they're meant to by the fashion police who make their living out of our ever-changing tastes, and the world somehow lost interest in highly decorated tiles some time after the Second World War. The Maws factory became a craft centre but the Craven Dunnill factory eventually closed before being rescued by the Ironbridge Trust. The Jackfield Museum is a worthy member of the Ironbridge clan, as it reminds you once again of the amazing range of important industries once existing in this tiny area.

Back on the Severn Way I followed the track down to the Boat Inn by the river where a black door marks the various floods recorded there. Top of the list is the 19 feet and 6 inches height of the floodwater that arrived on 1 November 2000. That mark is about 1 inch below the top of the door and shows that the whole ground floor of the Boat Inn must have been under water at that time, causing some discomfort to the local darts players I imagine. Opposite the Boat Inn is the Jackfield Memorial footbridge which was refurbished with lottery money and reopened in 2000, some time before the flood. It's an attractive green-painted metal construction and I took a slight detour from my journey to cross it in order to reach the second objective of my day.

Clay was still my theme, of course, for my next port of call was the Coalport China Museum on the opposite bank of the river. There had been potters and potteries in the Ironbridge Gorge area for many years before Abraham Darby (AbDab 3), the builder of the iron bridge, sold the land that is now Coalport to his brother-in-law, Richard Reynolds, whose son William built houses, warehouses and wharves on that land. The major industry was china manufacture at the Coalport China Company's factory which opened in 1796 and continued to produce high-quality china goods until 1925.

If you are of a certain generation, you will remember one of the first television panel game shows, *What's My Line?* It featured four panellists – grumpy Gilbert Harding, bubbly Barbara Kelly, bald-headed magician David Nixon and faded aristocrat Lady Isobel Barnett. Their task was to guess the occupation of a succession of guests by interrogating them about a mime that they did to illustrate their job. The most famous occupation, at least as far as I can recall, was that of saggarmaker's bottom-knocker and it is at the Coalport China Museum that you can discover what this job entailed.

The extensive museum explains all the processes involved in the making and decorating of chinaware and this is where you will discover the role of the saggarmaker's bottom-knocker. Saggars were rounded fireclay containers into which chinaware items were placed to protect them while they were being fired in the kilns. The bottom-maker's job was to beat the marl into an iron ring to form the base of the saggar.

Easy, eh?

Now I've no intention of boring you with descriptions of the range of china made at Coalport, mainly because I'm not especially interested in it. Yes, I know some of it is infinitely beautiful in its design, I know that the intricacies of painting must have required endless patience and I know that Coalbrookdale china is a very expensive collector's item nowadays. But either you like this stuff or you don't, and I'm just a Philistine on this matter.

Sorry, but if you're a real china fan, go and see for yourself. What I will tell you, because it amused me, is that the central process in china-making is design. Consequently, the Art Director is the most important member of staff. From 1899 to 1932 this post was held by one Thomas John Bott, as a result of which the Coalport Pottery became the Coalport Bottery.

Well, it would have done if I'd been around!

I will also point out that there is a fantastic Children's Gallery at Coalport where kids can disport themselves in a bouncy kiln, stacking their plastic saggars. There are also opportunities for dressing up in clothes of the period, for crayoning their own plate designs, and many other active models can be explored. On one wall there is a grainy black and white picture of youngsters working in the factory, with a chilling reminder that says: 'Young children worked at the Coalport China Works. Many worked for 12 hours a day, 6 days a week. Some did not go to school.'

It does rather put to shame that Thatcher-led idolisation of the Victorians, doesn't it?

I had to re-cross the Jackfield Memorial footbridge to get back onto the Severn Way for the remainder of my short day's walk. For the rest of my journey, the footpath follows the riverbank in parallel to a track where the Severn Valley railway used to run. It was easy walking and there's not a lot to see other than the glorious woods on either side of the Severn as it cuts through the valley. Where there are woods, of course, there is a plethora of bird life and this was no exception. Every stile I climbed over took me into a new field where pheasants and grouse scurried about, anxious about my approach, as they have every right to be. For, if you were a pheasant or a grouse, would you welcome the sight of a human? Not bloody likely, you wouldn't. You've been told since you were knee-high to a grasshopper by the elders of your family that all humans want to do is fire lead pellets up your backside, send one of their slobbering dogs to pick up your dead carcass, and then get you back home to eat you.

So I didn't blame them for scurrying into the deep ferns ahead of my approach. I'd have done the same if I saw a dinosaur come climbing over a stile and into my field. Or a giant panda. Or an orang-utan. Or a sloth. Especially a sloth.

The noise from some high oaks distracted me from this foolish train of thought as I took my measured strides through the dewy fields. The noise came from three large black cormorants squatting atop those trees and squawking into the light breeze. I thought of those three 'queer, black, ugly birds' in Wilfred Gibson's *Flannan Isle* who dive into the sea as the rescuers arrive at the deserted lighthouse to search for their three missing companions. I always think of that poem whenever I see cormorants beating their way upstream in their long flat flight. I often spot them from my window. When I first moved to Bridgnorth, I was surprised to see them, thinking my sighting was a birdwatcher's prize catch. Then a fisherman friend told me that there are growing numbers of inland cormorants and they are the biggest nuisances that fishermen have to deal with. I don't want to get into the hermeneutics of fishing here, or even my sniffy views on such, but what my friend told me was that he has known of fishermen shooting cormorants because they are such poachers of the precious fish stocks.

Oh, go on then, I will sound off a bit. I promised myself I wouldn't because the Severn is one of the major fishing venues in the country. Every day of my trek I passed little pegs on the river bank where fishermen had stations for their exclusive use. But just ask yourself this – if a fish-eating cormorant is hungry, where will it go to seek food? Correct, the place where fish are to be found. And since cormorants have yet to master the tricky art of purchasing Birds Eye fishfingers from the local supermarket, they're going to have to head for the nearest river, take a deep dive and grab whatever they can. Now if a fisherman is hungry, where does he go for food? Correct, into that wicker basket standing behind him on the river bank. In there, carefully wrapped in greaseproof paper next to his tin of maggots, he will find his delectable cheese and tomato sandwiches.

In short, I don't think that fishermen have got much by way

of natural justice on their side in this equation. Still, those three cormorants were probably right in keeping their distance and squawking out their warning. How were they to know that I was on their side?

The other segment of the worldwide bird community that decided to force itself on my vision that day was Canada geese. As I crossed yet another stile and came into yet another dewy meadow, I could see this gang of birds waddling along in formation at the river's side some 50 yards ahead of me. Canada geese were first introduced to Britain in 1665 as an addition to the waterfowl collection of King Charles II and there were only small numbers of them until the 1950s. Then, drawn perhaps by the music of Alma Cogan and Frankie Vaughan, they started appearing in greater numbers and there are now thousands of them. We're used to seeing them in their distinctive v-shaped echelons as they head back to Canada for the winter, honking high above us in the sky and we think that's pretty spectacular. But they're becoming a bit of a menace in places, especially around airports, because if they take off at the same time as a jumbo jet and crash into it they can cause one hell of a splat!

This gang were mustering, presumably, ready for their migration but they made it clear that they weren't yet ready for take off. There was one goose, a fat specimen who I imagined was their major-general, who began honking orders and the whole army of them marched off at full wobble into the middle of the field. Major-General Goose kept up his loud honking orders as he strutted around the edges of his retreating army, jostling recalcitrant privates into line. I could have sworn that there was a warning in there for me too – something along the lines of 'Don't mess with me, brother, or I'll get this lot to crap on you from a great height'. But I wasn't in the mood for argument anyway, so I hurried on through the field till I reached another stile.

There ahead of me spanning the Severn sat one of its hidden

bridges, the Apley Bridge. I'm calling it a hidden bridge because it is private and you're not supposed to cross it, since it leads to the privately owned Apley Hall. This Gothic mansion can be seen in its glorious position from a little bit further down the river bank, where it sits on the opposite hillside. It was built in the nineteenth century for the local MP and it has been suggested as a model for P.G. Wodehouse's Blandings Castle, since the comic author spent much time living near here in his youth.

Now this is the sort of thing that makes my blood boil, this 'private' bridge. I bet there aren't any private bridges over a major river in Russia, nor in France, nor I suspect in the US of A. It all just smacks of the class system that still undermines our country. Just because some old Frenchman laid claim to this bit of territory as his reward for helping William to subjugate the local Saxons, then handed it on, together with his genetic make-up, to his descendants, one of whom built this bridge, we're supposed to kow-tow to them still and keep off it. Well, I'm going to start a protest movement here and now.

'FREE THE APLEY BRIDGE!'

That's our slogan. Watch out for announcements in the national media for our annual convention, which will take the form of a squat on the bridge until the police are called to forcibly remove us. That should shake the buggers up, eh?

I was by now nearing the end of my day's journey. On the opposite side of the river were the red sandstone cliffs that betokened my home town's closeness. These cliffs are riddled with caves right down to and through Bridgnorth, many of the caves having been lived in for centuries. It's only in modern times that they have ceased to be dwellings and there are several older homes in the area built into the cliff face, thus using the hollowed-out caves as part of their property.

The last stretch of the river bank footpath runs alongside the Bridgnorth Golf Club course and as I walked I mused on my utter uselessness at this game. I have tried to play on a couple of occasions but have always been frustrated at my inadequacy at hitting the golf ball with a wooden club off the tee. Since this is the first shot you're expected to play and since you know that everyone in the clubhouse or, even worse, waiting behind you for their turn is watching you, this is not a particularly good inadequacy to have. So now I pretend that I can't afford to spend three hours of my life walking around a golf course, in order to avoid this acute embarrassment.

While I was passing the sixteenth tee, I noticed a bloke in an anorak approaching it, pulling his golf trolley behind him. There is a road that runs alongside the fairway just here and a fenced-off bike path beside it. The golfer teed off and hooked the ball in that direction. The ball went over the fence and bounced off the bike path onto the road, where it hit the tyre of a passing bus and was knocked back onto the fairway.

I stopped in amazement and blurted out:

'How on earth did you do that?'

'Ah,' he replied. 'You have to know the bus timetable.'

Sometimes the old ones are the best ones, eh?

It was time to head home.

12 Bridgnorth

When my wife and I first moved to Bridgnorth, we decided to join a local bowling club which is situated in a unique position on a tiny island known as The Bylet in the middle of the river. On our first visit to this club, while waiting at the bar to be served, I was greeted by one of the club stalwarts who enquired if we were newcomers to Bridgnorth.

'Yes,' I told him, 'but I've wanted to live here for a while. It's a wonderful spot, isn't it?'

'God's little acre,' came the smiling and sincerely meant reply.

And he was right.

Bridgnorth is, in my view, the most attractive of all the Severn-side towns and I'm not just saying that because I live here. It has been compared by other writers to Mediterranean towns sited on cliff tops, and even to Jerusalem or Gibraltar. It has been variously described as having the character of a city in miniature, as a town that has few equals in the country and as the most dramatically sited town in England. Pevsner describes the approach from along the river, north or south, as a 'happy surprise' and I think this is one of its truest qualities. For it is not just to those journeying from north or south that Bridgnorth makes its sudden dramatic appearance, but also to travellers from the industrial West Midlands to whom the town is all but invisible until they reach the brow of the ridge of hills that guards its entrance.

So what is so wonderful about Bridgnorth?

I'm going to try to tell you.

First, we have a castle. Well, sort of. Yes, it was one of those Normans, Robert de Belesme, who came here in 1101 and had a castle built on the high rock above the river. Now Our Bob was not the smartest card in the pack, since he sided with some of the Normans still in France against Henry I, but he did manage to get this amazingly big castle built. Leland, visiting in 1539, estimated that the castle covered more than a third of the town, although he did admit that much of it was by then in ruins. This was because Henry I besieged it a year after it was built and took control of it. And, in the way of such things, that wasn't the only occasion in which king and lords fell out and used Bridgnorth Castle as an excuse for a punch-up and bits off it got knocked down and were not always rebuilt.

Charles I called the view from the castle 'The finest in my kingdom'. Mind you, he had his head chopped off not long after so he didn't see many other views. And it was around this time when what was left of the castle was finally, but not quite wholly, obliterated. Oliver Cromwell (warts and all) besieged the Royalist army in the castle in 1646 and tried to dig a tunnel through the sandstone underneath the castle with a view to blowing it up. However, before he could complete the task, the Royalists surrendered, having set fire to most of the town on the top of the hill – not a very nice thing to do. The castle was subsequently demolished except for part of the keep tower which still stands, or rather leans, at an angle of 17 degrees (three times more tilt than the Leaning Tower of Pisa) in what is now the Castle Gardens.

Around the gardens is the Castle Walk, from where you get stunning views of the river and of the opposite side of the valley. This is presumably where Charles I stood gazing. This is certainly where tourists stand gazing. And this is where, after seven o'clock at night, teenagers come to drink their cans of Special Brew and to practise their snogging technique.

Beyond the gardens are two streets, surprisingly called East Castle Street and West Castle Street, which would have marked the extent of the original castle grounds. The properties in the former of these streets are gorgeous old Georgian houses dating back centuries, have long gardens that back on to Castle Walk and are where the local toffs used to (and still do) live.

Just beyond the end of Castle Walk you come to an amazing construction called the Cliff Railway. This consists of two carriages that travel on rails up and down a deep fissure cut into the sandstone in 1892. It's the only inland cliff railway still operating in the country and it regularly carries Bridgnorth citizens and visitors from the riverside up to the top of the town throughout the day. It's properly known as a funicular railway but we locals refer to it, in our everyday speech, as the 'vernacular'.

It's a remarkable experience to travel uphill in this contraption. You rise vertically some hundred odd feet in a matter of seconds and the view of the Severn valley as you climb is stupendous. The poet John Betjeman described his journey up the Cliff Railway as like 'being lifted up to heaven' and I wouldn't want to disagree with him.

Parallel to the Cliff Railway, cut into another fissure in the sandstone, are the Stoneway Steps, one of seven such flights of steps that give passageway up the steep sides of the sandstone hill on which Our Bob built his castle way back when. There are 115 steps on Stoneway Steps and they are cut in such a way that it is extremely uncomfortable to walk either up or down them. This is because they were designed, not for humans, but for donkeys, which were used to carry goods up from the river in the days before white vans were invented.

Halfway up the Stoneway Steps is the Theatre on the Steps, a former Congregational chapel that was converted in the 1960s and has been used by local amateur groups and visiting professionals since. I have to say this is a truly wondrous place, because I am at the time of writing chairman of the committee that runs this theatre, but I would say that it was anyway because I really believe it is. I can't think of another theatre in the country like it. It's run entirely by volunteers and without any regular financial support from local government coffers or from anywhere else. Everyone who visits, whether as a paying customer or as a paid performer, remarks on how wonderful it is.

So, when you're passing through, come and see a show!

We call the town at the top of the hill High Town in order to distinguish it from the area at the bottom of the hill known as Low Town. There's a lot of snobbishness about which part of the town you live in and it has led to fierce rivalries in the past. Mostly we're at peace with each other nowadays, though there's still occasions when Low Town scallywags roar downhill on their skateboards, just to annoy the High Towners.

The street they mostly do this on is known as Cartway and it was once the only route up from the river to the town. Cartway actually follows a bend as it climbs up the sandstone cliff face. In the past, when Bridgnorth was one of the busiest mainland ports in Europe, Cartway contained over twenty public houses and every other property was a brothel. There's only one pub there now, the delectable Black Boy with its chimney sweep inn sign, and all the other properties are now privately owned homes. As far as I know, none of them are brothels but the camp television presenter Dale Winton, who fronts the truly awful daytime show *Supermarket Sweep*, once lived in one of them.

Cartway is now full of rather twee residences and traces of its former glory are hard to find, though some houses still have the outside shutters that would have been closed to keep the donkeys from lurching against their windows with their heavy loads. Mind you, they may have been kept in case Dale Winton reappears with a bunch of screaming women shunting their shopping trolleys!

There may be brand new relationships opening up my world this year, though I'll probably be working harder than ever in the practical field. In late January I may experience unexpected pressures in my daily life. In April I may have fresh romantic encounters. In August I must keep a sense of variety to spice up my life and in December I am to use my powerful personality to get what I want. There will be a flare-up in Chechnya in January, crisis in the Balkans in June, a high-profile celebrity divorce in October and Maggie Thatcher will join the Labour Party in December.

These all-too-predictable predictions, except for the last which I made up, are to be found in that greatest of all astrological publications, *Old Moore's Almanack*, which has been published since 1697. You can also, courtesy of this fount of all wisdom, 'discover the wonder you really are!' from the Rosicrucian Order, purchase 'holy squares of divine magic' from Finbarr or 'get in touch with your own guardian angel' with the Angel Life Guild. Or you could purchase your own psychic supplies, start your own Wicca business (don't ask), have your runes cast, get relief from rheumatic pain, or seek personal predictions by phone from Old Moore himself.

This last I think is probably rather dodgy, since Old Moore, or Dr Francis Moore to give him his full title, died in 1715. The reason he features in this chapter is because, in case you hadn't guessed, he was born in Bridgnorth in 1657. He did actually qualify as a doctor and then travelled to London where he became the assistant to a well-known astrologer and almanac maker. Eventually he set himself up in business on his own as a physician, astrologer and schoolteacher – in those days there wasn't much distinction between the three callings. In 1699 he published his first almanac under a fancy Latin name, *Kalendarium Ecclesiasticum*, no doubt hoping to impress with his learning. This was mainly to support his trade as a pill-maker and pill-distributor, since all the predictions concerned the weather and what medicaments should be taken to avoid the worst excesses of the weather.

The following year he published the first of his astrological observations under the equally naff Latin title, *Vox Stellarum*, and that really was the start of the Old Moore nonsense. There's been an *Old Moore's Almanac* every year since but, just in case you were thinking that it had been continued by members of the Moore family and that I was being rather too precocious in denying the possibility of Francis Moore addressing your concerns when you phoned him, it was created after his death first by somebody with the exquisite name of Tycho Wing and then by the more prosaic-sounding Henry Andrews. Nowadays it is published commercially in Slough, its authorship anonymous in the best tradition of all quacks and mountebanks.

I've no idea whether Old Moore attended church in Bridgnorth but, if he did, it's quite likely that he would have worshipped at St Leonard's church where some few years before he was born the religious writer Richard Baxter was briefly the assistant minister. There's a pretty black and white house in St Leonard's Close with a plaque announcing that Baxter lived there and ever since I've lived in Bridgnorth I've wondered who on earth he was and why anyone should be bothered. Well, first, he wasn't very complimentary about the people of Bridgnorth whom he called 'a very ignorant, deadhearted people'. Then it turns out that he was one of the leaders of the non-conformist views of the church which seemed so terribly important in his day – a time when people kept inventing odd names for themselves like Levellers or Diggers or Ranters. Apparently what he liked more than anything was a good old argument and he was known to have spent whole days disputing with some other cleric about infant baptism.

Yes, Richard Baxter really knew how to live life to the full!

I'm being unkind, for poor old Baxter suffered for his preaching. He was imprisoned for keeping a conventicle (served him right!), meeting-houses where he preached were closed down, he was fined regularly for preaching sedition and, when he was seventy, he was tried before the notorious Judge Jeffreys and imprisoned after receiving a fierce verbal ticking off by the said judge.

I'm still not sure if any of this matters or if Richard Baxter is of any great significance in our history. I'm a little more sure of the impact of Bridgnorth's other famous resident, Bishop Thomas Percy, the author of *Reliques of Ancient English Poetry*. Now, you've just read that and thought bore, bore, bore, but hang on a minute, because much of our way of looking at things owes its origin to Percy's book. But just to keep you dangling for a little while as you wait for this world-shattering revelation, I want to tell you first about Bishop Percy's house. This is a lovely black and white timbered house at the bottom of the Cartway and is one of Bridgnorth's oldest buildings, having survived the Civil War fire that destroyed High Town. Thomas Percy was born there in 1729 and lived there till he was seventeen. In 1765 he produced his famous *Reliques*, which is a collection of medieval English folk ballads, including *The Ballad of Sir Patrick Spens*, *Robin Hood and Guy of Gisborne* and the King Arthur cycle. Percy came upon these ballads at the house of a friend of his in nearby Shifnal when he saw maids about to use them to light the fire.

So why does all this matter? Simply because Percy's collection of ballads was the inspiration for Wordsworth and Coleridge when they set about the revolution in English poetry and thought that became known as the Romantic Movement. And it's because of this that we all yearn to live in black and white cottages in the country, surrounded by fields filled with Highland cattle and sturdy yeomen in smocks and milkmaids all in a row, rather than in noisy, polluted towns and cities filled with loud music and blaring car horns and McDonald's fast-food emporia.

Bishop Percy's house is now a youth club. It stands imposingly, looking out on to the River Severn and features in every tourist leaflet about Bridgnorth you will ever come across. It's worth pausing outside to consider what emanated from it and how, in a curious way, it symbolises that folk memory we English seem to want to cling on to about our rural past, which in reality for the vast majority of people was dirty, squalid, laborious and unpleasant.

Bridgnorth is the northernmost of the Severn-side towns that, as charabancs and the first private motor cars became more popular between the First and Second World Wars, drew in the industrial workers of the Black Country and Birmingham seeking a weekend and holiday resort. Yes, even these denizens of the factory and the furnace were attracted by the Romantic notion of the countryside as the panacea for all evils, and they began to come in greater and greater numbers to the riverside for their rest and recuperation. Here their menfolk could fish to their hearts' content, their children could play safely in the verdant pastures, and their womenfolk could swap the kitchen sink for the much smaller caravan sink!

And still they come. Every weekend the car parks fill with Black Country folk, eager to visit a real street market, even though it's stocked mostly with stuff that's purchased originally from the heart of the West Midlands, to eat their Saturday ration of chips from the Hightown Grill, to induct their children into the ways of the 'vernacular' railway, and to get back in touch with their agricultural past. On spring and summer bank holidays, our wonderful town elders even lay on a fairground for them, so they can remember the joys of candyfloss, the excitement of carousels and the thrill of winning dodgy coconuts at the Aunt Sally. At such times, the gentle Shropshire accent is overwhelmed in the town's streets by shouts of 'Tricy! Coom 'ere! Be'ave yowerself or oi'll belt yer one' or, 'Darren! Stop pickin' yer nose or it'll drap aff!'

And yet I know why they come here, for I feel the same about the place. Every day I take a walk through the town centre, past the lovely old market hall in the High Street with its arched underway where local produce-sellers have traditionally sold their goods. Every day I look in wonder at the variety of architectural styles that have been preserved in the town and the unevenness of the skyline that their roofs produce – so different from the boringly ordered skyline of new towns and new estates.

The river, as well as being a Mecca for fishermen, is also used by our local rowing club, whose sleek boats powered gracefully by taut oarsmen and oarswomen glide past my window every weekend. Like many of Sabrina's towns, Bridgnorth has its own annual regatta when men in blazers and white slacks appear to marshal the young hopefuls from up and down the river in their races. And every year a charity raft race takes place where mad people of various ages and abilities build slightly dangerous rafts from plastic bottles and attempt to row them with the river's current until they reach the landing stage here.

And then there's one of the secret reasons for visiting Bridgnorth – its pubs. Old-timers will tell you that there used to be hundreds of pubs in the town and that they've all disappeared. Well, there are still more pubs per head of population here than in most parts of Britain, believe me. I really ought to keep the best ones secret because those of you reading this book will come flocking into town looking for them but I can't resist mentioning the Black Horse in Low Town, which has a most amazing selection of real ales as well as its own blue parrot, the Friars Inn in St Mary's Street, which has a lovely ambience, and the Bear in Northgate, where all the best people go.

Bridgnorth is a wonderful town, full of wonderful atmosphere, interesting architecture, excellent pubs and remarkably pleasant people. It's the sort of town where you can still feel safe smoking a pipe, or wearing baggy corduroy trousers, or whistling, or saying hello to perfect strangers.

But be warned! We have very strict immigration controls in place, so you are not very likely to be able to be part of all this wonderful life.

Sorry!

13 Bridgnorth to Bewdley

There are some things that we British are particularly good at, and one of these is preserving scraps of our past. Think of all those stately homes, castles, city walls, priories, abbeys and other ruins. Is there any other country that has so much of all this? And then, in more recent years, once we'd got all that really ancient stuff safely under lock and key, we turned our attentions to newer relics – those from our more immediate past. I'm thinking of the nostalgic yearning that led us to seek to preserve in aspic bits of our industrial history like redundant mineshafts, superannuated trolley buses and unwanted pottery kilns.

The Severn Valley Railway is an example of this. The line was built originally in 1862 to link Hartlebury in Worcestershire with Shrewsbury, some 40 miles away. This was in the great age of railway mania when people were putting down railway lines all over the place. This particular stretch was intended to provide links between Worcester – already linked by line to Hartlebury – Stourport, Bewdley, Bridgnorth, Ironbridge and Shrewsbury. The commercial rationale is not hard to determine when you consider that the River Severn had been used for centuries to transport goods and now this quicker means of transport could follow pretty much the same route. And it was not dependent on the amount of rainfall there had been, nor on the muscle power of men or horses pulling barges upstream.

Well, Dr Beeching saw the Severn Valley Railway off in his infamous rationalising of the railways a hundred years later. The line closed and the section from Buildwas to Bridgnorth was dismantled in order that the track could be used elsewhere. Two years later a small bunch of railways nuts in Kidderminster formed the Severn Valley Railway Society. With a judicious mix of public pleading, private finance and unlimited volunteer support, the restored Severn Valley Railway ran its first passenger service in May 1970, leaving Bridgnorth station at 14.00 precisely to the accompaniment of champagne corks popping. Since then, it has grown and grown to become one of the major tourist attractions in the area.

Trains on what is now commonly known as the SVR run every weekend of the year and daily at peak times between Bridgnorth and Kidderminster. There are also several special services, such as the popular Santa Specials that run over the Christmas period, and the trains and stations are frequently used as backdrops for period films and television programmes.

It is easy to be snooty about all those volunteers who shed their city-slicker suits at weekends to don the blue overalls that their grandfathers used to wear and then spend hours buffing up some rusty piece of metal or shovelling tons of gravel from point A to point B. I know, I've been critical earlier in this book. Like enthusiasts anywhere, they can be loud and voluble about their hobby and nowhere more so than in the Station Arms at Bridgnorth, where I am sometimes forced to go for a pint of Batham's bitter. When a group of them are waxing loud and lyrical about the joys of a West Country class 4-6-2 or a GWR 44-6-0, it's sometimes hard not to want to tell them to shut up and get a life.

But then I have to remind myself of the pains of travelling on our less than wonderful privatised railways at the start of the twenty-first century on those grim trains provided by the likes of 'Sir Richard Virgin'. And that's when I appreciate the joys of the Severn Valley Railway. Yes, I know that many of its workers are now paid but everyone involved is always so pleasant and so friendly that you wouldn't know it. Yes, I know that it's unrealistic to go back to having steam railways because of the pollution they create but many people just love the sound and sight of a steam engine coming into the station. So, though I have less than pleasant memories of travelling on steam trains as a youngster and getting soot in my eyes from opened windows, on balance I am a quiet supporter of the railway nuts who have preserved the Severn Valley Railway.

The line that the SVR takes from Bridgnorth to Bewdley is pretty much the same as the one that I took on the third day of my second week's walking, although my journey had been interrupted by a trip to see the Severn Bore in its full glory. But that story will have to wait for a later chapter.

In fact, the Severn Way path leaves Bridgnorth on the riverside through a tree-filled cutting just after passing by the railway bridge over the new bypass. I had taken the precaution of buying sandwiches from the wonderful Delo's Bakery in Low Town, served by the delightful young lady in her pinafore and dark blue overall, because I wasn't sure whether the pubs I was to pass en route would be serving food. There was a light drizzle throughout the day which had begun overnight and which made some of the path mildly treacherous. I had to step gingerly at times, particularly where the path was at the bottom of a slope and close to the river, as my boots threatened to slide me into Sabrina's gently flowing waters.

The SVR takes a much more direct southerly route out of Bridgnorth than the river, which executes a long loop to the east. A mile or so after leaving Bridgnorth I could see Quatford church spire high on the hill on the opposite side of the river. Quatford was the original site of Bridgnorth, if you see what I mean. The Danes built the first fortification here in 893. Alfred the Great's daughter, the warrior Queen Aethelfleda, also built a castle here, and then Roger de Montgomery built his Norman stronghold in the same place. Why? Because there is a good fording place here. Hence the name Quatford, though no one knows what quat (or, more probably, cwat) means. Until a few years ago, there was a ferry at the very same spot where this ford used to be. It was only in 1101 that Robert de Belesme upped sticks and moved everyone to Bridgnorth.

I found myself musing about these Anglo-Saxon settlers, as I passed by Quatford. So many of the place names in this area derive from the Anglo-Saxon settlers – Quatford, Arley (the clearing where eagles live), Highley (the clearing of Huga), Alveley (the clearing of Elvis?) – and yet we know so little else about them, because writing was not one of their great strengths. Those records we do have tend to have been written much later by baldy monks in Norman monasteries. A commonly held view, fed by generations of historians, is that Britain went through a period of barbarism between the times when the Romans cleared off back to Serie A and when the Normans arrived. I was brought up to call this period the Dark Ages, but, if it had all been so grim, why is it that so many of our place names derive from that period and have stuck, and that we actually call ourselves English? Above all, why is it that all our most profound and secret words – those used to describe the sexual act and the organs used in that act and to describe our bodily expurgations – come from the Anglo-Saxons?

I don't know. What I do know is that my route had now rejoined the SVR line, though I was to see no steam trains chuffing up and down the track that day because it was mid-week. The line was to be my companion for most of the remainder of my day's journey through the lush greenness of the Severn Valley. You can see why those railway nuts wanted to preserve it, for the slow journey through this picturesque vale is exactly what Wordsworth and his Romantic chums have made us see as truly beautiful.

I had been looking forward to reaching Hampton Loade a couple of miles further downstream and the site of one of the beautifully kept stations on the SVR line, because this is where the last remaining ferry on the Severn is situated. However, I was to be disappointed because the ferry – a wire rope stretched from one bank of the river to the other with a pulley attached which moves across the rope pulling the ferry boat with it – was not operating. It had been badly damaged in the floods of the previous year and, although it was being refurbished, its operators felt that the time to replace it with a newer version had really come. Some time after my call on the ferry, the landing stage was vandalised and the future of the Severn's last remaining ferry is in considerable doubt as I write.

This is a terrible shame, not just because of its historic significance, but because the ferry is the only way you can get to visit the two pubs on either side of the river – The Lion on its eastern bank and The Unicorn on the west. It was still too early in the day for me to seek sustenance in either, however, so I carried on down the river bank with the railway line as my constant companion.

There can be no greater dissimilarities between my next two stopping points, Highley and Arley, which are also stations on the SVR line. Highley town is actually half a mile away from the railway station that bears its name and is a sizeable village which owes its growth to coal mining. The Highley Mining Company arrived in 1878 to sink a mine shaft some 300 feet into the ground to get at the high-quality coal seam there. Subsequently, the company dug out many square miles underground and housed the miners in Highley, whose population exploded in the early part of the twentieth century. In 1935 a new colliery was opened on the opposite side of the river at Alveley, connected underground by a tunnel and over the river by the still extant footbridge.

I passed under this bridge and then took the short walk into the village itself because I wanted to see one of its treasures. One of the three parallel brick terraces in the centre of the village, built to house all those coal-blackened miners, is called Coronation Street to commemorate the 1901 coronation of Edward VII. The houses in the street are very much like those in their fictional television counterpart, being terraced dwellings with two rooms downstairs and two upstairs. Nowadays most, if not all, have been modernised but their exteriors look pretty much as they always have done. The residents of Coronation Street held celebrations in May 2001 in recognition of the centenary of their street.

I had a brief walk around the centre of Highley, half-expecting and indeed half-hoping to bump into Vera Duckworth or Elsie Tanner or Ken Barlow lookalikes, but, if there are any living there, I didn't see them, though I'm told there was for many years an Annie Walker living in Coronation Street. Even though the mines closed down in 1969 and the village has nowadays become more of a dormitory community for West Midlanders, its High Street still shows the evidence of its former working-class status. But Rita Sullivan with her padded shoulders wasn't serving in the newsagents on the corner and Roy's Café seems to have been displaced by the Highley Balti Indian Takeaway and the Jade House Chinese Takeaway.

Ah well, it was just a thought.

I headed back to the river and followed the Severn Way's slippery path and the SVR railway for a further couple of miles till I came to the very different Upper Arley, the first Severn settlement in Worcestershire. This pretty little village spans both sides of the Severn with a rather unprepossessing bridge, which was built in 1972 to replace the ferry that formerly joined its two parts. That ferry was a very ancient one, first mentioned in 1323, and for centuries this was a major crossing and resting point for the river traders, as is evidenced by the fact that it once had six pubs – the Valentia (named after Viscount Valentia of Arley Castle), the Crown famed for its cockfights, the Cock on the river bank near the vicarage garden, the Nelson (later the site of the village shop), the Harbour Inn on the west bank and a cider house called The Case is Altered.

But before crossing the footbridge, I took the short walk up to the very attractive Arley station. This was the site of the fictional Hatley station in the BBC sitcom appropriately entitled *Oh! Dr Beeching!* which ran for two series in the middle of the 1990s. This fairly dire show, relying heavily on the importing of a trio of actors – Paul Shane, Su Pollard and Jeffrey Holland – from the long-running holiday camp sitcom *Hi De Hi*, was set in 1963 at the very time when the infamous Dr Beeching, Minister of Transport, was about to announce his cull of the railways. I suppose it's ironic that *Oh! Dr Beeching!* was filmed at Arley since, as I've already explained, the Severn Valley line was one of the victims of that culling process.

Sadly, such irony does not make *Oh! Dr Beeching!* funny.

If only.

I retraced my steps to return to the river and cross the bridge, as the Severn Way path follows the eastern river bank from here into Bewdley. And, despite the damp, I sat on a bench overlooking the river and ate my sandwiches, throwing a crust or two to the swans below.

It was a further 3½ miles to Bewdley, going through thick woodland at first and, then, shortly after passing underneath the magnificent 200-foot single-span Victoria Bridge, made at the Coalbrookdale Works in Ironbridge, that carries the SVR line over the river, by the side of a grassy embankment that holds the Trimpley Reservoir. It's odd to think about this water supply, which provides Birmingham with clean water, because it originates, like the River Severn, on Plynlimon. The Elan Valley dams and reservoirs in mid-Wales were created in the middle of the nineteenth century, along with the pipeline that transported water from there to the Birmingham area. Joseph Chamberlain and his fellow civic leaders had realised that the growing population of the second city needed to get cleaner water and so they flooded these two Welsh valleys, shifting a hundred Dais and Blodwens out of the way with no compensation.

The pipeline crosses the river a bit further down and then I was into chalet country. Virtually all the way into Bewdley now was strewn with these holiday chalets – some with corrugated iron roofs, betraying their age, others of more modern wooden construction. They had names like Cherrywood, Hazelwood, Fernwood, Hollywood and so on. I thought this was rather odd since they all backed onto the same wood, which didn't appear to me to be that varied.

Finally, the footpath took me through a caravan park – I liked the name on one caravan, 'Edd & Flo' – and on to the bridge at Bewdley, where my day's journey ended.

Now that's where I would normally have left this chapter, in order to go on to expatiate upon Bewdley itself. But, after I had toured the sites of Bewdley, I caught a bus heading back to Bridgnorth and it turned out that I was the only passenger on this bus. So, instead of spending the journey making notes about my day's walk, I found myself in rather extraordinary conversation with the bus driver, who had clearly been anticipating some company. And, if it had to be this poor bedraggled hiker in a red cagoule, then so be it.

'You walked far?' he began, as he steered the bus round the narrow turns out of Bewdley.

'Just come from Bridgnorth today,' I said, with what I hoped was an air of quiet satisfaction without being braggardly.

'See any trains?' he queried.

'No, they don't run mid-week,' I answered, hoping that this was just politeness on his part and that he would leave me to my note-making sooner rather than later.

Some chance!

'I like them old steam trains,' my new friend continued. 'Been on that TGV, you know. Abroad. They say it's done a record 500 kilometres an hour. Mind you, there was no passengers. Still, makes you think.'

I grunted, to indicate that I was thinking but hoping he would realise that I wasn't really wanting a longer conversation.

'Mind, I don't like that tunnel,' he began again. 'It's a disaster waiting to happen, if you ask me. I'd rather take the ferry across the channel any time.'

How did we get from the TGV to the Channel Tunnel, I wondered.

'You know that Mont Blanc tunnel's still closed?'

I stayed silent. This conversation was heading in a direction I could barely comprehend.

'Been closed for months now. They say it may never open.'

I don't recall saying anything to encourage him further but presumably he took my silence as some form of approbation of his story.

'I tend to go round Lake Geneva myself. It's better than Chamonix, there's too many mountains to climb that way. You're always climbing. I go four or five times a year.'

It was no good. I really was hooked now and he knew it. He'd got me just interested enough.

'You drive coaches over there?' I queried.

'Yes. Take them white-water rafters. They're bloody mad, if you ask me. They go out in the freezing cold and they raft all day and then drink all night. I don't know how they do it, the mad buggers.'

I sat silent, listening to this tale. What had I said that made him think I wanted to hear all this? I'm not being unkind, because he seemed a nice enough sort of bloke, but I'd paid £2.40 in order to get to Bridgnorth on his bus, not to be entertained with his continental travels!

Still, the heavens opened as we were driving through the late afternoon countryside and I was glad I'd finished walking before the worst of the weather descended. And, although he kept up this stream of reminiscence all the way, it wasn't long before we were on the outskirts of Bridgnorth and I was able to bid him a fond, and I have to say grateful, farewell.

14 Bewdley

On this spot
on October Monday
the thirteenth nineteen
ninety five absolutely
nothing happened
d.g.

This tasteful plaque, on the outside wall of a house in Dog Lane in Bewdley just up from the riverside, may be accurate as far as that specific 'spot' is concerned but it is far from the truth as far as Bewdley itself is concerned. For this town, described by Pevsner as 'the most perfect small Georgian town in Worcestershire', was the birthplace of a man of whom Winston Churchill once said 'it would have been much better had he never lived'.

Stanley Baldwin, Prime Minister of the United Kingdom three times between 1923 and 1937, and leader of the Conservative Party throughout that time, was the person that Churchill spoke of. He also called him 'no better than an epileptic corpse' and 'an old turnip', while George Orwell called him 'simply a hole on the air'.

So, what had they got against our Stanley? And did he deserve this opprobrium?

The popular view is that Baldwin was one of the 'Guilty Men' responsible for not rearming Britain in the 1930s when Hitler's German rearmament was at its greatest. And, while there is truth in this fact, the reason why Baldwin refused to commit Britain to an equal rearming process was because he was engaged in an even greater enterprise – the creation of suburban gardens. Yes, if you find bra-less Charlie Dimmock and squeaky Alan Titchmarsh unbearably irritating, then just remember that, if it hadn't been for Baldwin and the drive to build suburban estates with their private gardens, we would not have had the need to invent them. And certainly not to fill primetime television with them and their digging, planting, squirreling, composting, pruning and so on. Not to mention the swinging of mammaries by the ginger-haired goddess of the garden.

Between the end of the First and Second World Wars, 4 million houses were built in Britain, almost 3 million of them in the 1930s. It was Baldwin's aim to create more Tory voters in this fashion. The vast bulk of this new housing was in the suburban estates that mushroomed on the edges of the major cities and towns of the country. The most common style was for smallish, semi-detached houses, each with its own garden plot with room for a garden shed and a greenhouse. And that's what started the stupendous growth in the British gardening fad among the lower middle classes.

There are currently fourteen general gardening magazines on sale every week in my local newsagents and, if you visit a garden centre (of which there are hundreds within 20 miles or so of my home), you'll find a further selection of specialist titles devoted to particular species – roses, fuchsias or clematis, for example. It's even possible that you're reading this book because you bought it in a garden centre, for they have now become major retail therapy centres for a certain generation of people who choose to spend their leisure time surrounded by the stench of rotten vegetation.

So if, like me, you have little or no interest in the following topics:

- the number of roses named after Shakespearean characters;
- colourful annuals that in no time at all are romping up your trellises;

- distinguishing a curvilinear greenhouse from a polygonal one;
- Alan's and Pippa's composting secrets;

then you can blame that good burgher of Bewdley, Stanley Baldwin, for overseeing the growth of suburbia between the wars and ensuring that each of the suburbanites received their own blessed plot of garden.

So, just to finish this little diversion, here's a really tasteless gardening joke.

A woman's garden is growing beautifully but the tomatoes won't ripen. There's a limit to the number of uses for green tomatoes and she's getting tired of it. So she goes to her neighbour and says:

'Your tomatoes are ripe, mine are green. What can I do about it?'

Her neighbour replies, 'Well, it may sound absurd but here's what to do. Tonight there's no moon. After dark go out into your garden and take all your clothes off. Tomatoes can see in the dark and they'll be embarrassed and blush. In the morning they'll all be red, you'll see.'

Well, what the hell? She does it.

The next day her neighbour asks how it worked.

'So-so,' she answers, 'The tomatoes are still green but the cucumbers are all four inches longer.'

What else is there to say about Bewdley?

Well, Pevsner was not wrong in his admiration for the Georgian town which really began life when the first bridge was built over the Severn in the fifteenth century. Thereafter, for the next 200 years, Bewdley grew in importance as a river port as the use of the Severn became more significant. Leland, visiting in Henry VIII's time, describes it thus:

> At sunrise, when the town is lit from the east, it glitters as

> if it were gold, for all its buildings are new. It has only three memorable streets. The first runs north and south, keeping to the bank of the Severn; the second is the fine, spacious market place adorned with good buildings; the third is the counterpart of the first, running north and south along the hillside.

Now when I arrived in Bewdley it was late afternoon and the weather was not such as would promise the sort of early morning sunrise that Leland spoke of. Still, I thought I'd explore its three memorable streets with the help of the Civic Society's Town Trail. The first of these, Severnside, runs alongside the river and is the bit that regularly gets flooded. Every year this is where the television crews come for their photo opps and their vox pop interviews with local residents in their wellington boots. This has become such a ritual that it's sometimes hard to know whether the television companies are actually revisiting Bewdley or merely using old film.

Many of the houses on Severnside are splendid seventeenth-century buildings, constructed with the prosperity that the river trade brought to the town. The site of the medieval bridge, destroyed in the 1795 flood, is clearly visible just before the modern Telford-designed bridge. There's the usual collection of scavenging ducks and geese and pigeons hanging around on the old slipway, often being taunted by the local skateboarding truants.

The 'spacious market place' described by Leland is now called Load Street and it still is the main thoroughfare through Bewdley. At its top end is the award-winning Bewdley Museum, situated in the old butchers' Shambles under the Town Hall. Here the crafts that were formerly part of everyday life in the Bewdley district are brought to life in the interesting displays. The influence of the surrounding Wyre Forest, exploited from pre-Roman times, is evident in the making of baskets, barrels, besoms and rope. The forest was a particular source of timber for charcoal-burning, which supplied the forges and furnaces of the Black Country. The museum is filled with the old implements of these trades – axes, saws, trenching tools, hammers and so on. And, although I could admire the collection and displaying of these artefacts and even more the accompanying videos of modern-day craftsmen demonstrating old techniques and crafts, I was left as I frequently am in these situations wondering why I should be interested. How much of any of this would I remember tomorrow or the next day? Would any of it really have any impact on my understanding of the world?

Maybe I was just turning into another old fart.

The Wyre Forest was also the source of the wood and hide used to make that archetypal Severn river-craft – the coracle – and I was actually interested in this. I'd read that there was a coracle regatta held each year at Bewdley, so I went to ask Dave who is a coracle-maker working at the museum.

'No, we don't have that now,' he told me. 'It's just one of those things. There's not enough of us now.'

'But you still make coracles here?' I asked.

'Oh, yes,' he answered, perching himself on a bench. 'Mostly for exhibitions now though. And some for research. We get a lot of school parties here and they're always interested.'

He showed me various of the coracles he had built to the different designs used on the River Severn, including a two-person model which looked as if you really needed to trust whoever you were in there with.

'Did you know Fred Davies at Shrewsbury?' I asked, keen to show him that I was no ignoramus on these matters.

'He died recently, didn't he? We've got one of his at the front of the museum,' he told me. 'Used to get paid £5 a year retainer by the football club.'

Dave was a blessing. He clearly knew far more about coracles than I had managed to discover previously and told me that they were mostly found in parts of the Severn where there had been the strongest Celtic influence, citing their similarity to the curraghs in Ireland.

'Traditionally they're made of willow or ash laths and covered with canvas impregnated with pitch and tar. They weigh between 25 and 40 pounds, so you can carry it on your shoulders. The old guys would walk up to 10 miles like that then drift down on the current looking for fish,' he explained.

'I was watching the video in there,' I pointed back inside the museum, 'and I noticed the funny way of paddling. Was that normal?'

'They always used a figure of eight movement. You hold the paddle in front of the coracle and steer it by twizzling it like a figure of eight,' he told me, miming the action as he did so.

Now I have remembered all of this, partly because of Dave's personal description but also because I was interested previously in this curious craft which was operated for centuries on the Severn and has only recently ceased being used. The coracle is not peculiar to the Severn – it was used all over Wales at one time, as well as in Scotland and Ireland, but it is something that pre-dates the Romans, the Saxons and the Normans who have been the dominant influences on our history. Its survival on the English Severn up until recent times is an interesting example of how conquering peoples never quite succeed in wiping every trace of their predecessors out of the picture.

I was thinking all this as I left the museum to continue my exploration. On the opposite side of Load Street is an old coaching inn, the George Hotel, where I repaired for some refreshment. The George has been at the heart of Bewdley affairs since at least the early seventeenth century and its modern appearance, both internal and external, shows its age. Of course, it has been through a number of transformations over the centuries but it seems to have always had a prominent part to play in local politics, being the place where voters were regularly bribed by Tory candidates and where Town Council meetings regularly adjourned to.

The George has had its share of famous visitors too. Eighteenth-century tragic actress Sarah Siddons, who made acting a legitimate profession for women and might be called the first truly modern 'star', is said to have played in the Assembly Room. The portrait *Sarah Siddons as the Tragic Muse* painted by Joshua Reynolds haunts our national consciousness to this day, though it is now housed in America. She was painted by all the leading portraitists of her day, including Thomas Gainsborough, in whose painting she looks very beautiful as she sits holding a golden muff.

Charles de Gaulle, then the large-nosed leader of the Free French, stayed in the George briefly during the Second World War. This latter visit is commemorated unofficially by the wooden panelling and mantlepiece in the rear dining room which were 'liberated' from nearby Ribbesford House, where Free French Officer Cadets were housed between 1942 and 1944. The story goes that de Gaulle rode his horse through the yard of the George, under its archway and out into Load Street to inspect a parade but who really knows? And who cares? You may remember him as the man who said 'Non!' to Great Britain's entry to the Common Market but most people know him better now as an airport.

I must confess this was not my first visit to the George. Its front lounge, formed from the old vaults bar, an office, the landlord's sitting room and parlour, is a splendid place. It is decorated throughout in a beautiful eggshell blue and cream, the vaulted ceiling with its pretty decorative mouldings being a particular feature. There are comfortable cushioned seats, wooden tables of various sizes and ages, a range of teas and gloriously unhealthy cakes, young waitresses who look as if they actually enjoy working there, and *no piped music*. And, of course, it attracts just the sort of person who might appreciate such an ambience.

While I was there, I witnessed two middle-aged and bespectacled businessmen discussing deals at one table with *no* laptop computers and *no* mobile phones! At another table were two elderly ladies of the blue rinse variety, clearly of an age where dietary concerns had long been discarded by the look of the chocolate fudge cakes they were getting stuck into. Next to me were some local young men, obviously friends with (and, by the sound of their conversation and the accompanying giggles, wishing to be more than this) two of the waitresses. It was a scene that could have been played out in any century. I always leave the George feeling better about the world; that day was no exception.

I went out into the late afternoon to finish my tour of this old town, past the elegant Georgian houses of High Street, which was the third of Leland's memorable streets. These tall houses with their hidden interiors betoken the wealth that once existed in Bewdley and made it the prosperous town it once was. The River Severn afforded a convenient landing point for all the goods brought up from Bristol as the country's ships scoured the world in the sixteenth and seventeenth centuries seeking commodities. In return, the trows that unloaded their goods would take timber from the Wyre Forest or, increasingly as these crafts developed, ironware from the Black Country back to Bristol.

The extension of High Street leads into Lower Park Street and it was here, at number fifteen, that Stanley Baldwin, the man responsible for Alan Titchmarsh and Charlie Dimmock, was born in 1867. I couldn't tell because of the high walls but it looked to me as if the house had only a tiny garden or none at all.

Ironic, eh?

Bewdley lost its pre-eminence in the late eighteenth century when its town councillors, no doubt well fortified from their visit to the George and thus overconfident, like all drinkers, in the wisdom of their judgement refused to allow Brindley's canal to connect up with the Severn. They called it 'a stinking ditch' but it was they who ended up as the stinkers, when the canal builders in 1772 decided to link to the river at Stourport a few miles further downstream. That was the beginning of the end for Bewdley, as traders realised they could transport their goods more rapidly to the growing towns of the West Midlands and further north via the canal network.

Bewdley has now become, like so many places on this stretch of the Severn, more of a dormitory town to the West Midlands conurbation. Its busiest times are, therefore, the commuting times in the early morning and early evening, and even those have shrunk since a bypass was built some years ago. It also shares with Bridgnorth and Stourport the function of being a Sunday trip away from the Black Country and Birmingham, and therefore an attraction to thousands. Bikers in particular have taken to using the town as one of the places where they preen themselves and their powerful motorbikes.

I'm not sure how many of these Sunday bikers are what are known as Bambis – Born Again Middle-aged Bikers – but some will be. These typically are men in their thirties and forties whose children have grown up, whose mortgages are nearly paid off and who are earning too much. Often they've had motorbikes when they were younger but just as frequently they lust for the throbbing excitement of a powerful engine between their thighs and the thrill of the open road. Yes, they suffer from having watched Dennis Hopper and Peter Fonda in *Easy Rider* too often, because there aren't any open roads in the United Kingdom any longer. That's because every Sunday they're filled with Bambis. You've seen them, in their brightly coloured leather outfits astride their equally colourful and highly polished motorbikes, when you're out for a picnic in the Datsun Sunny, roaring past you or doing wheelies on dangerous bends.

If you want to avoid these people, visit Bewdley during the week and go to church on Sundays. You'll stand a much better chance of getting to heaven too.

Remember those hilariously unfunny elephant jokes we used to crease ourselves laughing at?

> 'How d'you get four elephants in an Austin Mini?'
> 'Two in the front and two in the back.'

Or:

> 'What weighs 5000 pounds and wears glass slippers?'
> 'Cinderelephant.'

Well, just on the edge of Bewdley there is a place where elephants live. Now what are elephants doing in the middle of England? No, they're not telling bad jokes (though they might be, if we could only understand all that trumpeting). Nor are they waiting for the next Austin Mini to come along to take them back to Africa or India. No, these magnificent beasts, whose ancestors took Hannibal across the Alps and maharajas through their Indian territories, are stuck in the middle of the West Midlands Safari Park, which is a rather poor imitation of what someone thought African game reserves might look like. Blame the Marquess of Bath. It was he who opened the first of these excrescences in 1966 at his stately home of Longleat in order to find a new way of raising money from the peasants.

There are lots of them around the country now and this one at Bewdley used to be a lot more fun than it is now. The reason is that it no longer houses the gang of rhesus monkeys whose antics were always so entertaining and some of whom, if you were lucky, might attach themselves to your car in order to escape. Apparently there are still quite a few of these beasts out in the wild to this day but the safari park now concentrates on the likes of lions, tigers, deer, elephants and rhinos. Plus, of course, its fairground which has grown over the years and now features such wonders as the Congo Carousel, the African Big Apple Coaster, the Tanganyika Tea Cups and the Zambezi Water Splash to entertain the little ones. You can also buy hamburgers and chips from the Botswana Burger Company or authentic mementoes of safaris, like pencils or sticks of rock, from the African Queen Shop or the Jungle Bazaar (closed during quiet periods).

It's all just like going on safari in Kenya, isn't it?

The West Midlands Safari Park advertises itself as 'A wildly different day out'. Not for me it isn't.

Personally, I'd rather be a Bambi.

15 Bewdley to Worcester

When I left Bewdley the following morning, the weather had picked up again and it was a pleasant dry day with a light breeze blowing into my face as I walked. The Severn Way stays on the eastern side of the river, passing beyond the housing developments of the town and the local high school, whose playing fields were occupied by a group of squealing male and female adolescents playing what we call rounders but what the Americans call baseball. I don't suppose those pimply youths I saw jumping up and down on the grass and calling out excitedly as one of their number raced around the wooden posts saw themselves as future participants in the grandly titled World Series (in which only America teams compete). To tell the truth, they seemed more interested in the bits of each others' bodies that were revealed by their sports outfits. And so they should be!

It wasn't long before I was passing under the bridge that carries the Bewdley bypass road and allows Midlanders to live further into Worcestershire without having their daily commute hampered by the narrow streets of Bewdley's Georgian centre. Just beyond the bridge, and on the same side of the river as I was walking, is the huge sandstone cliff known as Blackstone Rock. At its base are a number of cave entrances which are all that remains of what was once a hermitage. I had read that these cave doorways looked like Norman arches but, try as I might, I couldn't see it. They just looked like natural cave entrances to me, though I noticed that inside one of them, someone had scrawled 'BAR' on a piece of timber hanging up. I was not to be fooled, though, so pressed on through the pretty woodland that skirts the Severn here.

Pretty soon I was into caravan land. This stretch from Bewdley down to Holt Fleet is probably the most over-caravanned part of the whole riverside; nay, of the whole country! This is where Black Country folk and Brummies have their second homes. This is where they come for their bank holiday weekends. This is where they expect to find all the comforts of home (Banks's beer, the Wolverhampton *Express & Star* or the Birmingham *Evening Mail*, fish and chip shops, people who speak like they do), together with the extravagances of being away from home (ice cream stalls, fairgrounds, Krazee Golf, candyfloss, boat trips).

Many of what I have called caravan sites are actually filled with huge mobile homes, though since they are all propped up on large concrete slabs they are in effect completely immobile. They are usually painted green in the daft belief that in this way they would merge more naturally with the surrounding countryside. They look rather like those things you see on building sites, where workmen in cement-stained overalls and yellow hard hats congregate for fags and cups of tea. Some of owners of these monstrosities attempt to personalise and domesticate them by planting little gardens around their perimeters. Others have erected little white wicket fences for the same purpose.

Other sites betray their origins in a different era. There's one particular one just outside Stourport which contains a number of small attractively built chalet homes, all different and all presumably erected according to the predilections of its original owner. These were created, I would guess, in the 1930s, before the age of mass mobile home excrescences and the caravan invasion. They look like what they are – small weekend homes, that melt naturally into their surroundings and welcome their inhabitants to weekend rest from the labours of the week in the industrial heartlands.

One of these is called Trinidad One, for reasons which I know not but which immediately set me to composing a petition and leading a march on Parliament to 'Free the Trinidad One'. And it was at the head of just such a march that I entered Stourport-on-Severn itself.

Stourport is the only town in Britain built because of the coming of the canals. As I've already mentioned, this was a direct result of the refusal of the good burghers of Bewdley to have anything to do with Brindley's 'stinking ditch'. This ditch was the Staffordshire and Worcestershire Canal designed to link the Severn with the Trent and the Mersey rivers and it was opened in 1772. The town grew rapidly thereafter, attracting brass and iron foundries, vinegar works, tan yards, worsted spinning mills, carpet manufacturers, barge and boat building, yards amongst other industries. Most of these have now gone, of course, although the vinegar brewery, now part of British Vinegar, still operates.

At the heart of the town is the lock basin, which nowadays is full of pleasure craft, for just north of here is the head of the navigable river, but was once the heart of the throbbing waterways industries. There are a number of still splendid buildings around the lock basin, none more magnificent than the huge Tontine Hotel, built by the canal company for the benefit of merchants and higher grades of employee. Sadly, the building is currently boarded up awaiting purchase by some latter-day entrepreneur who might just see the possibilities of opening a lap-dancing club in Stourport.

But before I reached the Tontine Hotel, I passed by the jetty where a large sign states 'NO BUMPING OR SWIMMING OFF THESE BOATS'. The boats in question are the pleasure steamers that sail up and down the river from here, carrying their freight of Brummie and Black Country weekenders on a booze cruise. To my left was the riverside park with its Krazee Golf course, featuring for some inexplicable reason a large concrete tiger, its kiddies' paddling pool, and its children's playground with an amusing set of musical metal slabs. Then it was under the 1870 road bridge to the real reason for Stourport's continued existence – Shipley's Fair, in all its glorious technicolour. Here you can ride on the dodgems, with greasy-haired John Travolta lookalikes leaping on and off the dodgem cars to collect your money, or ride on a mat belly-down and head first, like some mad winter Olympics sledger, down the belly-churning Big Slide.

There's always been a fair in Stourport, or at least as long as I can remember. It's this that brings the Midlanders flocking here with their children on bank holidays. They can dump the screeching little 'uns at the fair and slip into the nearby Bridge Inn ('Good Food, Cask Ales') for a couple of pints and a packet of crisps. Oh, go on then, make it three pints. Of course, it wasn't a Bank Holiday when I passed by and the fair was closed down. But I can never pass it without sensing the special noise and the smell that screams 'Fairground' at you.

On the opposite side of the river is the headquarters building of the Stourport Yacht Club, whose website has provided me, and I suspect many of you, my readers, with the following extremely helpful information:

> **Is it Left or Port?**
>
> For some reason, most people are worried about getting this wrong, so until it becomes second nature use LEFT or Right it's much safer. To help you try to remember use the following. The captain LEFT his RED PORT on the table.
>
> In addition, you could remember that RED and PORT are short words; whereas GREEN and STARBOARD are longer.
>
> Red is the colour used for the navigation light on the left hand side of a vessel, looking towards the bow. Green used on the right.

Got that?
Me neither!

A mile or so beyond Stourport I came to the first of the great locks that were built to control the flow of the River Severn. This one is called Lincomb Lock and it features a similar pattern to those later on downriver, with huge concrete cylinders bound together to prevent boats from going through, forcing them to steer through the narrow man-made lock. Here a lock-keeper is on duty from eight in the morning till late afternoon to control entries and exits. But there were no boats passing through that day and the lock-keeper seemed to be busy reading the *Mirror* for entertainment.

The chief interest of my late morning walk were the three hostelries on the opposite bank that I passed. First up was the Hamstall Inn near Astley Burf, which used to be known as the Cider House at Hamstall. This reminded me that I was deep into cider country now and that for many people in this part of the West Country cider, not beer, was the only serious drink. Julius Caesar is reported to have enjoyed a pint of British scrumpy when he made his brief visit to these isles in 54 BC but it was only after the Norman invasion that serious cider-making (and, I guess, serious cider-drinking) began to take off, as the French brought some of their home-grown apples to England and began cultivating their orchards, particularly in monastery gardens. It became a massive enterprise and by the end of the eighteenth century 10,000 hogsheads of cider – one hogshead equals 110 gallons – were being exported each year from Worcestershire.

I'd have liked a pint of scrumpy but there is no way of crossing the river just there, any more than there is at the site of the next hostelry which hove into view on the opposite bank a couple of miles later. The Lenchford Hotel's car park was full of similarly coloured blue vans, though I could not tell which company they were from. Obviously the drivers of these vans were indulging in one of those glories of the early twenty-first century – the corporate conference. Business management manuals, a relatively recent importation from the US of A, require companies to take a section of their workforce, usually middle managers, to some out-of-the-way hotel in the countryside for a spot of team-building. This might involve those selected in using 'techniques borrowed from the theatre to develop their creative teamwork', or 'utilising the science of personality and inter-personal relationship testing to help their understanding of team dynamics', or 'allowing thinking energy to be focused in one direction at a time for the purpose of consensus building'.

Crucially, this allows otherwise unemployable people to earn large amounts of dosh running such conferences and fills otherwise empty hotels at slack times of the week. This might be described as a win-win situation – the management consultants who run these conferences and the hotel managers clearly benefit, the company believes its employees will be better workers, and those attending the conference and listening to all this nonsense know to say nothing, 'cos it beats working for a living.

So, who pays? You and I, my friends. The so-called training costs are reflected in the price of whatever product or service emerges, and that's what we are paying for.

I suspect the management of the Holt Fleet Inn, the third of my morning hostelries, would rather have had a fleet of blue vans to deliver their customers than the rather weary looking figure that presented himself at their door just after half past one that day. I knew that the Holt Fleet Inn had once been the most popular resort for Black Country folk. As far back as 1901 a local journalist reported as follows:

> Holt Fleet is one of the most charming spots in Worcester, and it is sadly to be regretted that its reputation is being ruined by vulgar day trippers. Since the recent freeing of

> Holt Fleet Bridge from tolls, Black Country people have swarmed there in greater numbers than ever, and their ideal of a day's outing appears to be drunkenness and bad language. More than once, attention has been called to the disorderly conduct and rowdyism which have taken place. Extra police have been engaged, but the same order of things still unfortunately prevails. This summer, the place has been visited by thousands of Black Country people, and their carousals have pained, even disgusted those in search of fresh air and scenes of quietude. Last Saturday, there were disorderly scenes because the police rightly objected to the foul expressions of a drunken dray-man from the Black Country. His more or less drunken comrades took his part, and so excited and angry did they become that one landlord had to close his public house – the Wharf Inn. Eventually, six of them had to be arrested. The County Bench rightly convicted them on Tuesday but inflicted absurdly small fines. Severity is the only way of treating Hooligans.

Maybe the landlady thought I was one of these rowdies because the greeting I got as I opened the door was not exactly welcoming.

'Is there a separate bar?' I asked, for I had noted that the sign above the doorway indicated that this was the entrance to the lounge and restaurant.

'No,' she replied, looking at me disdainfully from her position by the fruit machine that she was sharing with the white-overalled chef. 'There's only a lounge and a restaurant.'

'Can't I get a drink here then?' I asked, for I was fair parched, having eaten my sandwich on the footpath some time earlier.

'What do you want?' she asked, casting me another disdainful glance.

'Just a pint of beer,' I answered, though I was beginning to lose hope.

'Oh, alright then,' she said and marched off to the bar.

I followed her into the lounge, ordered a pint of shandy and sat down. There were only two other people there, finishing their lunch, and they soon left. Apart from the landlady and the chef, who were continuing their conversation at the bar, I was the only customer.

Suddenly the phone rang and the landlady, looking harassed beyond belief, went to answer it, declaring to her companion:

'Ooh, it's all go in here!'

I had difficulty restraining my laughter. This did not look, in all fairness, the most stressful day in the life of this hotel. She, the landlady, did not appear to be under the same sort of duress as, say, a schoolteacher facing a class of adolescents or an airline pilot in turbulent weather or even a management consultant.

I just had to leave. I swallowed the last few grammes of my beer and did just that.

The Severn Way footpath leaves the river just beyond Holt Fleet, having crossed now to the western bank. It leads through the tiny hamlets of Holt, with its attractive Norman church and castle, and Grimley, which are separated by a huge quarry. Then it rejoins the river just before its junction with what used to be the Droitwich Canal, now silted up but to be reopened in the next few years.

Droitwich is only a few miles from the River Severn but its peculiar geological basis has meant that for centuries it was one of the most important towns in Britain, for underneath its soil lay a substance that, before the invention of the refrigerator, was an essential part of every household – salt. Spoiled as we are by modern technology, we forget how crucial salt was in preserving food, particularly meat. The saltway roads that led from Droitwich spread across the country and the coming of the canals sped that journey. The first person to think about connecting Droitwich to the River Severn by water was one

Andrew Yarranton, a local ironmaster, who in 1665 persuaded the burgesses of the town to sponsor his attempts to deepen the River Salwerpe so that larger boats could use it. His attempts came to nothing, however, and it was a hundred years before James Brindley was commissioned to build the canal that more or less follows the line of the Salwerpe.

I was following the river bank again now, passing Bevere Island where Worcester citizens used to flee from whichever invading force was attacking them – the Danes, Cromwell's New Model Army, the Plague, the Martians. There's another huge lock here, using the natural features of the river as it flows either side of the island. Shortly afterwards I reached the Camp House Inn, which appeared to be closed, and then over a stile which carried a sign saying:

WALK ON A RAINBOW TRAIL, WALK ON A TRAIL OF SONG
AND ALL ABOUT YOU WILL BE BEAUTY,
THERE IS A WAY OUT OF EVERY DARK MIST
OVER A RAINBOW TRAIL.

I have no idea who placed this sign there. I'm not actually sure of my reaction to it. When I first saw it, I have to say I was moved without really being able to put my finger on why. As I write it down here, I am even more unsure. It could be seen as sentimental claptrap, couldn't it? The sort of verse you might find in a Rod McKuen or a Patience Strong poem. I don't know. But I will say that, after the treatment I received in the Holt Fleet Inn, it cheered me up and reminded me that there are good people out there.

As I approached the built-up area, a large stone on the river bank welcomed me to the City of Worcester. There ought to be more of these. Every town and every village on the Severn should have a stone like this on its river bank, facing the oncoming walker or cyclist and welcoming them into its environs. On the eastern bank I could see the grassy racecourse, which is often the first place to flood when the Severn bursts its banks, and beyond it the spire of the cathedral. A rowing eight made its way steadily upstream as I reached my destination for the day and crossed the aptly named Sabrina Bridge.

Sabrina had been my companion all the way and the footbridge named after her took me in the late afternoon into the Faithful City itself for the final stages of this second week of my trek.

16 Worcester

'Dead – and never called me Mother.'

I'm sure you recognise those immortal words. You may even recollect that they come from that famous Victorian melodrama, *East Lynne,* written by Mrs Henry Wood. What you almost certainly won't know, however, is that Mrs Henry Wood was born in the shadow of Worcester cathedral, or that her father was a prosperous owner of a glove factory, that being the chief industry of the city in those times.

Now, I'm not especially interested in Victorian melodrama or in Mrs Henry Wood but I am curious about gloves. Where have they all gone? When I was younger, everyone seemed to wear them. I certainly did anyway, and all my family. And I'm pretty sure all my friends and their families did too. In fact, I used to own several pairs – a swashbuckling pair of leather (probably simulated) gauntlets for cycling, a rather swish pair of lambskin ones for when I was cutting a dash with the ladies (as they still call them on Radio 2) and a common or garden pair of woolly ones for knocking about in. But now? Nothing. I've still got a pair of grey woolly things somewhere at the back of the car, just in case I ever have to open the bonnet and look inside the engine as if I knew what I was looking at, or for. But I never ever wear them – or any others.

And I'm convinced that this is not an uncommon experience. Unless you are a cricket wicketkeeper, a football goalkeeper, a cross-country skier, a mountain-biker, a golfer, a boxer or a surgeon, you almost certainly won't have a need for a pair of gloves. Of course, you might choose to don some fancy ones to show off in – a long white silk pair for opera-going, perhaps, or a skimpy fishnet pair for sexual allure. But, in general, gloves are no longer an essential clothing item, even in winter. Now that we all wear multi-coloured fleeces made from polythene bottles (so I'm told) or waterproof anoraks, we don't need gloves because we keep our hands permanently in our pockets for warmth. So that, I fear, has also put an end to the possibility of reviving that quaint set of etiquette rules about glove-wearing which began in Charlemagne's time.

What about this, for instance:

'Gloves were not worn by men or women when taking the hands of partners in the dance.'

OK, so maybe that's understandable but what about this:

'The act of picking up the glove of one's lady-love was a sign of deep devotion. Many lovers sought, as sole favour, permission to pick up the lady's glove, and return or retain it.'

Well, I suppose it beats 'Fancy a shag?', which I heard called out in Worcester the afternoon I was there.

And then there's this:

'Elegants of the 15th century carried both gloves slung in the waist- or pouch-belt.'

The elegants of Worcester that I saw as I strolled through the city that early evening were certainly not carrying gloves slung in their belts. If anything, they were more likely to have mobile phones strapped there. And in Worcester there is a law that all mobes have to play the opening bars of Elgar's *Pomp and Circumstances March* as their call sign.

As far as I'm aware, there are no glove-makers in Worcester today. One of the largest glove-making businesses in the days when everyone wore gloves was that of Fownes Gloves, which merged with Dent's Gloves many years ago. Dents is now located in Warminster, Wiltshire, and it is there in its museum that a collection of rare gloves once belonging to the Fownes family can be seen. These include such wonders as a gauntlet supposed to have been worn by Sir Walter Raleigh (no doubt, to avoid getting nicotine stains on his fingers after he'd brought tobacco back from America, or maybe to protect his fingers when he was inventing chips with the very first potatoes seen in England), a glove worn by Charles I, another belonging to the Empress Josephine of France and the Coronation Glove worn by Queen Elizabeth I. What interests me is why they've only got one of each glove – has some other Glove Museum, in America maybe or more likely Hong Kong (well, they do have a Museum of Toilets there), got the other ones? Is there an illegal worldwide trade in gloves?

I think we should be told.

Fownes' factory on the City Walls Road was converted into Fownes Hotel in 1985. So nowadays, if you are so inclined, you can have your wedding reception in the hotel's restaurant which was the former glove works dye shop; your guests can while away their time waiting for your arrival in the former boiler house (now the library), or adjust their attire in the Stuart Suite (once female sewing rooms – why were Worcester women being sewn up?); and after the celebrations everyone can do what I almost did that evening – strip off and relax in the hotel sauna (once, most appropriately, the fur room!).

Oh, and Mrs Henry Wood never wrote that immortal line – it is from one of the many stage dramatisations of her *magnum opus*.

Since I've mentioned Elgar, this is as good a point as any to deal with Worcester's most famous son – the man responsible for all those Hooray Henrys and Henriettas who wave their tipsy Union Jacks at the Last Night of the Proms when the band (and that's all they are really) launch into *Land of Hope and Glory*. And he didn't even like the words that were written to accompany his *Pomp and Circumstances March*!

Edward Elgar was born just outside the city of Worcester in 1857. His father was a piano tuner and church organist who later ran a music shop in the shadows of Worcester Cathedral. Young Eddie thus grew up surrounded by music, whether from the shop, or from accompanying his father on piano-tuning trips to country houses, or from sitting beside him as he played the organ every Sunday in St George's Catholic church. He also got pally with choristers in the cathedral and through them borrowed scores from its ancient music library. After leaving school, he got involved in numerous musical activities, including taking the post as conductor of the staff band at the County of Worcester Lunatic Asylum.

This latter prompted Our Eddie to marry his mum, or rather his mum-substitute – Alice Roberts, daughter of a major-general and eight years older than himself. She it was who drove him on to compose his greatest works, the *Enigma Variations*, the *Dream of Gerontius* and the *Pomp and Circumstances Marches*. The enigma of the first of these works has been the subject of endless speculation since it was first performed. You see, not content with expecting his listeners to work out which of his friends or family were being portrayed in each musical *Variation*, Elgar let it be known that there was another 'dark saying' at the heart of the music and then never revealed what it was. It was well known that he loved puzzles and crosswords and suchlike, so the hunt for the melody which he claimed was counter-pointed in the *Variations* has gone on and on. On its way it has taken in *God Save the Queen*, *Rule Britannia*, Bach's *Agnus Dei*, Beethoven's *Pathetique* Sonata, and *Auld Lang Syne*.

Now does any of this really matter? When we get to the Pearly Gates, will Saint Peter ask us if we know what the enigma is at the centre of Elgar's musical composition? I think not.

However, His Archangelship might well ask if we knew who composed the world's very first football chant and the answer to that one – surprise, surprise! – is Edward Elgar. Among his many friends was the Rector of Wolverhampton and Elgar, a keen spectator of Worcestershire cricket and at Worcester races, was also a frequent visitor to the Wolves' stadium. Here he apparently overheard a fellow spectator on the terraces say 'He banged the leather for goal' and set it to music. You won't be surprised to know that it failed to catch on. It doesn't have that resonance, does it? Not like 'Ooh ah, Cantona' or 'You're a bastard, referee.'

Elgar's great love was the Three Choirs Festival, where he played violin as a young man and where he conducted the first performance of the *Enigma Variations*. The Three Choirs is Europe's oldest music festival, commencing in 1715 and rotating annually around the cathedrals of Worcester, Gloucester and Hereford. All his life Elgar would make sure he attended the Three Choirs, though he never sat down to watch and listen. Instead, he preferred to wander around the cathedrals like Banquo's ghost, no doubt surprising any cleric who was up to no good in the cloisters or spectators snoozing in the shadows.

A statue of Edward Elgar holds pride of place at the top of Worcester's High Street. He looks rather forbidding, with his hands clasped behind his long frock coat and his huge Stalin-style walrus moustache. It's hard to imagine him as the insecure young musician who constantly felt undervalued because he was a mere tradesman's son and who craved success and prestige.

Bet he'd enjoy hearing all those Worcester citizens' mobes ringing out his *Pomp and Circumstances*!

Just beyond Elgar's statue stands the cathedral itself. It is a magnificent building, like all those monuments from the Norman Conquest. And, just as I feel in all its sister cathedrals throughout the land, although I can admire – nay, I am gobsmacked at – the sheer size and majesty of the building and its architecture, I have real difficulty in reaching an understanding of how several generations of people could hold the vision over three centuries to build it. Yes, I know that most of those who did the real work were little better than slaves. But can you imagine their modern-day equivalents in their torn Levis and ancient Iron Maiden T-shirts setting off every Monday morning in their battered white Ford Transits to build a cathedral? And keeping at it, father and son and grandson and great-grandson, for 300 years?

It beggars belief. I suppose that's what I'm in awe of when I stand in the nave of some cathedral like Worcester and gaze up at the intricate carvings, the carefully crafted beams, the delicate tracery and the vaulted roof. The Christian faith must have been really strong in those guys who designed and built them. Can you imagine anyone nowadays asking us to believe the words of some book about flatulent goat-herders with no teeth which has been translated by people with bad haircuts and funny beards?

Well, I suppose someone like David Icke might!

There are two features of Worcester Cathedral I feel you really should know about. The first is that it contains the tomb of King John. Yes, everybody's favourite Bad King. And that's simply because he was the one who outlawed Robin of Loxley and turned him into our dashing hero, Robin Hood (Kevin Costner), with his band of Merrie Men romping around in Sherwood Forest, getting one over on the wicked Sheriff of Nottingham (Alan Rickman), and getting another one over Maid Marian (Marilyn Monroe or Sabrina). In fact, poor old King John was so bad that his barons made him sign away half his power on to Magna Carta.

John must have known he was a baddie because the legend is that he left instructions that he was to be buried in Worcester Cathedral between the tombs of St Oswald and St Wulfstan, two of the founder bishops of the cathedral, so that he might sneak into heaven beside them when the last trump was sounded. When the tomb was opened at the end of the eighteenth century, it was found that he had even taken the trouble to disguise himself by being incarcerated in a monk's cowl.

And, poor sap, he died too soon to know the secret of

Elgar's enigma!

However, there is an even more interesting piece of stonework herein, which is worthy of some of your time.

Can you guess the connection between Maggie Thatcher, Lord Longford, Sir Edmund Hillary and the Duke of Norfolk? No? Well, they are all members of The Most Noble Order of the Garter, the oldest and most important of the chivalric ranks in Britain, founded in 1348 by Edward III. There are only ever twenty-four Knights of the Garter at any one time. They are appointed by the Queen and meet up for a party once a year, when they are expected to dress up in their blue, red and white velvet clobber. In particular, they have to wear their blue garters just below the left knee (and on the left arm for women) with the famous legend on it 'Honi soit qui mal y pense', which means something like 'Honey, don't think bad of me, just 'cos I dress like this'.

But why do they wear this blue garter? And what has it to do with Worcester Cathedral?

Pin back your earholes and I'll tell you.

There is a memorial in the cathedral to the Countess of Salisbury. According to Daniel Defoe it was she who, while dancing with Edward III at Windsor Castle, dropped her garter. Edward, who like most royals was having a bit of the extra-maritals with the aforementioned Countess of S., picked it up and decided that such a trophy should be the emblem of his new order of knighthood.

The only trouble with this is that Defoe had got the wrong Countess of Salisbury. The one whose memorial is in Worcester Cathedral died long before Edward III was born. In fact, she wasn't even a proper Countess of Salisbury, but merely adopted the name on her second marriage.

Didn't I tell you that Defoe was notoriously unreliable?

Still, it was too good a story to omit. So I haven't.

Speaking of royalty brings me to the moment in history when

Worcester really put itself on the map, so to speak. You see, for reasons which will become a bit clearer shortly, Worcester was the site of the final act of the English Revolution, which showed the way to the French and the Americans, who took another hundred years or so to copy us, and the Russians, who, because of the cold weather, took a bit longer. As a result of what happened at Worcester in 1651, King Charles II set off on his momentous flight through England to his eventual escape to France and Oliver Cromwell (warts and all) became the first and, so far, only civil leader of the United Kingdom. The curious thing about all this is that it is Charlie's flight, including his time stuck up an oak tree at Boscobel and his hiding in various priest's holes, which has come to be part of our cultural hoard of legends, and we learn little about Cromwell and the English Revolution in our schooling.

Anyway, let's run through the story behind the Battle of Worcester which, as I've already indicated, was the decisive battle in the Civil War of the mid-seventeenth century. Cromwell was a reluctant revolutionary. He had no creed, other than his firmly held Christian beliefs, and preached no revolutionary slogans. He was driven to lead the English Revolution by the excesses of Charles I, who sought to rule without recourse to Parliament, which he had suspended, and to raise taxes to prosecute his own private wars. To counteract this unpopular monarch, Cromwell invented his New Model Army, which took on and beat the king's armies. Eventually – such is the way in revolutions everywhere – Charles was brought to trial and was executed in front of the baying crowd outside the Banqueting Hall in Whitehall in January 1649.

There's a superb display about all this in the Commandery Museum in Worcester, including an opportunity for you to participate in the trial of Charles and decide on his fate (though it's a bit too late to make any difference!).

After this, Oliver might have believed his job to be over but, of course, there was more to come. The son of the dead king, also called Charles, had been lurking in France for some time, being kept warm by a succession of French mistresses (he was later kept warm by Nell Gwynne with her lovely round oranges and by Frances Stuart, who with helmet and trident was engraved as Britannia on the coinage of the realm for the next 300 years). Now he decided to raise an army in Scotland to march into England and reclaim his throne.

Eventually, Charles II and his Scottish troops reached Worcester and, overcoming some feeble resistance, took the city where they encamped ready to fight Cromwell's army. What he hadn't reckoned with was Cromwell's cunning plot to cross the Severn south of Worcester by building a bridge of boats. This gave the Parliamentary troops an unexpected advantage, which they drove home by marching on the city itself. After a number of bloody skirmishes, the city was taken within the day of 3 September 1650 and Charles was forced to flee. And that, my friends, as they say in Hollywood, was the end of the Civil War and the beginning of rule by Parliament, led by the Lord Protector, Oliver Cromwell (warts and all).

If central casting were to look for someone to play God's Irishman, they would probably end up with Richard Harris. If they wanted someone to play God's Englishman, as Cromwell is sometimes known, they would probably end up with someone like Ricky Tomlinson. Somehow or other, central casting got this mixed up for the film of *Cromwell*, where a wartless and unblemished Harris glowers under his eyebrows at Alec Guinness's Charles I, whose doe-eyed innocence is modelled, I take it, on the spaniel that bears his name.

I think it's a shame that we don't have an affectionate portrait, in paint, word or film, of the Lord Protector whose actions changed the course of history. Whatever his political mistakes, Cromwell never became a corrupt, power-drunk, bloodthirsty megalomaniac, running a regime of terror, like so many of the revolutionaries around the world who came after him.

Both the Labour and Conservative parties in recent years

have sought to win the votes of the mythical Midland Englanders, whom they have styled at different times as Mondeo Man or Worcester Woman. Is it too much to hope that one day Mondeo Man and Worcester Woman might actually come to acknowledge the part played in the creation of these parliamentary parties by Oliver Cromwell?

Without him, Neil and Christine Hamilton would never have existed.

Come to think of it . . .!

My wife was due to collect me in Worcester but she got delayed, so when she did arrive we decided we would eat in the city before returning home. We chose a place we'd been to once before – a former church which has been converted into a café bar, now called RSVP, serving a variety of beers and a reasonable selection of food. It is a quite splendid building and, I have to say, is probably one of the best uses for a church that I have come upon. If you can't feed people's minds with spiritual things, then let them feed their bellies with French fries and Theakston's is my motto. Long live the revolution!

After I'd told her about my day's journey, I thought I would quiz her on her knowledge of Worcester. She is not a native of these parts and I was curious to know what the word Worcester evoked in her mind.

'It's where Worcester sauce comes from,' was, surprisingly, her first thought. 'Isn't it? There must be some connection, surely.'

This allowed me to display my stunning erudition on the matter.

'Spot on,' I replied. 'It was invented by a certain Mr Lea and a certain Mr Perrins here in Worcester, surprise, surprise! But do you know why?'

She shook her head. I took this as a desire to know more.

'Well, back in the early nineteenth century a Worcestershire toff tasted some sauce in India and commissioned Mr Lea and

Mr Perrins, two tame chemists, to reproduce it. What they produced tasted like dog poo, so they bunged it in a cellar and forgot about it. When they came upon it two years later, it tasted wonderful and it's still made to that original secret recipé,' I delighted in telling her.

'And there's Royal Worcester porcelain,' she added. 'Wasn't that something to do with Queen Victoria?'

I nodded and was ready to show off my knowledge again but she pressed on before I could.

'Not my cup of tea, to coin a phrase,' she said. 'It's far too decorative for my taste. Still, each to his own. Oh, and there's the cricket ground by the cathedral, isn't there?'

'Yes, I used to come here to watch,' I began to reminisce. 'The cricket field was always flooded in spring and you always wondered if the water would disappear in time for the season. Of course, it always did and the grass was always brilliantly green at the start of the season and there was that gorgeous smell of new-mown grass all around.'

'I went to watch Lancashire once with an American visitor,' my wife cut into my reveries. 'Have you ever tried to explain cricket to someone who's from a country where they don't play it?'

'All that business of in and out!'

'And legside and offside,' she interjected. 'And why a match can go on for five days. And as for lbw! Don't even try.'

We paused to nibble at our meals.

'It's a bit of an odd thing for a grown man to do, isn't it?' I said. 'I mean, all that dressing up in white clothing and fastening pads to your legs, so you can't run fast, and helmets, so your head sweats even more than it might normally in warm weather.'

'It's better than football,' she admonished, giving me a meaningful glare.

'D'you know what the Worcestershire badge is like?' I quizzed her, changing the subject quickly. And then, without giving her the chance to reply, said, 'It's three pears. Worcestershire is pear county, you know. It's where they used to make perry. I've never tasted it, have you?'

'Of course!' she said. 'Is the Pope a Catholic?'

I declined to answer. My wife's experiences with a range of alcohol products is not part of this narrative. It was time to leave.

17 Worcester to Tewkesbury

Pausing on Worcester Bridge, which has stood solid since John Gwynn built it in 1781, and looking down at the River Severn as she wended her gentle way underneath it and past the cathedral, it was hard to believe that only a year earlier the bridge was flooded and the road closed to traffic. Television pictures showed firefighters in their waterproofs giving piggyback rides to stranded pedestrians as the waters swirled beneath their wellington-booted feet. Jet-skiers practised their art on flooded riverside meadows. The army was commandeered to run a bus service over the bridge in its lorries. It is surprising how quickly we can forget all this. On the wall below the cathedral, a short way along the footpath that runs from below the bridge, there are markers for every flood for centuries, the highest one being for 1770. I guess the 2000 plaque is still being readied – it certainly will be higher.

The riverside footpath I was chirpily waltzing on that morning as I began the third stage of my Dance with Sabrina would have been some 16 feet under water back then and not the lovely tranquil path it is now. This is a favoured walk of Worcester citizens and visitors alike, beside the walls of the Old Palace and the cathedral, with myriad swans sailing in their stately pomp upon the river. Across the river is the county cricket ground where such Worcestershire luminaries as Don Kenyon, Tom Graveney, Ian Botham and Graham Hick have held sway in their time. In my memory I could still hear the click of bat on ball, the swelling roar of the crowd, and the West Country burr of John Arlott commentating on the first match of the cricket season when Worcestershire played an overseas touring team.

Soon I was leaving the cathedral behind and crossing the footbridge at Diglis Locks, where the Worcester and Birmingham Canal meets the river. Shortly after that I could see where the River Teme flowed into the Severn. It was here in 1651 that Cromwell's troops, under the command of one General Fleetwood (commonly known as 'Mac'), built their bridge of boats to allow the New Model Army to cross both rivers and from the south attack Charles II's Scottish not-so-super troopers.

I hummed a few lines of Elvis Costello's *Oliver's Army* to myself. This is something I do for no apparent reason and often with no obvious connection between the tune I hum and anything in the immediate vicinity of me or my life. I actually have never understood the lyrics to *Oliver's Army* but that hasn't stopped its hook line burying itself in my unconscious and awaiting its opportunity to leap into my mouth as it did just then. And, in this case at least, there was some connection. Though heaven knows what!

Two miles or so out of Worcester I came to the old village of Kempsey, which has a recorded history going back to Roman times. Here was one of those places to ford the river and therefore an inevitable site for guarding against incursions from the Welsh boyos. Later the Anglo-Saxons built the settlement's first church and, later still, three kings of England (two Henrys and an Edward) called in for a glass or two of cider, though Henry III probably had to beg for his, since he only got to Kempsey as a prisoner of Simon de Montfort.

But the story I like best about Kempsey concerns the supposed visit of the famous highwayman, Dick Turpin. Now everybody knows of the legendary Dick, if only through his scurrilous adventures portrayed in *Carry On Dick*, where the eponymous hero is played by the louche Sid James. In this story, however, Turpin concocts a plot to rob Lord Coventry, then resident in Kempsey, by holding up his stagecoach and accepting a cheque for 30 guineas in lieu of a framed miniature portrait of Coventry's lady-friend. The cheque he then cashes at the home of Lord Coventry's agent. The unlikely story is told in *Berrow's Worcester Journal* but, just because this august newspaper is the oldest in the world, having appeared every week for over 300 years, this doesn't make its stories any more likely to be factual than, say, those in today's edition of the *Sun* or *The Times*!

Still, it amused me to recall this tale as I strolled along the river bank, passing Kempsey's church on my left-hand side. This was the straightforward part of my morning trek, for shortly afterwards the Severn Way deviated away from the river again and through some poorly waymarked fields. There was the almost compulsory herd of young bullocks guarding one such field, all of whom gazed at me in hopeful anticipation of some sport. It was raining now and I had donned my red cagoule, as if I knew to expect these creatures. But I wasn't in the mood for a tussle with them, so I took a brisk turn across a different field.

The detour I chose probably added half a mile to my walk as I headed directly for the river bank again, but the detour around Cliff Wood a mile or so further on was ridiculous. The Severn Way footpath is forced to make this mile-long deviation, presumably because the local landowner doesn't want oiks like me tramping through his forest. As I trudged around this offending piece of woodland, aware of hunger pangs gnawing at my stomach, I couldn't help but hope that Dick Turpin or his modern-day counterpart would come upon this Worcestershire worthy and exact an appropriate penalty.

Fortunately, as I once again rejoined the river bank, I could see no bullocks waiting to charge me but I could espy the tower of Upton-upon-Severn's Pepperpot and knew that food and ale were within reach.

Try as it might to be otherwise, Upton-upon-Severn is chiefly lodged in the common consciousness because of something that didn't actually happen there. I'm talking about that classic scene – surely one of cinema's most memorable moments – in the 1963 Oscar-winning film, *Tom Jones*. You know the one – it's where Albert Finney, as the eponymous hero, enjoys a gargantuan feast with the woman he has just rescued from rape: 'but her cloaths being torn from all the upper part of her body, her breasts, which were well formed, and extremely white, attracted the eyes of her deliverer'.

And all the time the two of them are eating each other lasciviously with their eyes as much as the food on the table with their mouths. The extended food orgy, culminating in the slavering biting and sucking of juicy Worcestershire (presumably) pears, leads inevitably to the bedroom in this wonderful film whose epithets usually include 'bawdy', 'ribald', 'boisterous' and 'lusty' – favoured terms of film critics when they're short of words for historical romps.

In Henry Fielding's masterpiece, *The History of Tom Jones*, this momentous scene is clearly placed at the White Lion Inn in Upton: 'a house of exceeding good repute, whither Irish ladies of strict virtue and many northern lasses of the same predicament were accustomed to resort in their way to Bath'.

Now, I suppose times have changed somewhat but I saw no Irish ladies of strict or, for that matter, of unstrict virtue, sadly, and there were certainly no northern lasses of any predicament at the bar when I called for my lunch-time repast. And, although my pint of Brakspear's and ham-and-apricot sandwich were certainly very palatable, they were taken without the coquetting of some flighty lady, whether Irish or northern, on the opposite side of my table. Nor was my brief visit interrupted, as Tom Jones's was, by the sudden appearance of his true love, Sophia Western, in flight from the marriage arranged by her father in order to find Tom, or later of Sophia's father, Squire Allworthy: 'My daughter's muff!' cries the squire, in a rage. 'Hath he got my daughter's muff!'

Good question, Squire.

No, my lunch was taken quietly and without interruption, in the company only of two thirtysomething travelling salesmen swapping tales of skiing, fast motor cars, even faster motorbikes and their golf handicaps. The only other inhabitants of the lounge in this loveliest of pubs were an elderly couple who munched their sandwiches in silence and in apparent ignorance of each other. At length, the woman left the room to seek the toilet. When she returned, her husband inquired of her thus.

'You alright?'

'No,' she answered abruptly.

My ears pricked up at this, ever-ready antennae sensing diversion.

'Are you going to the lavatory?' he pressed.

'I've just been,' she replied witheringly.

Both were speaking at considerable volume. I guessed there was a certain shared hearing difficulty – not to mention listening difficulty or attention deficit disorder.

'Oh,' Victor Meldrew said, for by now I had identified him as the prototype of the television sitcom character played memorably by Richard Wilson. 'You alright then?'

'No,' she barked.

There was a pause as Victor M. took this in. He knew what was coming. They'd had this battle many times before.

'What's the matter then?' he barked.

'You,' she snapped. 'You haven't spoken to me since we came out. What's the point of coming out if you're not going to talk to me?'

Now I had some sympathy with him at this point. After all, what he'd wanted was a quiet pint in a good pub and he'd probably thought she'd enjoy the day out too so he'd suggested she joined him. No mention of conversation. Just a quiet drink and a sandwich. And now here she was expecting him to be a combination of Michael Parkinson and Claire Rayner.

'Oh,' he said again – it was one of his better phrases. 'I'm going to the toilet. I'll see you in the car.'

And with that they both got up and left in their separate directions.

I finished my own sandwich but, bearing in mind what happened to Tom Jones, I did avoid the pears.

The irony of all this is that the filming of that classic scene in *Tom Jones*, clearly set by Fielding in the White Lion at Upton, was done in west Somerset where the entire film was shot on location. So poor old Upton's one claim to worldwide fame is somewhat tarnished by the vagaries of film-making. And poor old Albert Finney, who received the first of his five Oscar nominations for his masterly performance as Tom, has still never won an Oscar.

The White Lion also features in the lead up to the Battle of Worcester described earlier, for it was because Prince Rupert's Royalist troops got drunk and fell asleep there one night that they missed the small contingent of eighteen Parliamentary soldiers crossing the bridge and seizing the church. Subsequently, 12,000 of Cromwell's men crossed the bridge at Upton on their way to what was to prove the decisive battle in the Civil War.

The bridge is, of course, largely why Upton exists. When Leland called, it was a wooden one, but by the time Celia Fiennes called 150 years later, riding side saddle, it had been replaced by a stone one – the only one in her day between Worcester and Gloucester. Cobbett came to stay nearby with a friend of his but was more concerned to rant about the bankers of foreign origin ('greedy, mercenary, selfish, unfeeling wretches') who had started buying up the great estates in the county. However, he did note the lushness of the grasslands in the area, munched by Leicester sheep and Hereford cattle, and also remarked upon the absence of turnips!

Since the decline in the river trade, Upton has become less significant on the national map. Its place in the busy river trading of the sixteenth, seventeenth and eighteenth centuries, together with earlier stages in its history, are well displayed in the town's attractive heritage centre, housed in what is known locally as the Pepperpot – the oddly shaped tower that is the sole remaining part of Upton's medieval church.

Nowadays, Upton is best known for its annual Oliver Cromwell Jazz Festival, held over a June weekend, when bands with names like The Stackyard Stompers or Bob Kerr and His Whoopee Band play traditional New Orleans jazz in a variety of venues around the town. Quite what Oliver Cromwell would have thought of it I hesitate to think but you can be sure that, for that weekend of the year at least, it is the cavalier spirit that abounds in Upton-upon-Severn.

I think the stretch of river bank I walked along south from Upton-upon-Severn is probably one of the most attractive stretches of the whole Severn Way. The path through riverside pastures is clear, the stiles are all in eminently good repair and the grass is such that it is nowhere overgrown, making walking so much more comfortable. Add to that the sight of Upton's church tower receding gently behind me, of the Malvern Hills shadowing me on my right-hand side as I walked, and the gently flowing Sabrina, dappled with occasional sun through the showers, accompanying my every step on the left, and it was hard not to be lulled into a sense of tranquillity.

Or maybe it was just the two pints of Brakspear's in the White Lion.

An hour after leaving Upton, I passed under the concrete stilts that carry the M50 motorway over the flood plain and was aware of the sounds of shooting. You will know of my morbid fears of farmers and guns, so you won't be surprised to learn that my heart began a-fluttering immediately. However, as I pressed on past the motorway, I realised that the shots were quite regular and seemed to emanate from a cluster of people standing together on a grassy bank two fields away. As I looked in their direction, I also became aware that there was a huge straw construction some distance from these people and, since none of them was shouting oaths at me and my body was not punctured with bullets, I made the not unreasonable assumption that the straw construction was some kind of target they were shooting at.

Then I saw a clutch of small boys in rugby jerseys and baggy shorts trotting reluctantly out on to a wet field and realised from my map that I was passing Bredon School, a minor private school. Clearly the age-old skills of rushing around in silly clothes in the rain and shooting rifles at imaginary foreigners were still necessary in preparing a future generation for running the British Empire.

No sooner had my heart, reassured by this realisation, resumed its normal beat than it was jumping about again. I was going through a field of sheep, when they decided to follow me in what I thought was a very threatening manner. Their leader, a Manichaean specimen with an evil glint in its eye, started the chant of 'Four legs good, two legs bad' (in sheep-speak, of course, in which I happen to have some expertise) and suddenly they were all pounding along behind me.

I tried my usual trick of turning to face the advancing throng and shouting 'Boo!' at them, and 'Piss off!' but they weren't impressed at all. They kept coming even faster. That blasted George Orwell, I thought to myself as I made a bolt for the stile at the end of the meadow, may he rot in hell!

Was I glad to find myself shortly afterwards away from the river and on a road crossing the Mythe Bridge, an attractive single-span bridge over the Severn built by Thomas Telford in 1826, and entering Gloucestershire on the outskirts of Tewkesbury?

And was I glad to find my room for the night at the Malvern View guesthouse where the kindly proprietors, Helen and Ron Gracey, took my wet socks and boots off to dry overnight and showed me the quickest route through the town to my intended dining place, Ye Olde Black Bear?

This claims to be the oldest public house in Gloucestershire and who am I to disbelieve it? It stands just beyond King John's Bridge over the River Avon which merges with the Severn here at Tewkesbury, making it an obvious point for a settlement. For centuries traders with packhorses laden with salt from Droitwich crossed the Avon here and turned towards Bristol, stopping no doubt to wet their whistle. Ye Olde Black Bear has been serving ale since 1308 and much of the interior of the pub shows little change from its original state. The front room has a wonderful ceiling, made of leather embossed with Tudor roses and green and gold fishes, believed to be the work of Italian craftsmen working at Tewkesbury Abbey.

At the rear of the pub where I went to have my dinner of lasagne (in honour of the Italian craftsmen, of course) is a dining room which has a very fine seventeenth-century carved overmantle and two horseshoes tacked onto the wall. This room used to be the stabling area and these horseshoes are reputed to have jumped across the room more than once. There are also tales of a little old lady dressed in black (they always are, aren't they?) who sits in one of the other bars but who disappears when anyone speaks to her. She wasn't there that evening as far as I could tell, not even after my third pint of the excellent Wadworth's 6X bitter, served by the teenage barman. The only other people in the dining room were three middle-aged men who were planning the annual general meeting of some association they belonged to. Much as I strained my ears to discover the nature of this association, I was unable to hear anything of substance. All I picked up were stray phrases like 'new committee' and 'resigning' and 'any other business'.

I love this kind of stuff. It's the essence of our democratic way of life. No, I don't mean annual general meetings, I mean all the plotting and planning that goes into them, because democracy doesn't just happen. Ask anybody who's been involved in any kind of association, club or society whose officers are elected and they'll tell you that it's one hell of a job to get people to stand for office. And this is just as true whether it's the Little Piddling Long John Silver Impersonators' Society or a branch of the Labour Party. So those who care have to meet to plot who they will persuade to stand as Assistant Secretary B (toilets). And it can't be just anybody. Oh no, it has to be someone who is (a) gullible enough to believe that you're doing them a favour and (b) wise enough to turn into a paragon of public-spiritedness after being elected. Otherwise, you might just get that old fart who you managed to get outvoted from last year's committee and who keeps saying 'Point of order, Chair' when you're only on the third line of the minutes of your last meeting.

Believe me, I know about all this. I've been the gullible one who felt flattered to be invited to stand for office. And I've done the plotting to ensure the right succession.

And that's why the National Association of People Who Are Scared of Farm Animals (NAPWASOFA) has now only one member.

I am all its officers and all its members. My word is law.

Baa!

18 Tewkesbury

I am a semi-trained killer.

For obvious reasons, I have kept quiet about this for many years but, since it now seems unlikely that my country will be calling on me in my sixtieth year to use this particular little-known skill, I feel I can now publish this information. You see, every Thursday for seven years while I attended The Grammar School, I was required to dress up in itchy khaki jacket and trousers, to polish my heavy black boots with the bottom of a toothbrush until I could see my face reflected in them, to paste vile-smelling gungy-yellow blanco onto my webbing belt and puttees, and to wear a black beret at a regulation angle. I was then given a .22 rifle and made to march up and down in a rank with my similarly attired fellow pupils, while older boys shouted at us. Occasionally, we were taken to the rifle range, where we were instructed in loading and unloading our rifles, and then given bullets to fire at distant targets from a testicle-crushing, lying down position. Once a year all of us were taken in buses to Cannock Chase, where we were divided into two armies and had to engage in a mock battle, the rules of which none of us ever understood and which always ended up with a fire being started on Cannock Chase by the flare from a Very pistol.

See what I mean about being a semi-trained killer?

Scary, eh?

But that's not all. Most boys, if they managed to stay in The Grammar School until they were eighteen, got promoted in this Combined Cadet Force. At the very least, they became sergeants, but the real keenies became sergeant-majors and quartermaster-sergeants, and various other offices which I have now forgotten. These seemed to entail wearing, for some godforsaken reason, a red sash diagonally over the uniform jacket and carrying a stick, which also seemed to allow you to shout louder and nastier than anyone else. Nowadays this would be considered bullying but then it was called character building.

Anyway, I only reached the dizzy heights of lance-corporal, because I had cunningly become one of the only two people who could operate the school's 16-millimetre film projector. Just as I entered the sixth form, somebody convinced the powers that be in the school's cadet force (i.e. teachers dressed up to look as silly as the rest of us), that being able to set fire to Cannock Chase with a Very pistol and being able to miss targets with .22 rifles might just not be sufficient to help us save our country in the event of a nuclear bomb dropping on us! So, for the next two and a half years, every Thursday Lance-Corporal Bibby retired to the science lecture theatre in order to thread onto the projector's spools the black plastic film which demonstrated how people were to behave in the event of nuclear attack. Yes, this was an early version of *Protect and Survive*, in which the witless citizens of Britannia were advised to climb inside brown paper bags to ward off the threats of radiation. And every Thursday afternoon some new group of hapless khaki-wearing boys received this wonderful instruction while I sat next to the whirring film projector and smiled at my luck.

So, not only was I a semi-trained killer but I now became an expert on surviving nuclear warfare as well.

It is this extensive knowledge of military thinking that now enables me to write about the Battle of Tewkesbury, which introduced to the world Hunchback Dick or Dick the Turd or Richard III, however you wish to remember him. More of him anon.

The Battle of Tewkesbury was really won by accident. It happened like this. The year was 1471 and the descendants of the original Norman invaders were still arguing the toss about which of them could call himself King. Top of the pile at this time, theoretically, was Henry VI but only because he had a battleaxe of a wife called Margaret who was a sort of precursor of our more recent Margaret (i.e. Thatcher, Baroness of Handbagging). The former Margaret, in order to demonstrate that she really had a feminine side, always wore a red rose fastened with a safety-pin to her plate armour and, because her husband Henry once had a hotpot on his travels in the north-west of England, she appointed herself head of the House of Lancaster. That's why the red rose is the special emblem of Lancashire to this day.

Now, if you're going to have a proper argument about who should be king, you need someone to set up in opposition. And, as luck would have it, there was a more than suitable candidate lurking in the country. His name was Edward and he had the good sense to be the son of the recently killed Duke of York, so, just to show Margaret what for, he started wearing a white rose every day on his battle tunic. Pretty soon everyone was doing it – Margaret's army all wore red roses, and Edward's wore white. Hence the Wars of the Roses. This, of course, helped enormously in battle because it was much easier to identify who was on the same side as you and who wasn't.

Anyway, back to the Battle of Tewkesbury.

What I haven't mentioned so far is that Edward had already had a shot at being king ten years' earlier – in his case he was Edward IV. And, furthermore, he had imprisoned Henry in the Tower of London (a favourite trick in those days) but he forgot about battleaxe Margaret. She arranged for Edward to be chased out of England and for poor old Henry to stop auditioning for bit parts in *Porridge* and get back to being king. Edward, however, being 6 feet 3 inches tall, was not likely to take this lying down. Before you could say Plantagenet, he was back in England with his army sporting their red roses, reclaiming his throne and ready for another fight.

Margaret was looking for the same thing and Twekesbury, although it had never done any harm to anyone, seemed a good enough place so the two armies pitched camp there for the night, preparing themselves for the next day's punch-up. Edward, as well as being very tall, was a bit of clever so-and-so when it came to tactics in battle and, seeing a wood on the edge of the battlefield, was worried that it might be used by his opponent as an ambush. So he sent 200 soldiers to scour the wood for the enemy. Of course, there were none there and the 200 did what most soldiers given a chance to skive would do – they sat down in the wood, had a flagon or ten of cider, played some cards and waited for the fuss to die down. If they'd waited another 200 years, they could have had a good smoke of their pipes as well but Sir Walter Raleigh hadn't yet been to America to discover tobacco, so they had to make do with the local scrumpy.

Come the next day, they wandered out onto the battlefield, much to the surprise of the Lancastrians, who thought all the red roses were somewhere else. That moment, amazingly, determined the outcome of the battle. Edward retained his title (and his Lonsdale belt), Margaret fled but was later captured and several of her supporters foolishly tried hiding in Tewkesbury Abbey, only to find that Edward's soldiers couldn't give a monkey's about respecting that sort of sanctuary. They were hauled out of the abbey and executed in the marketplace.

Oh yes, and the commander of Edward's left-wing troops was the nineteen-year-old Richard, Duke of Gloucester, who would a few years later become Laurence Olivier croaking:

> Now is the winter of our discontent
> Made glorious summer by this sun of York

and a source of parody for ever after.

One of the Lancastrians who had tried hiding in Tewkesbury Abbey but had been butchered for his pains was also called Edward. He was the Prince of Wales, the youngest son of Henry VI and the last of the Lancastrians. He is buried in the abbey in an unmarked tomb and it is quite possible that he was killed by the aforesaid Laurence Olivier lookalike.

Tewkesbury Abbey is one of the finest buildings of its kind in Britain. Even to a heathen like me it has an awe-inspiring appeal. Although Leland attributes its origins to two Mercian princes with the unlikely names of Odo and Dodo, its real growth began in the late eleventh century when one of William the Conqueror's mob, Robert Fitzhamon, dug the first foundations. Well, probably not him personally, you understand, but him metaphorically. It was originally a Benedictine Monastery, built to house the monks who worked and worshipped there, but it also became the parish church for the townspeople as Tewkesbury itself grew. This was a smart move that ensured its survival, as you will see shortly.

The first things you are struck by when you enter the abbey are the gigantic Norman pillars, fourteen of them in all, that support the roof, each of them rounded and rising to a height of over 30 feet. They are the tallest of such pillars in the country and are a genuinely dramatic sight as you look up towards the choir. It was in this part of the abbey that the townsfolk were allowed to worship.

At the business end, i.e. where the monks prayed and where the great and the good came to try buying their way to heaven, there are a number of interesting features that are worth more than a momentary pause. There's the infamous Kneeling Knight – a full-size effigy of Lord Edward Le Despenser – which adorns the top of the chapel bearing his family's name. He looks harmless enough, dressed in what looks like the medieval equivalent of a Spandex jump-suit and wearing the latest style of pointy-head helmet, as he kneels in prayer. But why are his eyes open? I was always taught you had to shut your eyes when praying, so was our Edward making a serious mistake here? I think we should be told.

Another noble whose memorial is in the abbey is the Duke of Clarence, a major player in Elizabethan times who featured in a Shakespeare tragedy. Clarence was another victim of Richard the Third, who found his brother a pain in the butt. 'False, fleeting, perjured Clarence,' was Richard's actual description of his dearly beloved kinsman. Shakespeare, drawing on an old tradition, had Clarence murdered at Richard's command by a couple of dodgy characters, innovatively known as Murderer 1 and Murderer 2, by drowning him in a 'butt of malmsey-wine', although for these two murderers this was quite easy since they had already stabbed him to death first. This was a bit of a waste of fine booze, because Malmsey wine was a rare delicacy brought over from the vineyards of Majorca, where nowadays the cream of British youth go to get smashed on lager and cheap vodka products.

Then there's the Milton organ, which is not as old as the abbey nor an original creation of the abbey. And John Milton, as far as we know, never visited Tewkesbury and certainly he never played the organ there. No, the story is somewhat different. The organ is genuinely ancient, being built for Magdalen College in Oxford in 1631. During the Commonwealth, Oliver Cromwell, presumably because he was fed up with listening to Radio 2 all day, had the organ moved to Hampton Court Palace. There, so it is said, he had his Latin Secretary, John Milton, play for him some Reginald Dixon numbers instead of wasting his time writing all those daft poems that no one would ever read. The Tewkesbury Abbey elders of 1736, being quite perceptive chappies, heard that this organ, by now returned to Oxford, was up for sale and realised that this would make a good tourist attraction. So they bought it and it's been here ever since.

Finally there's the macabre monument to the last Abbot of Tewkesbury, John Wakeman. Following the fashion of his day, he prepared an effigy of his rotting corpse, covered with vermin, as a memento mori. Despite this extravagance, the grave below is believed to be empty, for Abbot Wakeman left Tewkesbury and his cenotaph behind to become the first Bishop of Gloucester. Now there is an interesting story behind all this, for John Wakeman as well as being Abbot at Tewkesbury was Henry VIII's chaplain at the time of the dissolution of the monasteries. It seems very likely that this allowed him to seek special dispensation for Tewkesbury Abbey, presumably on the grounds that it was really just the local parish church (see above). Anyway, the abbey was sold by Henry VIII to the townsfolk for £453, none of the monks were harmed – indeed they all received very good pensions – and Wakeman became Bishop of Gloucester.

Nice work, eh?

Maybe it was the surprise of all this that made the Kneeling Knight open his eyes in astonishment!

Tewkesbury itself is an attractive town with loads of medieval timber buildings along its three main streets. It grew in prosperity because of its riverside position at the confluence of the rivers Avon and Severn and was an important port in its day. It continued to prosper right into the nineteenth century, being a major stopping-off point for stagecoaches. The coming of the railways in the middle of that century brought about its decline, for the line from Birmingham to Gloucester bypassed some way to the east. Ironically, it was the construction of another type of transportation route, the M5 motorway, in the 1960s which has led to its increased economic prosperity in recent times.

Cobbett came through Tewkesbury in 1826, finding it 'a good, substantial town'. He comments on the agricultural prosperity he had ridden through, particularly the endless flocks and herds, and wonders what happened to all that meat. This gives him the opportunity to rant on about nearby Cheltenham which he calls one of the 'devouring Wens'. Cheltenham, according to Cobbett, is a place where:

> East India plunderers, West India floggers, English tax-gorgers, together with gluttons, drunkards, and debauchees of all descriptions, female as well as male, resort, at the suggestion of silently laughing quacks, in the hope of getting rid of the bodily consequences of their manifold sins and iniquities.

You get the feeling that he didn't approve of Cheltenham, don't you?

Charles Dickens must have also visited Tewkesbury in its stagecoach days because he has Mr Pickwick and his companions call in at the Hop Pole Inn, which still stands, though I have to say it is not quite as top-notch as it sounds in Dickens's description:

> At the Hop Pole at Tewkesbury they stopped to dine; upon which occasion there was more ale, with some more Madeira, and some port besides; and here the case-bottle was replenished for the fourth time. Under the influence of these combined stimulants, Mr Pickwick and Mr Ben Allen fell asleep for thirty miles, while Bob and Mr Weller sang duets in the dickey.

Duets in the dickey was presumably a popular number of the day. If not, I hesitate to guess what Bob and Mr Weller were up to!

As well as the timber and brick buildings on its main streets, Tewkesbury boasts an unusually high number of alleyways. There were once about ninety of them, built at right angles to the main thoroughfares because of the pressure for housing in the restricted area that the town occupies between the two rivers. By opening up these alleyways, it was possible to build more dwellings with access to the town. Eventually, the alleys became rubbish dumps and thus major health hazards, as they acted as conduits for cholera and diphtheria in the nineteenth century. Nowadays there are just thirty alleyways left, with names like Crooked Alley, Fletcher's Alley, Chandler's Court and Old Baptist Chapel Court. This last leads to what is claimed to be the very first Baptist chapel in England, now open to visitors with no curator checking up on you. Beyond it is the burial ground and beyond that the Mill Avon waterway.

The Mill Avon is a channel originally cut by monks from the abbey in the twelfth century to provide water power for the mill and so that barges could carry grain from the mill down to the Severn and then onwards north or south. Leland claims it was built in 1475 by order of the Duke of Clarence but accounts of the Battle of Tewkesbury show that there was deep water at the mill four years earlier. Anyway, the Duke of Clarence would have been too busy at the time being 'false' and 'fleeting', so I suspect Leland had had a bit too much Malmsey when he wrote that.

Whatever, Tewkesbury is a gorgeous little town, another of Sabrina's secrets. It has many splendid buildings, it has a wealth of historical associations and it is the home of the legendary Companions of the Black Bear whom you are going to meet shortly.

What more reason could you want for visiting?

19 Tewkesbury to Gloucester

Over breakfast next morning I asked Ron and Helen Gracey how they, with their distinctive Scots accents, had come to be in Tewkesbury. They told me they had only been here for the past eighteen months and that this was their first venture into the bed and reakfast trade. They had left Hawick on the Scottish borders thirty years ago and previously had worked in America and in Wales in other businesses.

'When's your busiest time here?' I asked.

'When they do the battle re-enactment,' Ron replied. 'It's spectacular. There's over a thousand people involved in the battle. All in proper costume and everything. Mind you, most of them stay in tents, like in the times of the battle, but some stay here. We had a couple last year who'd got soaking wet in their tent one night and came here to dry off.'

'So you only get a few from the re-enactment staying here then?' I asked.

'Yes, but there's also thousands of visitors who come to watch everything,' he answered. 'Mind you, the busiest time is the Cheltenham Gold Cup meeting. At that time of year you can't get a B & B or hotel room for love or money within a 20 to 30 mile radius of Cheltenham. We could charge what we wanted for that period. Mind you, we don't.'

Now I knew something about this re-enactment because, while researching Tewkesbury before my walk, I had discovered that it is organised by a group calling themselves the Companions of the Black Bear. I had emailed them to find out more and received this reply:

The group lurched into life early in 1984, to do a re-

> enactment. It has gone through several metamorphoses since then. There are currently about 15 active members, though active is a relative term. No one ever formally joins, or formally leaves, so there is a growing band of old grey bears, and an occasional bear cub. Hope this answers your questions.
>
> Steve

Wanting to know more, I replied as follows:

> Thanks for getting back. Are there really only 15 of you to do a whole battle? Do the 8 always beat the 7? Or do you have reinforcements from somewhere? How did you 'lurch' into life? Was it a spontaneous lurch or was it an individually inspired lurch? Or did 1984 seem a particularly appropriate year to look back in history?
>
> I'm planning to walk down the Severn this summer and will be visiting Tewkesbury as part of this. Maybe you'll be in the Black Bear when I call?
>
> Bob

Steve Goodchild then sent me a much fuller account of the activities of the Companions of the Black Bear, who, I'm sad to say, were not in the Black Bear the previous evening, which may have had something to do with my not telling them that I was visiting. Although, when I think about it, maybe those three men plotting the AGM were . . .

It seems that the group began life in Tewkesbury but has now established links with other re-enactment groups throughout Europe and they attend each other's events. The Famous Fifteen now spend so much of their time organising the Battle of Tewkesbury re-enactment that they have no time to participate themselves. Let me share with you some of the instructions that battle participants have to observe:

- Keep spears, bills, staves or other long weapons at a low angle during engagement.
- Crow-scarers will not permitted on the battlefield
- Loose arrows at an angle not less than 45 degrees to the ground. Do not shoot directly at other participants.
- Always remember the people you are about to hit are fellow enthusiasts here to enjoy themselves just like you.
- Once the battle has finished the King will be presented to the public and then all the dead will rise and process around the arena then march into the authentic camp then on my signal fall out to enjoy the night's entertainment.

This all sounds like a load of fun, particularly the bit about the dead rising up and processing around the arena, and I was only sorry that I couldn't have done my walk in July to coincide with this festival. I have to admit that, prior to listening to Ron, I had thought that these people must be mad to dress up in funny old costumes and then pretend to fight each other. I still don't understand their motivation but I can see that, as a spectacle, it must be remarkable and I'd like here and now to offer myself as a future participant, if they'll have me.

But I insist on being the future Richard III. With the limp that was developing in my right ankle, I was already halfway towards a decent impersonation.

I had to wait for the shops to open in Tewkesbury that morning because of this ankle. I had reasoned that I needed some of that magic spray stuff that footballers get given by those fat men in baggy tracksuits who wobble onto the field of play when summoned by the referee. So I sat on a bench outside Tewkesbury Abbey, with my boot and sock removed, spraying Deep Heat onto the offending ankle, in the hope that it would do the trick. Then I limped off down the lane that led me back to the riverside once again. That was where I saw the first sign that said 'NO ELVERING'.

You might think this is a warning against engaging in some unlawful pursuit on the river bank – nudist leapfrog, for instance, or impersonating Richard III. But I knew this was warning me against catching elvers and I was to see many more 'NO ELVERING' or 'PRIVATE ELVERING' signs during the day, for this is the stretch of the Severn where the elvermen come to fish with their strange nets. Only the elvermen have a licence to catch elvers along these stretches of the river and they guard the secret of where the best place for their treasured catch is.

Elvers begin life as eel larvae, drifting from their birthplace in the Sargasso Sea for three years across the Atlantic Ocean till they end up by some miracle of nature in the Severn Estuary. The elver season lasts from the middle of March until the end of April and during that time countless thousands are caught and sold to elver stations. From here they are exported live to Europe and Japan for the restocking of their waters. Elvering has been a part of river life around here for centuries, but it is now carefully regulated because of the scarcity of these baby eels.

Not much fun being an elver, eh?

I have, to the best of my knowledge, never eaten eel. I don't believe I have ever seen an eel. And I certainly wasn't going to see one that day, not just because of the 'NO ELVERING' notices but because I was here at the wrong time of year.

Henry VIII banned the taking of elvers from the Severn and Elizabeth I made this order a fixed law. After the Commonwealth, the ban was reintroduced by Charles II and remained in place until 1778, when presumably the royal palate had become sated with elvers and sought its satisfaction in some new delicacy – black pudding, possibly, or chicken tikka masala.

Not being a royal, I doubt if I will ever know. Or, for that matter, care. 'Let them eat elvers' is my advice to the monarchy and its offspring.

Not much more than a mile out of Tewkesbury, as I went through wet-grassed meadows, I came to the remarkable village of Deerhurst, which I wanted to visit. Deerhurst has two Anglo-Saxon buildings – the Priory Church of St Mary and Odda's Chapel. Both are unique and I just had to see them.

The Priory Church apparently dates from the seventh century and there are all sorts of Anglo-Saxon features still inside it – carved wolf-heads, herringbone masonry, pointy windows and a carved limestone font, discovered 100 years ago on a local farm being used as a drinking trough. It is believed that this was the main church of the Hwicce tribe and that kings of that same tribe were buried here. Sadly, the only recorded event we know of happening here was when in 1016 King Edmund Ironside met with King Canute of Denmark to sign a treaty defining the boundary between Saxon England and the Danelaw. Shortly after that, of course, Canute went to sit on his throne in the sea to order the waves back.

He should have stayed at Deerhurst and eaten up his elvers.

Odda's Chapel is a very odd thing altogether. It was only identified as an important Anglo-Saxon relic during repair work in 1885, having been attached many years earlier to a medieval timber-framed farmhouse where it served as the kitchen. It is, typically of its Anglo-Saxon origins, very plain inside but the windows are quite clearly Saxon, as is its chancel arch. An inscription stone indicates that this was Earl Odda's royal hall, built around 1056 – some ten years before William conquered.

Oddest of all was the fact that I was minutes later walking through a grassy field back towards the river bank, trying to envisage how this tiny community had once been central to affairs of state in England, and I could not, in all honesty, do so. Sometimes, however vivid your imagination, it is difficult to make sense of history. This was one of those times.

The trouble was, I think, that my aching right ankle still had me in Richard III mode. So, I hunched my back and declaimed: 'A horse! a horse! my kingdom for a horse!' Well, it does you good sometimes, even though I got some strange looks from the two middle-aged women out walking their dogs who passed me in the opposite direction. Mind you, as I approached a pub called the Coalhouse Inn a mile or so further on, I became worried that they had phoned ahead about me. For, climbing over a stile and heading in my direction were two tall blokes in some kind of heavy green uniform wielding chainsaws. 'Had they been sent to restrain me?' I wondered in momentary panic.

'I surrender,' I called out, holding up my hands to demonstrate my state of utter cowardice.

They looked at me bemusedly and it turned out they were merely employees of Gloucestershire Wildlife come to clear some of the overgrown footpath. I felt simultaneously chastened and relieved.

Perhaps I should have eaten up my elvers.

Perhaps, unknowingly, I had.

Eventually I came to a pub called the Red Lion where the Severn Way footpath was temporarily diverted because of a landslip at Wainlode Cliff, whose marly earth is particularly susceptible to such erosion. In fact, several old barges have been sunk into the river at the base of the cliff to try to prevent further erosion, and warning posts steer boatmen to the other side of the river. I had also been told that the stretch of the footpath from Sandhurst to the edge of Gloucester was closed because of foot-and-mouth restrictions, so the next stage of my journey was inevitably to take me inland from the river.

In fact, the footpath that led me over Sandhurst Hill was one of the pleasantest parts of my journey. It is a clearly defined track and from time to time lovely views of the Severn snaking below you come into sight. The fields were full of maize and also full of game birds. And when I say full, I mean teeming. I have never seen so many game birds in one place. Pheasants, black grouse, red grouse, partridge, the lot. They were everywhere, pecking at the ground, looking up as they sensed my approach, then taking off in that short-barrelled flight that they have.

There's a bench on top of Sandhurst Hill, put there by the Tewkesbury Walking Club, and I paused there briefly to ruminate on these game birds. Really, the Creator of the Universe was most unkind when these birds were made. I mean, their design is all wrong, isn't it? Their bodies are too stubby, like little barrels, to be borne aloft quickly by their little wings. So, when they take off, they have difficulty gaining much height and leave themselves open to being easy targets for men with guns. I suppose they had a better chance before the invention of gunpowder, when our ancestors were reliant on catapults or variations of such, but nowadays they're just easy meat.

A little while later I passed through the little village of Sandhurst, where I was greeted by a man pruning the yew tree in the churchyard.

'Are you crossing the Severn?' he asked.

What kind of fool question was this? Wasn't it obvious that I was walking down a road which ran parallel to the river but was half a mile from it?

'No,' I replied. 'I'm following the Severn Way footpath. But it's closed round here because of foot-and-mouth.'

'D'you think it'll rain?' he asked.

Now this was getting seriously daft. Who did he think I was? Michael Fish or somebody?

Normally I'm quite enamoured of surreal conversations but I was anxious to get on my way, so I didn't deign to reply, pretending that I hadn't heard him and soon I was back on the riverside again and entering the outskirts of Gloucester. It was approaching two o'clock and I was in need of sustenance, so I made my way towards the city centre and followed two men down an alleyway into a pub, where I ordered a pint of shandy and a sandwich.

The pub was called the Fountain Inn and it was full. This was clearly the pub frequented by the city centre workers of Gloucester. I could tell by the way they ranged themselves along the bar that these people come here every day and that they each have their own special spot. In the Fountain, the favoured position is standing at the bar. In this way you can eat your lunch, drink your beer, converse with your colleagues and simultaneously keep an eye on anyone else coming into the bar. Another major attraction of this position is that you are able to include the bar staff in your chit-chat, particularly the feisty landlady of the Fountain who gave as good as she got in the verbal jousting.

There was a particularly loud group of four middle-aged men at the far end near to where I sat. They all wore dark suits, they all had beer bellies resting against the bar, and they were all eating and drinking more than they should have been doing if they were to be able to do honest work that afternoon. There was also a lot of laughter – raucous and hearty – emanating from the group and their reddening faces smirked with constant amusement. I knew, simply from their poses and the looks on their faces, that they were seriously engaged in the ancient pastime of Telling Dirty Jokes.

Now, I don't know if other cultures have this tradition but it is a major feature of the lives of many males in English-speaking countries. In fact, in some all-male circles, it is almost a rite of passage to gain acceptance by telling a dirty joke. The rules of these jokes are very complex and it is only possible to understand them by observing prior to participating. Inevitably, they contain reference either to bodily functions normally not mentioned or to the male and female sex organs, usually in their Anglo-Saxon terminology. The preferred way of telling such a dirty joke is by lowering the head and the voice, thus drawing your hearers in conspiratorially closer, until the punchline releases everyone to a gale of ho-ho-hoing.

I have a major fault in my genetic design. I rarely, if ever, find dirty jokes funny. It's not that I have any squeamishness about their subject matter or that I get upset at the treatment of other races or of women that is a common feature of many of these jokes. No, it's just that I don't think it very funny to say 'And he had shite all over his trousers', as I caught the conclusion of one of these dirty jokes in the Fountain that lunch time, and which caused the most enormous amount of cheek-jiggling guffaws and wobbling of stomachs imaginable.

As I left the Fountain Inn, I noticed that I was passing through a courtyard into an alley that took me out on to the main street. In that alleyway was a notice which informed me that this was a very old pub, supposedly dating back to 1255. Its most famous incident was when:

> The King is said to have shown his contempt for James II and the Stuart cause by riding his horse up a shallow flight of stone stairs leading to a room where a local Jacobite Society, sympathetic to the deposed king, held their meetings.

This must have been William of Orange, later immortalised in Northern Ireland as King Billy, but what on earth he was doing in Gloucester, heaven only knows.

Later that same afternoon, after visiting the cathedral and the docks, and stopping briefly to purchase a copy of Bill Bryson's *Down Under* (which I was pleased to find at a reduced price), I found the guesthouse I was staying in. Here I was welcomed by a barking dog pretending to be fierce who then rolled over and demanded tickling as I was welcomed in by the landlady's daughter who said he was 'as hard as soft cheese'.

While hunting in my room for somewhere to put my clothes, I opened a door of what I had taken for a wardrobe to find a washroom and toilet. There was another optical illusion inside. On a shelf was a glass containing what looked like something small, dark and unpleasant. I tried to tip it out over the sink but nothing happened and it was then I realised it was one of those trick glasses with some plastic substance that looks like water in the bottom of it. And sailing delicately in this 'water' were, I saw as I inspected more closely, three miniscule penguins. Don't ask. I didn't. It seemed a time for quiet acceptance of life in all its infinite variety.

After a subsequent shower and change of clothes, I began to feel almost human again and set off to find somewhere for an evening meal. My choice was the Tall Ship just by Gloucester Docks, where my beer was served by the inevitable teenage boy with a basin-cut and my pork steak was served by the inevitable teenage girl with a ponytail. I had gone there because I had seen a big-screen television advertised and had hoped to find a comfortable place to watch that evening's football match between Manchester United and Deportivo La Coruña. But it was not to be. Instead the teenage barman directed me, together with several other men who had been lured in by false promises, to another pub called Baker Street two blocks away.

So that's where we all duly trooped. Baker Street is actually on the corner of Baker Street and some entrepreneur has come up with the subtle scheme of milking this coincidence by hanging a pub sign featuring the head and pipe of the great Sherlock. That, however, is the only connection for the interior is little more than a rather tacky beer-hall. Inside there were about 150 people, all staring goggle-eyed at two huge television screens or at three smaller monitors. All but two of these people were male. They were mostly aged between twenty and thirty-five. All wore T-shirts, jeans and trainers. All of them were drinking lager. Nearly all of them were smoking. It was a normal night out in Gloucester.

As for the match, well, we all leapt with excitement when Paul Scholes scored a superb goal just before half time, only to be totally deflated when Deportiva La Coruña scored twice in the last few minutes to win the match.

In the gents afterwards, a shaven-headed bloke standing next to me, said:

'I'm so pissed off with that result, I can't piss.'

'That's what happens,' I said, 'when you live your life vicariously and pin all your personal hopes and aspirations onto the back of a team of footballers. Why don't you take up some serious hobby like elver-fishing or Richard III impersonating? You'd feel much more fulfilled. Your life would be enriched and you'd no longer have bladder problems.'

Actually I didn't say any of that. I merely grunted non-committally. You never know what you might be letting yourself in for by acknowledging someone in the gents of a strange pub. I just zipped up and left.

To be honest, I'd had a particularly poor evening. The food was average, the beer was average, the company was less than enthralling and Manchester United had lost.

I should have stayed in my room and read Bill Bryson.

20 Gloucester

Most people when they hear the name Gloucester, if they think of anything, think of two things – Dr Foster and Double Gloucester cheese. I'll come to Dr Foster later. The cheese is so called because it is made from the full cream of both the evening and the morning milkings. This makes it a full-flavoured cheese and a durable one, which keeps well and travels well. It has been made for over 1000 years and cheese buyers, in order to test the strength of particular cheeses, used to jump up and down on them.

Now that's not the only strange thing they do with cheese in Gloucester. Every May, on a knoll known as Cooper's Hill just outside the city, crowds gather to watch the ancient sport of cheese-rolling. This is, of course, not something you can do with American Kraft cheese slices or with those squishy French Camemberts. Oh no! What is needed for this sport is a good old circular Double Gloucester cheese, 4 inches thick, 12 inches in diameter, and weighing a solid 7½ pounds. Cooper's Hill is a grassy slope which stretches for about 300 yards and has an angle of 45 degrees. This makes it extremely difficult to run down and that's where the sport comes in.

At a given moment, the cheese is sent on its way down the hillside, rapidly followed by up to 100 pursuers – generally young, mostly male and indubitably mad. This is a highly dangerous sport, for the cheese is travelling at 40 miles an hour and can do serious damage if it hits you in the back. Because of the steepness of the slope, you can also very easily be felled or tripped. In 1998 the competition was cancelled because there had been so many racers who were injured in the previous year's race – twenty-seven in all, mostly with broken arms or legs. The winner that year, a local postman, finished with a broken arm but wasn't bothered by this, since he'd won three years before having broken the other arm.

The winner of the race to the bottom of the hill gets to keep the cheese and this is still one of the few sports invented in Britain at which we can confidently say that we are the leading exponents in the world. In fact, a campaign is currently underway in Gloucester to have cheese-rolling recognised as an Olympic sport. It won't be long, of course, before the Aussies take up the sport, create a national academy to train up their youngsters in it, and then comprehensively beat us. But for now, we can all bask in the reflected glory of our success in this as yet little known sport.

Another food that Gloucester is known for, or at least used to be known for, is lampreys. These are long scaleless river fish which used to be common in the Severn around Gloucester and were considered to be a delicacy. It was usual in earlier times for kings of England to hold their Christmas Councils at Gloucester, because it was close to their favoured hunting grounds in the Forest of Dean. In fact, it was at his Christmas Council of 1085 that William the Conqueror order the compilation of the famous Domesday Book and simultaneously created the term 'jobsworth', as thousands of clerks scribbled into their chapbooks details about everyone then living, muttering into their beards: 'I'm sorry. It's more than my job's worth to ignore those three tythes but thank you anyway for the offer of your daughter's maidenhead. Just send her along to my quarters and I'll see what I can do.'

Anyway, the custom developed for the citizens of Gloucester to present a lamprey pie to the king each Christmas and this custom lasted until Victorian times. Henry I, of course, as we know from our history books, died from 'a surfeit of lampreys', but he was unable to punish the people of Gloucester (a) because the lampreys were the dastardly French type and (b) he was dead. A hundred years later, however, King John fined the men of Gloucester 40 marks because 'they did not pay him sufficient respect in the matter of his lampreys'.

Ah, diddums!

Nowadays lampreys have become scarce in the Severn and are a protected species, so they cannot be fished. So, when you stay in Gloucester, you have to make do with cheese. But please don't try and race one down a hillside!

In the Mel Gibson film, *Braveheart*, where an American actor saves Scotland from the wicked English, there is a minor character who is a gay prince. Remember him? Mincing around and lisping for all he's worth? Well, that prince was Edward, the first English Prince of Wales, who was later to become Edward II and whose tomb is in Gloucester Cathedral.

What's it doing there? Well, it's one of the better stories of the English monarchy, showing them in all their gory greatness.

Edward's father was also called Edward (they weren't very imaginative about names in those days) and was known as Edward Longshanks, because of the size of his – wait for it – legs! He was also known as 'The Hammer of the Scots' because he united England and Scotland by defeating the Scots in battle. He also chopped off the head of Llewellyn ap Gruffydd, who thus became headless and the last Welsh Prince of Wales. Unfortunately for him, but fascinatingly for us, Longshanks was so busy beating up Celts that he failed to notice that his young son had fallen head over heels in love with his tutor Piers Gaveston. Even when young Edward was married off to Isabella of France, he preferred to spend his wedding night in Gaveston's bed. Now most people would have taken this as a warning but the king, long in the leg but a bit short in the brain, thought that exiling Gaveston would do the trick.

It didn't, of course. As soon as Longshanks was dead and young Edward installed as king, he brought his lover back from France, made him a duke and let him run the country. The barons, who were the other top dogs of the time, weren't struck with this idea so they had poor old Piers murdered. But, once a queen, always a queen, and Edward took another lover, Hugh Dispenser. The barons liked him even less and, to show him what they thought of him, they had his testicles chopped off and burned before his eyes.

Then, to really show him what's what, they decapitated him.

Oddly enough, the Gay Prince was not feeling so gay now, especially when in 1327 he was himself imprisoned in Berkeley Castle, not far from Gloucester. Here he was thrown into a pit with loads of dead animals, forced to eat rotten food and made to drink foul water. When that didn't kill him, a more ingenious method was devised. His jailers inserted a straight cow horn with the point removed into Edward's bum, then pushed a red-hot poker through the cow horn and into the body, burning out his entrails. This killed him while leaving no marks on his body, making it appear as if he had died of natural causes.

Neat, eh?

And you thought the royals were harmless old eccentrics?

In fact, Gloucester Cathedral also has mementoes to another couple of unfortunate royals. First up, there's a stained glass window showing the coronation of the boy king, Henry III, in the cathedral in 1216 – the only English king since the Norman invasion to be crowned away from Westminster. It didn't do him much good, mind you, because during his reign he suffered the indignity of being imprisoned by Simon de Montfort (yes, he was the Henry who was taken as a captive to Kempsey) and he is now generally considered by historians to have been a Poor King.

Then there's the effigy of Robert, Duke of Normandy, resplendent in his Manchester United red bib over his chain mail. Robert was the eldest son of William the Conqueror but made the mistake of playing away on a crusade when his father died, so missed out on the inheritance of England and had to make do with Normandy. Then, when he tried to reclaim what he thought was his birthright, he lost in battle to his younger brother Henry I and was stuck inside Cardiff Castle where he died.

It's a strange pose that his sculptor has chosen for Robert, with his right arm across the front of his chest and his right leg, with toes daintily pointed, similarly planted across his left leg. He looks really as if he's auditioning for a part in *Riverdance* or some such thing, though one of the cathedral guides told me she thought it was supposed to represent him in a state of readiness for battle.

Mind you, it's not just the royals who get themselves into a pickle from time to time. Gloucester Cathedral has also recently been the excuse for a bit of a ding-dong between two groups of the God Squad. In the right corner, we have a couple of Evangelicals from Gloucester who announced their intention to stage a protest if the proposed filming of scenes for the first *Harry Potter* story occurred in the ancient cathedral. In the left corner is the Dean of Gloucester Cathedral who professes himself a fan of the Harry Potter books and has given permission for the filming.

The Evangelicals are Paula and Derek Clare and they run a Christian goods shop called New Day, which sells board games like 'Redemption – at last an alternative to Pokemon', 'Pilgrim's Progress – Adventure to the Celestial City' and 'Catechumen – a Stunning 3D Spiritual Warfare game'.

Stunning stuff, eh?

It's the witchcraft in *Harry Potter* that's the cause of their anxiety and they are not alone. There are loopy groups in America trying to ban J.K. Rowling's books from children's eyes. Haven't they heard of what happened in Germany on Kristallnacht?

I asked another of the cathedral guides what had happened to the Clares' proposed protest and he told me they'd held a silent vigil outside the cathedral while the filming was taking place and then they'd gone home, no doubt to a slice or two of Double Gloucester. This guide showed me the part of the cloisters used as the entrance to Hogwarts School in the filming of scenes for *Harry Potter and the Philosopher's Stone* which has now taken place at Cloucester Cathedral. The film has become a huge success, making even more money for Ms Rowling and selling even more copies of her books. D'you think that my mentioning all this here might just make my book a cult?

Somehow I doubt it.

I'm a bit hesitant to focus here on an other representation of evil in Gloucester but the greatest amount of newsprint mentioning the city in recent years has been about Fred and Rose West, the notorious murderers of 25 Cromwell Street, dubbed by the press the 'House of Horror'.

Over a period of twenty years, the Wests tortured and murdered at least ten young women, including their own daughter Heather, at this unprepossessing house in the middle of Gloucester. Their victims arrived in several ways, some to work as nannies, some picked up on the streets, some abducted. All were subjected by both the Wests to depraved sexual acts, involving sadomasochism and bondage, before they were casually murdered and their bodies dismembered and buried under the patio or in the cellar. It is a chilling story.

When police arrived at 25 Cromwell Road with a search warrant in September 1994, they were looking for Heather, the Wests' daughter who had been reported missing and whose supposed whereabouts was the subject of local gossip. The first bones they found as they began digging up the garden were not those of Heather but of another victim of the Wests. As police continued to find the dismembered bodies, Fred West confessed to the murders but for some strange reason denied charges of rape. Altogether nine bodies of young women, including Heather, were found in the grounds of the House of Horror, together with the bodies of West's first wife and her child and the body of his pregnant mistress discovered in a field near to a trailer park where he had lived previously. In every case, the fingers, kneecaps and toes had been hacked off and were missing – the Fred West signature.

In December he was charged with twelve murders but on New Year's Day 1995 at Winson Green Prison in Birmingham, when the guards were having lunch, Fred hanged himself with strips of bedsheet. The following November Rose West was convicted of ten counts of murder and sentenced to life imprisonment. She will never be released.

Curiously, this whole story resurfaced just as I was about to set off on my walk. Channel 5, a minority television channel, announced that it was to broadcast a programme which featured the tape-recordings of Fred West's interviews with the police. There was considerable disquiet about this from sections of the population, especially the Gloucestershire police and surviving children of the Wests.

How did Channel 5 come to be in possession of these tape-recordings? I wondered. Was this normal practice with the police? Is there some law which dictates that the tape-recordings of police interviews become public property after a certain number of years, rather as the proceedings of government do?

It seems that the fault lies with the person who was the Official Solicitor at the time. This person, one Peter Harris, sold the rights to make a television documentary about the mass murderer Fred West. These rights included various types of archive material including recordings of police interviews, and West's pornographic home videos. Harris's idea was that money raised from this sale would go to West's younger surviving children. In effect, the Official Solicitor had arranged it so that the West children would profit from their father's murders, including that of one of their own sisters. In fact, none of them wanted to know.

Fred West was born a few months before me. I have tried to comprehend the mind of someone close to me in age, but cannot. West came from a poor farm labourer's family and left school virtually illiterate. He seems to have grown up with few behavioural constraints. He quickly fell into petty thieving and indiscriminate sexual activity. By the age of twenty, when I was midway through my university course, he had been convicted as a petty thief for stealing a watchstrap and cigarette cases from a jewellery shop and as a child molester for getting a thirteen-year-old girl pregnant. I had pals who stole records from Woolworths, though they were never caught, and I had a friend who courted an under-age girl and later married her. So maybe our life experiences weren't that far apart at that stage.

But by 1967, when I was pursuing further professional qualification in London, Fred West was married to his first wife, Rena, was bringing up two children and had carried out his first murder – Anna McFall, his mistress. And that's where we part company. I know he had limited intellectual ability, I know his work in a slaughterhouse may have inured him to blood and death, I know that two falls in his teenage years may have caused some brain damage, but I cannot understand how a person can brutally murder another and, not content with that, continue to murder, for pleasure it appears, for many more years as part of some ritual of sexual gratification.

25 Cromwell Road was dismantled some time after the police investigation and the trial of Rose West were completed. It still, however, attracts the occasional visitor, curious about what went on there.

But not me. I did not visit Cromwell Road that evening. I can only record this gory story that happened in Gloucester. I cannot understand it.

And I didn't watch the programme on Channel 5.

Defoe, recording his (or possibly one of his spies') visit to Gloucester, described it as 'an ancient middling city' and added that the 'stone bridge over the Severn and the cathedral is all I see worth recording of the place'. Celia Fiennes found it 'a low moist place', while Cobbett was very exercised about the use of the cathedral as an 'Opera-House' with its 'assemblages of player-folks, half-rogues and half-fools'.

None of them mention Gloucester Docks, although there has been an inland port there for centuries. The Romans, naming the place Glevum, built a fort here almost certainly so that they could carry goods up from Bristol. The Saxons certainly continued this usage and it was granted the official status of a port by Elizabeth I in 1580. Its real growth, however, occurred in the mid-nineteenth century, after our travellers came to call, when the Gloucester and Sharpness Canal was opened. The huge Victorian warehouses that still surround the docks are testament to its busyness at this time as a place for storing large quantities of grain and timber.

In the 1980s a regeneration programme was launched in the docks area to make it into a tourist attraction. There is still much to do but the basic shape of that development has produced a mixture of museums, restaurants and cafés, and specialist shops. That's what the glossy says at any rate and that's what I went to investigate in the late afternoon.

There are three museums at Gloucester Docks – the National Waterways Museum, the Soldiers of Gloucestershire Museum and the Robert Opie Museum of Advertising and Packaging. Now, you can see why the first two are appropriately sited but you may ask, as I did, who Robert Opie is and what he has to do with Gloucester. The answer is that, like Andrew Logan and his Museum of Sculpture in Berriew, Robert Opie has nothing to do with Gloucester. He seems to have been an avid collector from his teenage years, his eureka moment occurring when he bought a pack of Munchies from a slot machine and realised that it would make a good item for a new collection tracing the history of advertising and packaging.

Sad, eh?

Now I'm sure there is a fascinating social history behind all this but, to be honest, I just thought it was a load of nostalgic rubbish and I didn't see what it had got to with Gloucester. Anyway, it was closing shortly, so there was little point visiting it. And given my known antipathy to all things military, you won't be surprised to learn that I also avoided the Soldiers of Gloucestershire. So it was the National Waterways Museum that got my entrance fee.

This is in the splendidly preserved Victorian pile known as Llanthony Warehouse which was once used to store huge quantities of corn. It's an extensive museum, housed on three floors of the building, which tells the story of Britain's canals. There are all the elements you'd expect to find in a modern museum – video films, touchscreen information points, cut-away examples of canal boats and other canal equipment, as well as models and interactive displays. Much of the information was already familiar to me but I was intrigued to learn of the women volunteers who were recruited to crew canal boats during the Second World War. The advertisements for such volunteers stressed the need for 'women of robust constitution' only to apply, so it was amusing to learn that they were christened 'Idle Women' after the IW (for Inland Waterways) badge that they wore.

The best fun I had, though, was with the Canal Investment game played on interactive touchscreen displays. This is a very clever way of helping visitors to appreciate the development of the canals from their late eighteenth-century beginnings through to their virtual demise after the last war. Through judicious investment with the share package I was given as part of my entrance ticket (and a certain amount of working knowledge of which canals had been successful), I was able to realise a profit of £2876 over a 150-year period. Not bad for someone whose financial skills are not normally considered to be specially sharp.

Afterwards I resisted going to Dr Foster's pub for a beer and, instead, had a cup of coffee in one of the quayside cafés while watching the numerous tourists who have been attracted here, and reflected on why I was for some reason disappointed with Gloucester Docks. It's not just the Robert Opie Museum; it's not the cheap tat (pencils, dolls, tea towels, etc.) that's for sale in the shops; it's not that the Waterways Museum isn't about all waterways as I'd expected but only about canals. It's something to do with the fact that the place doesn't have an obvious heart. You sort of wander in from the car park or from the street and you follow the signs to the place you're most interested in but none of it really hangs together. And, although you can cruise down the canal on a boat, Gloucester Docks doesn't really feel as if its existence as a port is what is driving the current commercial venture.

Maybe it needs some tall ships. Maybe it needs to tell the story of the whole docks area better. Maybe it needs some more imagination in its development.

Or maybe it just is, as Defoe wrote all those years ago 'an ancient middling city, tolerably built, but not fine'.

And Dr Foster, who came here in a shower of rain?

Ironically, this is a reference to Edward I or Edward Longshanks, whose son was entombed in Gloucester Cathedral after his excruciatingly painful death. Apparently Edward on a visit to the city fell into a muddy hole and vowed never to go there again. And he didn't.

But why he was rechristened as Dr Foster, I haven't the faintest idea.

(Except that Longshanks doesn't rhyme with Gloucester!)

21 Gloucester to Slimbridge

I left Gloucester the next morning feeling decidedly glum.

Reasons to be glum in Glevum:

1. The Severn Way footpath half a mile out of the city was closed off by a tall metal gate with a notice from British Waterways announcing maintenance work but offering no alternative route.
2. Having then decided I would follow the Gloucester and Sharpness Canal, I discovered that there was no towpath for the first stretch because it was overgrown with weeds.
3. I had stupidly drunk one pint of beer more than I had planned in Baker Street the night before and had woken with a headache.
4. I had only had cereal and orange juice for breakfast because that was all that was available, which I had known when booking the guesthouse. However, instead of buying something more substantial at one of the several Gloucester shops I passed on my travels, I kidded myself that I didn't really need anything more filling and I would be fine. That was a lie.
5. My rucksack was definitely heavier than it had been the previous two days. All I could put it down to was my purchase of Bill Bryson's *Down Under* to read on my journey – travel not only broadens the mind, it also burdens the body.
6. Manchester United had lost and I still carried some of the collective gloom of Baker Street.
7. Despite the Deep Heat treatment and despite the fact that I had only walked for half of the previous day, my ankle

was seriously playing up.

Eventually, I found the canal towpath and set off determinedly (and limpingly) down it. I knew that parts of the Severn Way footpath were closed off on that day's journey because of foot-and-mouth restrictions and I had already decided to miss out the long loop known as the Arlingham Peninsula because it was a 9-mile stretch that I just couldn't fit into my planned daily routine. This meant that, to add to my general dystopia about Gloucester, I was leaving it via some tough-sounding places like Tuffley, Quedgley and Hardwicke rather than the softer-sounding Hempsted (maybe a drugs farm), Elmore (a Blues Brother) and Lower Rea (brother of Chris).

I don't really know why Gloucester exists. It felt like a place that had developed with a clear *raison d'être* as a major port and docks but had continued to grow for no apparent reason after the docks ceased operation. Its city centre is largely nondescript, apart from the glorious cathedral tucked away and the redevelopment of the dockside area. It seemed to take forever to get away from Gloucester, as it appears to have spread in a southerly direction, first by building endless industrial estates and then by building houses. I couldn't wait to get out of it.

Maybe it was Gloucester itself that had made me glum.

'Did you see the one in March?'

'No, but I were at Newnham in '97 when that big 'un came through.'

'I've got a photo of the one in March.'

'How high does it get here?'

'Oh, you'll see. It can be nearly 30 foot high.'

'Well, I've never seen it that high at Minsterworth.'

This was some of the conversation I had heard at one of the parts of the Severn Way that I missed while I walked down the Gloucester and Sharpness Canal towpath. It was the stretch of river opposite the village of Minsterworth, which had been the site of my visit midway through the week before. I had interrupted my walk in order to witness one of nature's marvels – the Severn Bore, which I had read was to be at its pre-eminent height on the day of my visit.

I was amazed when I got to the small car-parking area by the old ferry just beyond the village of Minsterworth to find the place already busy. I had not planned to get there early but it was just as well I had, for, by the time the Bore itself arrived, the crowd of thirty or so that I found on arrival had been supplemented by about sixty more adults plus a coach-load of primary schoolchildren.

I couldn't believe it. Where were all these people from? Why weren't they at work (this was a Wednesday morning)?

As I listened to the cheery conversations, I realised that many of these people were addicts – they turned up for every big Bore of the year. This was their major spectator sport. They were mostly older people, all suitably kitted out in waterproofs and warm clothes, and their conversation about past Bores witnessed told me that the river wasn't the only source of bores.

The actual Severn Bore is caused by a high spring tide, coinciding of course with a new moon. This rides upstream against the flow of the river. It begins in the Severn Estuary but can first be sighted about 15 miles south of Gloucester and it then races at almost 20 kilometres an hour up to Maisemore Weir just north of Gloucester where it peters out. Its height is normally about 6 feet above the normal height of the river and you can hear it coming like an express train. According to legend, it was stirred up by the goddess Sabrina who would vent her anger by riding the tumultuous waters against their natural flow.

'Here she comes!' came a shout from one of the elderly bores who were blocking my view by raising their cameras up to their faces. I dodged underneath someone's arm and caught sight of this amazing surge of brown water as it roared past me. Ahead of it and in its immediate wake were, not the goddess Sabrina, but two motorised rubber dinghies, each with a complement of people waving to us on the bank.

And then it was gone. And all of us started drifting back to our cars, all smiling happily. It was all very curious. All these people's lives had somehow been made better by seeing the Severn Bore. Even curiouser I saw, as I drove further down the road, there were hundreds of other people emerging from their different sighting spots on the river bank in exactly the same glazed-eyed, smiling satisfaction. I would guess that I saw upwards of 500 people in that short excursion. And that's not counting all those further north of Minsterworth or south of a pub called fittingly The Severn Bore, where I stopped and turned back.

Why did they all do it? I asked myself. Why did all these people come out of their nice comfy homes on a damp Wednesday morning? Why weren't they all watching *Richard and Judy* with a nice cup of cocoa?

And, even more problematically, why was I there?

Fred Rowbotham, a former engineer of the Severn Water Board, suggests in his classic book about the Severn Bore that it is because we in Britain have virtually no spectacular natural phenomena that this gives the Bore its fascination. He calls it a 'relentless moonchild that glides, sweeps and crashes its way upstream', which I think is very apt.

I was glad I'd seen it, though I wished in my selfishness that it had been less like a football crowd that I'd had to manoeuvre through in order to see it.

The Gloucester and Sharpness Canal, whose towpath I had chosen to follow that morning, was completed in 1827 and its main purpose was to bypass the River Severn, whose shifting sands as it changed from estuary into river had made it a treacherous reach for centuries. It is a very wide and deep canal, cut deliberately so in order to facilitate the passage of large ships to Gloucester Docks, thus giving good access to the Midlands and the north of England. Though used mainly by pleasure craft nowadays, it still maintains a human presence at each of its bridges, where bridgekeepers' cottages stand. Many of these have a quaint neoclassical frontage with fluted pillars guarding their front doors.

I have to say that the walk along the canal towpath that day was not one of the most inspiring. However, it achieved what I wanted it to achieve, which was to get me well on my way, without having to work out which bits of the Severn Way footpath were open and which were closed. So its bypassing status served me as well as those tall ships that once sailed up and down its length.

The only person I saw all morning was an odd character on a bike who passed me. He wore shorts, brown brogues, cerise ankle socks and jam-jar glasses. He greeted me with a cheery 'Not a bad day, is it?'

Well, it was actually. It was dull and grey but I didn't want to offend so I grunted something non-committal.

A mile or so further down the towpath I came upon him again, skimming pebbles into the canal, his bicycle dropped in the damp grass.

'Not a bad day, is it?' he said again, grinning fiendishly at me.

Now I don't know if it was just the hangover from Gloucester that made me wary of him for I'm sure he was just an innocent simpleton but I decided against taking any chances. I increased the speed of my limp and moved away from him as quickly as I could, glancing furtively over my shoulder from time to time to check that he wasn't coming after me at full speed on his bike with a bloody axe in his hand.

You can't be too careful in Gloucester.

By lunch time I had reached the village of Frampton-on-Severn, which boasts the longest village green in England – a stretch of green sward over half a mile long with three ponds. This is known as Rosamund's Green after 'Fair Rosamund' who was Henry II's bit on the side and who later became the inspiration for a famous painting by Dante Gabriel Rossetti and of a folk song. Rosamund's real name was Jane Clifford and she allegedly was born in Manor Farm which overlooks the village green. In Rossetti's painting she looks with her long ginger tresses and her apple-red cheeks a bit like Fergie, the former 'Duchess of Pork', which may not be too flattering to either of them. In the song she is discovered in flagrante delecto with good old Henry by his queen, Eleanor of Aquitaine, who then poisons her rival and thus turns her into a legend.

You can read about this on the back of the menu of the Bell Inn, a splendid Georgian building on the edge of the green, where I repaired for my lunch. A sign outside boasts of the pub's speciality of locally-produced sausages, so, after missing out on my breakfast cholesterol, I just had to order the sausage and mash with three types of sausage – the Frampton (pork and stilton), the Gloucester (traditional pork) and the Arlingham (pork, leek and ginger).

While waiting for my meal and drinking my pint of fulsome Shepherd Neame Masterman beer, I noticed some of the other customers. The village has a reputation for being a bit posh and when I heard one group of people loudly ordering expensive wines from the cellar and another group of Americans ordering salmon and champagne, I got some sense of this. The two older citizens sitting closer to me, however, were clearly not impressed by the behaviour of this wealthy clientele. I had difficulty understanding them at first because they both spoke with a distinctive Gloucestershire burr and one had no evident teeth. Eventually, however, I tuned into a snatch of their conversation.

'Couple o' lovebirds in tharr,' said one of them, who sported a baseball cap at what he probably thought was a rakish angle.

He pointed into the other bar where he had come from a few minutes earlier.

'Oh ar,' replied his companion, the toothless one (I have to confess I was guessing at his words).

'Left 'em to it,' said baseball cap and took a swig of his beer.

'Oh ar.' This was a man, I could tell, of considerable philosophical wisdom.

''E might as well 'ave 'ad 'er across the table,' concluded the wannabe Yankee Dodger, turning in his seat to wink conspiratorially at me.

Now, I don't know why I was being brought into this conversation and, believe me, I was very glad not to have to collude with their crude and lewd observations, for just then my sausage and mash arrived. I have to say this was excellent – the flavours, the textures, the mix, all were perfect. I felt better than I had felt all day. The Gloucester glumness was shunted away into the background and I was looking forward to the next few miles of my journey which would take me to Slimbridge.

Just before leaving, I went to the toilet and there, in the corridor outside the ladies' loo, were the two lovebirds of the earlier conversation, deep in each other's arms and throats. I could see now what my Yankee Dodger friend had been talking about. They were in that first flush of a relationship where they couldn't get enough of each other. I made my way quickly into the urinals.

I don't know their marital status but they were not two adolescents, these lovebirds. I left wondering if (and secretly hoping that) there was a Queen Eleanor stalking them with a surprise potion of strychnine.

The official route of the Severn Way for the next part of my journey south of Frampton-on-Severn actually followed the canal towpath, so I walked the length of the huge village green and rejoined the footpath at the wonderfully named

Splatt Bridge, where a large boat made to look like a Mississippi paddle-steamer and named the *Oliver Cromwell* was moored. For the first time for some while I could see the Severn to my right as it made its way through the huge sandbanks that separate the river from its opposite shore by up to a mile at times now. Three miles further and I was limping across Patch Bridge to explore Slimbridge before turning into the place where I was staying that night.

May Cottage, the home of Peter and Sue Gibson, was to provide me with a welcome rest that evening. Peter is a retired engineer, Sue is a teacher of horticulture and son Mike, who was also staying with them that night, works for the Department for Environment, Food and Rural Affairs (DEFRA). It was a conversation with him later that evening over our supper in the nearby Tudor Arms which gave me the clearest information I'd yet garnered about foot-and-mouth disease and its effects. Mike had only joined DEFRA (then the Ministry of Agriculture and Fisheries, or MAFF) in February of this year, just as the disease began to catch hold. Since then, he had been involved in sorting out the problem in north and south Wales and in the Gloucestershire area.

'You name it, I've had to do it,' he told me, as we supped from our pints of Gloucester Old Spot beer, bought by his father Peter ('spending the profits!' he joked). 'Burning carcasses, disinfecting farms, shooting stray sheep up on the hills, putting up and taking down notices, the lot.'

'Where were you in north Wales?' I asked, curious as to whether our paths might have crossed.

'Near Welshpool,' he said and my ears pricked up. 'Little place. The whole valley was full of it. Place called Berriew.'

'I was there,' I cried. 'There were some suicides round there, weren't there? Farmers. I don't suppose you were flavour of the month, were you?'

'To be fair, I've found all the farmers I've had to deal with, when you explain to them what's got to happen, very understanding and reasonable,' Mike answered. 'I like the Welsh farmers. They're good people. But they've had a tough time.'

'So how do you think it spread so rapidly?' I asked.

'It's pretty clear that it came from abroad initially,' Peter told me. 'Then it spread down the M6 because of stock being transported in uncleaned wagons.'

So Ceiriog Hughes's modern counterpart at the Caersws railway halt had been right, I thought to myself.

'So what's the answer?' I asked. 'The country can't keep having these crises in our food stocks, can it?'

'It's the government subsidies that are to blame for farmers overstocking,' Peter said. 'Have you had any problem getting meat the last year? No. Have you had to pay any more for it? No. And that's because there were too many cattle and too many sheep being bred and farmers were getting huge subsidies for doing that. It's daft. Mind, there's some farmers who've been rescued from bankruptcy by the compensation they're getting because of foot-and-mouth.

'Yes, I've heard that everywhere I've been,' I nodded agreement.

'And we're too fastidious about obeying Common Market regulations in this country,' Peter continued. 'In France you can buy anything at a farmers' market and you're not telling me that all those cuts of meat have come from animals killed in an official abattoir. We're just too law-abiding here.'

I hadn't heard this argument put before and I turned it over in my mind as I went to the bar to fetch more drinks. As I did so, I was aware of a gang of twelve to thirteen youngish women taking up several tables at the opposite side of the room from us. As I returned from the bar, carefully balancing three foaming pints of Gloucester Old Spot, I saw that they had formed a circle and had all produced identical pieces of paper which one of them – their leader, I presumed – was using as her aide-memoire. Yes, it was their agenda. And yes, this was democracy at work again. This was a meeting but what of? I couldn't really hear anything of what they were saying because of being in conversation with Peter and Mike, so I had to speculate. Was this, I wondered, the Slimbridge Theosophical Society? Or the Michael Howard Appreciation Association? Or the Gloucester Old Spot Breeders (Female Branch) Club?

Who knows?

But I slept sounder that night for knowing that they existed.

22 Slimbridge

I know it's very 1960s but, whenever I think of Slimbridge, that Manfred Mann song *Pretty Flamingo* comes high-stepping through my brain. And yes, I know, the lyric is distinctly non-PC, with its 'crimson dress that clings so tight' to a young woman likened to a preening flamingo. And yes, it conjures up all sorts of sexual sensations that are enough to cause someone of my age to have a heart attack unless I foreswear them here and now. But it's because of the flamingos that Slimbridge is particularly famous, for all six types of flamingo to be found in our world are visible there in all there flamboyant pink glory.

And why are they there? Because that's where Peter Scott founded his Severn Wildfowl Trust in November 1946. It's now known as the Slimbridge Wildfowl and Wetlands Trust and is only one of several such sites in the United Kingdom. But none of these would have happened – indeed, the whole conservation movement probably would not have happened as it did – without the influence of this man who at various times was a wildlife artist, a champion ice skater, a world-class dinghy racer and a war hero.

Peter Scott's younger life was bedevilled by the reputation and fame of his father, Scott of Antarctica, who in 1911 died of starvation, exhaustion and frostbite 11 miles from the South Pole depot where supplies awaited him and his three companions who also died. It's the stuff of legend now, isn't it? Those images of the icicle-encrusted adventurers freezing to death in their little tent with no food, and of Captain Oates setting out alone with those immortal words, 'I may be gone some time', knowing that he would perish but maintaining his stiff British upper lip while doing so. And then there's that irony that we know that Roald Amundsen, the Norwegian explorer, had beaten Scott and his team to the South Pole anyway, so their deaths seemed even more pointless!

Not that any of this bothers the British National Party, whose newsletter *Spearhead* is proud to lionise Captain Oates as an 'inspiration to others, in this selfish, greedy society of today, to rise above the contemporary worthlessness of modern Britain, to show once more to the world that the true spirit of our nation is not dead.'

So now you know why the BNP is set on a suicide mission!

Peter Scott was three at the time of his father's death. For the next thirty-five years, his life was overshadowed by the tragedy and dominated by his mother who lavished all her love and affection and ambition on her fatherless son, even after she had remarried. It was just as well that they were toffs – his mother, Kathleen, descended from Byzantine emperors and Moldovan princes, his father, Robert Falcon, the Great British Hero and adventurer. Peter was named after Peter Pan, whose creator James Barrie was a family friend and his godfather. He was encouraged to call Prime Minister Asquith, another friend of (and probably lover of) his mother, 'Squiff' on his visits. He sheltered from German bombers in 1914 in a cupboard shared with Marie Rambert, the founder of the famous ballet company. And the likes of George Bernard Shaw, Franklin Roosevelt, Rudyard Kipling and T.E. Lawrence (soon to be 'of Arabia') were regular callers at his mother's London home.

A bit like my home life really!

Somewhere in the middle of all this, the young Peter Scott developed a fascination for the natural life around him, beginning with the common boyish curiosity about caterpillars and butterflies, tadpoles and frogs, lizards and newts, but broadening into an enthusiastic interest in wild birds. And it was bird life, in particular, that was to come to dominate his existence and for which he is now known and remembered.

His fascination with birds, and particularly geese, led him to buying a deserted lighthouse in the Wash area of East Anglia, where he set about capturing the essence of birds in flight in his painting. For it was as a painter that Peter Scott initially made his reputation and one of those paintings, *Taking to Wing*, subsequently became one of the most popular bird paintings of the twentieth century, reproduced endlessly on table-mats, coasters, prints, scarves, underpants and so on.

Another but lesser known painting of Scott's, but one with a fascinating story, was for the front cover of Paul Gallico's best-selling novel, *The Snow Goose*. The story drew its inspiration from a real goose that Scott had become attached to and the hero in Gallico's story is modelled on Scott himself. The model for the cover painting was Elizabeth Jane Howard who became the naturalist's first wife and subsequently the second wife of the rebarbative novelist Kingsley Amis, thus having the misfortune of becoming stepmother to dyspeptic novelist Martin Amis.

Now I have discovered, after extensive research in my local pub, that there are two attitudes to wild birds. The first is represented by my friend Graham.

'They're a bloody nuisance. They wake you up at some ridiculously early hour of the morning with their bloody dawn chorus in the spring and summer,' he says. 'Then, when they've got you out of your bed and eaten all the bits of toast that you've burnt because you were still half-asleep and that you've chucked out into the garden, they crap on your car or on your head. And it never washes off the windscreen of your car. How do they do that? Make it so adhesive, I mean?'

Graham would prefer the universe to be staffed by more malleable creatures like sheep, for instance, or Vietnamese pot-bellied pigs.

The second attitude is portrayed by my other friend Harry. He is a member of the Royal Society for the Protection of Birds (RSPB) and always carries his Zeiss binoculars in the glove compartment of his car, in case he should spy a Lesser Spotted Purple People-Eater somewhere in the sky on his travels. On a bad day, when Theakston's Old Peculier is controlling our debates, Harry thinks that Graham should at the very least have his tongue cut out but preferably be made to eat rat poison.

'You're a complete philistine,' Harry will say, his face acquiring a tinge of red as he grows in anger. 'It's people like you who are responsible for the fact that forty-nine different species become extinct every year on Planet Earth. Do you realise there were once 268 different species of bird native to this country alone? That there were twenty-three different types of sparrow, fifteen types of woodpecker, forty-one breeds of flycatcher? And now where are they all? Gone, or most of them at any rate, because of people like you.'

I swear Harry makes these figures up. Occasionally I vow to check them out when I get back home but always forget. Life's too short anyway. But you know the type that Harry is. Graham, when there's only the two of us there at the bar, calls him a Hen Harrier, which he thinks is very funny. What he doesn't know is that, when *he's* not there, Harry calls him a Greylag Goose, which *he* thinks is terribly funny.

I sometimes wonder why I have friends like this.

But I digress. Peter Scott was of the Harry ilk. In fact, if it hadn't been for Scott, there wouldn't have been a Harry ilk, at least not in the way that we know it. For it was Peter Scott's championing of the conservation of bird species, particularly those whose habitat was wetland areas, that led to many of the developments that we now take for granted. What began in 1946 on the wetland banks of the River Severn at Slimbridge with a few geese of different species – Lesser Whitefronted, Redbreasted, Beans, Ruddyhead, Greater Snow and others – became the heart of the conservation movement that Scott spawned. They are all there still, along with hundreds of other species of wetland birds – ducks, geese, swans, moorhens, coots from all over the planet – all happily pursuing their lives in a cared-for environment of pools and reeds and marshes, enclosed by fencing that keeps out unwelcome foxes and other predators. And there are strongly constructed and plentiful hides from which visitors can look out over the old sea wall to the Severn Estuary where more birds gather in their little gangs to fish for sustenance, to rest on their migrations or simply to crap on the golden sandbanks.

Slimbridge is a very special place, still adhering to the tenets on which it was founded by Peter Scott. It is not over-commercialised. There is no fairground there but the young children I saw were obviously enjoying their exposure to the birds dwelling therein. There is no pushy insistence on guided tours, but you can get help from one of the volunteers if you want it. And the signposting around the site is helpful, informative and at times thought-provoking.

And those pink flamingos! So delicate, so shocking pink, so pretty!

The Manfreds did have a point.

Peter Scott came to Slimbridge because of a flock of Whitefronted Geese that came every year from Russia to winter on the saltings on the nearby bank of the River Severn. I'm sure he would have been intrigued to find that the place that has come to be associated with his name is also noted for being the birthplace of a man who many argue was the father of the modern English language.

Just think of 'let there be light' or 'the salt of the earth' or 'the signs of the time' or 'the spirit is willing, but the flesh is weak' or 'eat, drink and be merry' or 'the powers that be' or 'fight the good fight' or 'a prophet has no honour in his own country'. These and many more words and phrases that are part of our everyday speech are all from the English translation of the Bible done by William Tyndale, who was born in Slimbridge in 1494. His version was the first direct translation from the original Hebrew into English but what made it particularly significant was that it was the first Bible which could reach a wide audience because it came at a time when multiple copies could easily be made on the Gutenberg printing press. Mind you, fathering the English language didn't do poor Tyndale much good, for he was burned at the stake – another Middle Ages barbecue that went wrong!

Tyndale should have realised this was the likely outcome of his efforts because there was a law which proscribed the translating of the Bible into English. Much safer to keep to the Latin version, said the priests, because this meant that nobody could understand it and its interpretation could only be done by them. Once ordinary folk got access to the Bible, the priests argued, their own power and influence would rapidly disappear. They could not continue the selling of indulgences for the forgiveness of sins or bartering the release of loved ones from purgatory. People would begin to challenge the Church's authority if the practices of the Church were exposed to what was really written in the scriptures.

As if!

This sort of thing has always gone on, of course. The true believers are always, according to them, the ones who tell you that they and they alone can understand the truth of the holy books. That's why the pope still denounces birth control and why women have to keep themselves covered up in Islamic countries. That's why Mao Tse-tung invented the Cultural Revolution and sent all the intellectuals out into the fields. That's why Bill Clinton tried for so long to claim that being given a blow-job by Monica Lewinsky did not constitute having sexual relations. It's all so much baloney. It's done to retain power.

So Tyndale's lifelong desire to translate the Bible into English was a threat to all those in power at the time. And none more so that the king himself, roly-poly serial adulterer Henry VIII, who in 1526 when Tyndale's translation of the New Testament first appeared was still married to Catherine of Aragon and still to invent his own religion in order to get his own way with the marriage laws. Knowing of all this animosity to his plans, Tyndale chose to fight the good fight in Germany. It was there at Worms that the first English New Testament was printed in an edition of 18,000 copies, which were smuggled into England in bales of cotton and sacks of wheat despite the opposition of the Church and of Henry himself.

Nowadays they would smuggle Bibles by stuffing them up their bums or swallowing them whole but this was the sixteenth century, remember. Folk weren't so sophisticated then.

Eventually, of course, the powers that be got Tyndale. He was betrayed by someone he had taken for a friend, tried for heresy and burned at the stake. His last words, reputedly, were 'Lord, open the King of England's eyes'. And miraculously that's exactly what happened, for three years later in 1539 Henry decided that Tyndale's Bible was A Good Thing and a copy of it was distributed to every church in the country to be chained to the lectern. The King James Bible created in the seventeenth century retained about 90 per cent of Tyndale's translation and it is that Bible which was the standard one used in churches throughout the English-speaking world for the next 400 years.

A prophet has no honour in his own country indeed (at least, not when he's alive)!

I went to visit the church of St John the Evangelist in Slimbridge village that afternoon because I had read that there was a screen to William Tyndale there and I was curious to find out what other evidence of the great translator's origins there might be. The church originates from the thirteenth century and, although it has been added to and altered over the centuries, essentially it is the same place that the young William Tyndale must have, presumably, been taken to as a child. Sadly the church was locked. A notice on the door directed me to a house on the opposite side of the road where

I might obtain the key, but it too was locked and no one answered my knock.

So I gazed at the church and thought about Tyndale. I tried out some of his phrases – some of those phrases that have become embedded in my and every other English-speaking person's word-hoard. At first I merely mouthed them, then, increasingly overwhelmed by the thought that Tyndale himself had worshipped here, I spoke out loud.

'Fight the good fight,' I called.

And, rolling my tongue around inside my mouth to moisten it, I shouted:

'A man after his own heart.'

It was very satisfying, if a bit loopy, to be behaving thus but I decided on one more:

'Eat, drink and be merry,' I cried, waiting for the words' echo to die in the otherwise silent churchyard.

And then I left to do just that – to eat, drink and be merry at the Tudor Arms beside the Gloucester and Sharpness Canal.

23 Slimbridge to Littleton-upon-Severn

A weak sun greeted me that morning, echoing the increasing cheerfulness I was feeling, despite my aching ankle.

Reasons to be cheerful in Slimbridge:

1 Sue Gibson's garden at May Cottage, which I gazed at as I waited in the conservatory for my breakfast. It is a wonderfully constructed garden with lots of gentle curves and unexpected moments. That September morning it was bright with late summer roses beneath the grapevine cleverly encouraged to grow around the window and with purple fuchsia bells by the espalier apple trees trained to act as a fence. It was lovely.
2 Peter Gibson, mine host at May Cottage, who was more of a companion than a host, full of openness, interest and conversation.
3 Breakfast à la P. Gibson which consisted of dry cured bacon from a local piggery ('I know which pig it came from!'), a choice of fried, poached or scrambled eggs ('I know which hens laid them!'), plus tomatoes and mushrooms, all washed down with a cafetière of flavoursome Colombian coffee.
4 The early morning sunshine that lit up the garden.
5 Being mistaken for Ian Botham at the Patch Bridge by two British Waterways workers who were fixing something in the mechanism of the bridge.

Yes, there was definitely a spring in my step, a jauntiness in my joints, and a larkiness in my limp that morning as I strode down the canal towpath in the direction of Sharpness. Even the light rain that began to fall after half an hour did little to dissipate my high spirits. I was soon passing the tiny village of Purton, once the home of large numbers of salmon fishermen, and passing along the narrow strip of footpath between the canal and the ever-widening Severn estuary.

Approaching Sharpness, you can see for yourself why it was thought necessary to build the Gloucester and Sharpness Canal. The estuary sands at low tide look dangerous enough, but at high tide, of course, they would be invisible and would have required exceptionally careful navigating by larger craft. The broad stretch of the canal provided a much safer and more reliable passage to Gloucester, and the scene must have been spectacular back in the early nineteenth century with those tall-masted ships sailing up and down and those sailors in *Treasure Island* costume calling out 'Ahoy there, me hearties' and 'Avast behind'.

There's the ugly remains of a broken-backed stone bridge on the towpath around about here. It's all that remains of the Severn Railway Bridge that used to carry trains over the river. It was apparently a spectacular bridge that took four years for the Severn and Wye Valley Railway Company to build, though it only carried trains one way from Berkeley on the east bank to Lydney on the west. The bridge was dismantled in 1960 after two oil-tanker barges, swept up river by the floodtide on a foggy night, crashed into it and demolished two of its spans.

Sharpness itself, a mile beyond Purton, owes its existence to the canal, for it was here that larger craft were to leave the treacherous reaches of the Severn Estuary for the milder waters of the Gloucester and Sharpness. What more obvious place could there be for a dock? Telford was responsible for designing the original 1827 dock but that was soon found to be inadequate as more and more ships needed passage on the canal, and a new dock was constructed in 1874. This could accommodate vessels of up to 7000 tons. It's a much quieter place now, of course, and, even though it's still used as a container port, it appears to have been colonised by the pleasure boat fraternity from the evidence of the huge number of such craft in the marina I passed through.

The people who descend on this marina on summer weekends suffer from an incurable disease known as nautical narcosis. This turns perfectly respectable folk whom you might be happy to invite into your home to share peanuts and pretzels into gibbering idiots with an inability to use common words, such as *up*, *down*, *left*, *right*, *front* and *back*, but to replace them with gibberish. They also seem to think that navy blue blazers are always fashionable, that turtleneck sweaters look good on humans as well as on turtles, and that lamps made from tiny ship's wheels are crucial to the continuation of the human species.

They are, in short, best avoided, and I was glad that none were visible as I passed through the Sharpness marina.

The Severn Way footpath took me on a slightly curious route around the Sharpness Docks and through a small housing estate until I regained the riverside on the flood embankment, which was to accompany me for much of the remainder of my journey. First, however, I headed inland along the Berkeley Pill inlet, after negotiating the usual field of young bullocks who had presumably been forewarned of my approach by their upstream cousins and decided to trot after me at increasing speed, into the ancient town of Berkeley itself.

Berkeley Castle, the scene of Edward II's terrible murder, was built in 1067, thus making it one of the earliest monuments of the Norman invaders. Although it was rebuilt several times in the following two centuries, the massive grey building that stands today is essentially that of 1350. Just off the great staircase leading to the keep is the small gloomy room, supposedly in which Edward II had a red-hot poker stuck up his backside. The historian, Holinshed, claimed that the shrieks of the king were heard in the town of Berkeley, but this isn't very likely because the walls of the castle are far too thick. Descendants of the Berkeleys have lived in the castle for ever and have been visited by at least sixteen English kings and queens. It was the site of the meeting of the rebellious barons before they leaned on King John to sign the Magna Carta and it has been pretty central to affairs of state since the days of William the Conqueror.

Leland, on his 1542 tour of the West Country, was not very impressed with Berkeley, calling it 'not a town of any size', although he recognised its good position. I on my 2001 journey down Sabrina was also not very impressed but for a different reason. You see, after leaving Gloucester, the Severn Way does not go through any large towns and I had foolishly not taken enough cash with me so needed to find a bank. Peter Gibson had assured me there was a bank in Berkeley – where else would all those royals have gone for their petty cash? – so I had assumed I would be able to resolve my temporary cash flow problem therein.

Well, there *is* a bank in Berkeley, a branch of the NatWest in fact, but it does not have a cashpoint hole-in-the-wall facility as I had hoped. So I duly trooped into the bank to see if there was some way my chequebook or my piece of coloured plastic would release some of my funds. Again, no luck. I was told that the only way I could get cash would be to go to the Co-op.

Can you imagine this? The only bank in a town of 2000 people doesn't have a cashpoint and tells potential customers to get their cash from the Co-op?

'Can you let me have 50 quid from my card?' I asked the woman at the till in the Co-op, proffering my bit of plastic.

'You have to buy something first,' she answered, barely looking up at me.

'But they told me in the bank you'd be able to give me some cash back,' I explained carefully, though I could tell from her lack of enthusiasm that this scene had been played out many times before. 'I thought banks were places that dealt in money. They do where I come from anyway.'

'Don't know about that. But here you have to buy something first if you want cashback,' she repeated in a monotone that I was already beginning to get irritated by.

'But I don't want anything,' I said desperately. 'Can't you just swipe my card through your machine and give me 50 quid?'

'We're not allowed to do that,' she said. 'You have to buy something first.'

It was no use. She had been too well trained in her response. I clearly wasn't going to get anywhere. So I gave in and made a purchase.

I've still got the packet of chewing gum I bought. I found it the other day in the pocket of my cagoule. I didn't want it then and I don't really want it now. I don't use chewing gum but it was the cheapest purchase I could make in order for the woman in the Co-op to release some of my funds. What would Robert Owen have thought about the use of his beloved Co-op for international finance transactions?

It beggars belief.

However, I did now have the cash to go into Berkeley's other major claim to fame – the Edward Jenner Museum, dedicated to the man who discovered the vaccination that prevented smallpox. Jenner was born in Berkeley in 1749 and, after studying in London, returned home to practise as a doctor. Smallpox was one of the most feared diseases of his time, responsible for killing up to 20 per cent of the population of the country. Jenner became intrigued with country folklore which claimed that those infected with cowpox could not then catch smallpox. So he decided to experiment in a way that nowadays would have him banged up in Strangeways.

First off, he persuaded a local dairymaid, one Sarah Nelmes, to come to his surgery alone. Then, instead of doing what some in the medical profession did (and still do) and taking advantage of her, he extracted some matter from a cowpox sore on her body. Next he persuaded another local youth named James Phipps to become deliberately infected with this cowpox stuff. The boy duly caught cowpox but, when he recovered, Jenner then tried to give him smallpox but found he was inoculated against it. Eureka! Vaccination discovered at long last and a justification for those little weals at the top of my left arm.

This all happened in 1796 but within a few years the practice of vaccination had become standard practice and the disease of smallpox has now been eradicated worldwide, thanks to the pioneering work done by this famous Gloucestershire doctor.

The Edward Jenner Museum is housed in what used to be his home, his study much as it was when he died and the thatched hut in the garden where he vaccinated the poor for free likewise. A good exhibition shows the importance of Jenner's work and brings you bang up to date with modern developments in immunology.

It is impressive and I left Berkeley in a better spirit than I had been a short while previously, full of admiration for the massive good one human being can do for the rest of the species.

It was not to last.

There was another foot-and-mouth closure just out of Berkeley, which I knew about and had planned to circumvent. This meant that I was unable to follow the regular Severn Way path past the Berkeley Power Station, the first nuclear power station to be built in the United Kingdom, in 1962, but since 1989 in the process of being decommissioned by a German company called NUKEM. You might, incidentally, be interested, as I was, to know that there is a computer game called Duke Nukem 'featuring realistic environments, goofy monsters, and an arsenal of creative weapons'. You can, apparently, 'Duke it out with up to eight players on a LAN, or play head-to-head through a direct modem connection'.

Tempting, eh?

Anyway, I bypassed the power station (Nukem and all) and followed a minor road to a crossroads at a place called Willis Elm, where my map told me I could cut off to meet with the Severn Way again a mile further away at Severn House Farm. No sooner had I turned right in this direction than I was confronted with a red notice forbidding me, and anyone else for that matter, from proceeding down this lane of pain of death! (Well, £5000). Foot-and-mouth restrictions, it said, were still in place here.

Now my limp was really quite pronounced by now after four days of walking and particularly after the past 2 miles on the tarmac. I was also pretty cheesed off that my careful planning had been wasted and that this route, which I had believed to be possible, was not so. With my good left foot I stamped the ground in exasperation and swore a loud oath.

Then I saw that there was a telephone number on the red notice with an instruction to ring the Gloucestershire County Council Rights of Way Department in case of difficulty. Never again will I curse the mobile phone. I had carried one with me at my wife's insistence and now I had a genuine reason to use it.

'Why can't I go down this road?' I demanded of the female voice that sweetly answered my call after I had explained precisely where I was. 'I checked your website and it said I could rejoin the Severn Way at the farm but how can I get to the farm if the road is closed?'

'Just a moment, sir, while I get my map open at the right spot,' answered the patient lady from the Rights of Way Department.

There then followed a short pause in which I envisaged the ludicrousness of this situation with the two of us staring at identical maps while communicating telephonically.

'I'm afraid that's the boundary,' she replied eventually. 'You'll need to go along the road to Upper Hill and take the track there.'

This would mean another 2 miles on the tarmac. My right ankle was already protesting.

'What would happen if I ignore this sign?' I asked, suddenly emboldened.

'I'd have to report you, sir.'

'And then?'

'Then you could be fined up to £5000 or transported to a penal colony in Australia.'

'Even if I said you had the loveliest voice I'd ever heard?'

'Yes.'

'Even if I said that the sound of your voice makes my heart go pitter patter.'

'Yes.'

'Even if I said I was madly in love with you and wanted you to have my babies?'

At that point she slammed the phone down. Oh dear! I thought. They'll get me for sexual harassment now as well!

In the end I decided that I didn't fancy being recolonised to Oz, so I followed her advice and took the hard road to Upper Hill but decided against the farm track there or any of the other footpaths marked on the map. I was in no mood for exploring and thought the surest way of reaching the riverside again was by following the road for another wearisome few miles to Shepperdine and the promise of some sustenance at the Windbound Inn mentioned in the *Severn Way Guide*. About 2 miles from Shepperdine, the air suddenly began to freshen as the sea breeze from the estuary began to blow across the fields. In one of these fields, behind a sturdy metal fence, was a large bull, chewing nonchalantly.

I summoned up all the venom I could muster, remembering all those beasts that had threatened me at various stages of my journey, and shouted at him.

'Bastard!' I called. 'May your seed fall on stony ground!'

The bull didn't even look up.

The Windward Inn was open, although it was mid-afternoon by the time I got there. My luck had changed for it had only reopened three days earlier after being closed for some months for extensive refurbishment. It is an unusual venture, being a café bar serving food and drinks between nine in the morning and five in the afternoon. Its manager and its chef both greeted me and told me about their plans. I was only too delighted to give them my custom (the usual tuna sandwich and pint of shandy), because they made me feel very welcome and there were none of the usual old caps swapping prejudices at their bar. Instead, there was a small group of mentally handicapped people from the sheltered accommodation provided in the upper part of the building by an organisation called Headwinds. It is an extraordinary and, I think, unique use for a former pub to be put to and I approve of all those who sail in her. Good luck to them!

So, body fed and watered (or should it be shandied?) and spirits raised again, I climbed up on to the flood embankment. The Windward Inn is exactly 200 miles from the source of the Severn on Plynlimon. I paused momentarily in the pleasant afternoon breeze and gazed back up the mighty river, giving a silent salute to Sabrina. Then I turned and set off for the last part of my day's journey.

About a mile south of Shepperdine is Oldbury Power Station, another of the Severn's nuclear installations. Oldbury has produced electricity since 1967. On a typical day, it will supply 435 megawatts, which is enough to serve a city one and a half times the size of Bristol. In order to sustain it, it needs 70 million litres of water an hour and a huge tidal reservoir sits in the estuary to provide this. As I walked past the length of its perimeter fence, I looked in at the huge edifice and for the whole of the 5 minutes it took me to walk past it I saw not one person. I wondered if Gordon Brown's policy of reducing unemployment had been too successful and maybe there was only one person in there running the whole caboodle. Maybe it was some spotty adolescent computer geek. Maybe it was the fiendish Dr Strangelove. Maybe it was . . .

The radiation must have been getting to me. Or maybe it was just my prejudices again. I was three when Hiroshima burst apart in that mushroom cloud. I grew up watching the Campaign for Nuclear Disarmament marching on television newsreels. Chernobyl was a recent and potent fact. I had never taken my children to the Lake District for fear they would be contaminated by Windscale before it was renamed after some sticky tape.

Then I looked the opposite way into the Severn Estuary and saw the extensive bird life – redshanks, herons, curlews, shelducks – all pecking sustenance from the sandy shore and obviously healthy. And there were lots of rabbits scurrying in the fields and dunes as I passed by. I really ought to examine these prejudices of mine a little more closely.

Mind you, those rabbits are visible at night because they glow green!

The Severn Way diverts from the embankment just after the power station to lead you up the Oldbury Pill and through the village of Oldbury-on-Severn, with its pub, its church and its equestrian centre. This diversion is really quite unnecessary, however pleasant Oldbury-on-Severn is (and it is) and I wished I'd known that I could have stayed on the embankment.

Anyway I didn't. I followed the guidebook's instructions rigorously until I came back to the riverbank and a short while later I was turning inland again through the late afternoon dusk to my final resting place in Littleton-upon-Severn.

My bed and breakfast was lovely, more like a flat attached to the side of the house than a bedroom, and my hosts were charming and friendly. I took tea with them and made polite conversation but I really was quite tired after walking for about 18 miles that day, much of it on roads. So I excused myself, showered and took a cat nap for 30 minutes before slowly limping down to the village pub, the splendid White Hart. If ever a pub deserved to be the last stop on a journey (well, almost, but you know what I mean), then the White Hart is it.

First, it serves a wonderful array of real ales – Young's Bitter, Young's Special, Young's Waggledance and Smiles' Best. I had to have the Waggledance, didn't I? Then there is an excellent menu and it's not the usual pub grub of chips and burgers. I ordered the Chicken Sizzler – a dish of half a chicken with garlic, prawns, vegetables and fries, which was brought hot and sizzling to my place by a middle-aged, generously proportioned woman from the kitchen. The barmaids were both over twenty years old and I mean that as a compliment, after being served so frequently on my journey by scrawny ponytailed teenagers. The furniture was such as you might expect of an old pub – old wooden pew-style settles with variously sized and shaped wooden tables. There was an old open hearth with logs piled beside ready for cold winter nights. The ambience was wonderful.

By eight o'clock, of course, the White Hart was full. Okay, the clientele was almost exclusively white, middle class and middle aged – I guess Littleton is a commuter village for Bristol – but so what? It just goes to show that there is a customer base for high-quality pubs like this. Lots of breweries attempt to create this ersatz traditional pub feel by ripping everything out and starting again. They always feel phoney. This pub has succeeded because it has used genuinely old materials. I was not surprised to learn later that it had won an award from the Campaign for Real Ale as 'Refurbishment of the Year'.

As I polished off my Chicken Sizzler, my eyes took in a couple sitting just to my right by the bar – he a thirtysomething Hooray Henry in big baggy Royal Navy-style blue jumper with a permanent frown on his forehead, she a drop-dead gorgeous twentysomething with long silky hair and tight jeans who laughed appreciatively at his tales. What did she see in him?

I pushed my plate away and reflected. Tomorrow I would complete my Dance with Sabrina. Tonight I was sitting in this wonderful pub, after eating a wonderful meal and drinking three pints of wonderful beer. In just over three months I would be sixty and, though my legs were weary and my feet were sore, I felt brilliant! I could not believe that I was in the last part of my life and that some time, sooner rather than later, my bodily parts would completely wear out or my mind would cease remembering and then start having illusions about what was happening.

When would I stop looking at a gorgeous young woman and thinking of her as an object of sexual desire, even though I knew that social constraints (not to mention my beer gut, white hair and wrinkles) prevented me from saying so? When would I become unable to enjoy real ale or a Chicken Sizzler (another one had just wafted past my table)?

The eternal verities.

Tomorrow I would complete my Dance with Sabrina.

Tonight I would have another pint of Waggledance.

24 Littleton-upon-Severn to Severn Beach

The last cooked breakfast before the food police resumed control of my diet was especially tasty and set me on my way from Littleton-upon-Severn in good heart. It was only a short stretch down a track and across fields to get me back on to the embankment above the Severn estuary, which glittered in the early morning sunlight. It was a beautiful late summer Friday morning, probably the finest day of my whole Dance with Sabrina. What a glorious accompaniment to my last few limping miles!

In no time at all I was in the grounds of the Severn View Service Station with its superb views of the magnificent Severn Bridge that stretches across the Severn here to Beachley and then continues across the mouth of the River Wye into Chepstow. In that clear morning light I could see both rivers clearly and I thought about old George Borrow visiting the source of both that Victorian morning way back when and about the more recent morning when my wife and I had almost visited the source of the Wye before finding the wooden poles that indicated the start of Sabrina's journey.

This part of the world is known as Aust and it has been the site of the crossing of the Severn for a very long time. Many locals still refer to it as the Old Passage, because until the bridge was built in 1966 it was where the ferry service operated from. Aust is supposedly named after St Augustine who in 603 met with the leaders of the Celtic Christians here to persuade them to acknowledge the pope's supremacy. There are all sorts of stories attached to this meeting, including one that I'm partial to in which the cunning Celts show the mighty Roman up when he fails to get up from his chair to greet them. As a result, Augustine was unsuccessful in seeking to convince his Celtic counterparts and so he did what all good members of the God Squad used to do in those days (and still do in Northern Ireland) – he threatened to have them duffed up.

There's another legend attached to Aust concerning a couple of the historicals we've met earlier in this story – Edward I (a.k.a. Longshanks or The Hammer of the Scots) and Llewellyn (a.k.a. Prince of Wales when that meant something). Apparently Edward had invited Llewellyn to a conference to discuss certain domestic difficulties – you know, this is my land/no it isn't/ yes it is/who says/my dad's bigger than yours etc. – but Llewellyn refused to cross the Severn. So Edward set sail for the Welsh side which so impressed the Welshman that he waded into the water and carried Edward ashore on his shoulders.

Now what was all that about?

And why did somebody or other bother to record it all?

The Severn Way footpath takes you on a footbridge over the M48 just here and shortly after that passes the amusingly named Cake Pill and into a military firing range, which fortunately was not in operation that day. The path follows the embankment again here and I could see from quite a distance a figure approaching me. He was pushing a bicycle and when our paths crossed, we both paused and exchanged pleasantries. He was a man in his mid-forties, wiry but not looking especially super-fit.

'You going far?' I asked, after we had agreed it was good weather (this is how the English always begin conversations with strangers).

'No, just out for the day,' he answered. 'You?'

I grinned. This was what I had been waiting for – a chance to brag a bit.

'I'm just on the last stretch of the Severn Way,' I said proudly and proceeded to give him a blow-by-blow account – summarised, of course – of my three-week journey.

'I haven't done the Severn Way,' he told me. 'I've done the

Pennine Way a couple of times a few years ago, and the Three Peaks, and the Coast to Coast, and Hadrian's Wall. Have you done any of those?'

This was not what I had expected. I had thought to get gasps of amazement at my effort. Now it seemed the boot was, if you'll excuse the pun, on the other foot. I had to confess I hadn't done any of those walks and that this was actually my first long-distance walk.

'Have you met lots of other people on your walk?' he queried.

'No,' I said. 'To tell you the truth, you're the first person I've met on the path. I put it down to foot-and-mouth. And I deliberately chose September because I didn't think it would be as busy.'

'You never do meet anybody,' my new chum explained. 'I know there's supposedly hundreds do the Pennine Way every year but I've only met half a dozen people when I did it. And I've never met anyone on the other walks. The books tell you to avoid August but, to be honest, I just don't think there's that many people doing these long-distance footpaths at all.'

Could this be true? I found myself wondering. Was it all just some great conspiracy to con people into believing we were a nation of long-distance walkers? Could it be that only I and the compilers of the *Official Walkers' Guide* would actually ever walk the whole of the Severn Way?

'Anyway, enjoy the last stretch,' my chum said, as he pushed his bicycle off and got ready to move on. 'Severn Beach is just over there. Not far now.'

And so we parted, he for his day's cycling and I, slightly confused, for the final few steps of my Dance with Sabrina.

The new Severn Bridge, carrying the M4 over the river which is at this point some four miles wide, was opened by the current Prince of Wales, Charlie, in 1996. One thousand men and women were engaged in its construction which had to take into account a 14-metre tidal range, an 8-knot tidal flow and winds of up to 100 miles an hour, hence its unique windshielding design. It is estimated that half a million sausages were served in the staff canteen during the bridge's construction and, if those sausages were laid end to end, they would stretch from Cardiff to Birmingham.

This latter piece of useless knowledge comes to you courtesy of the Severn Bridges Information Centre which is tucked away underneath the new bridge and which otherwise contains much useful and interesting information about the crossing of the Severn at this point. It is believed that the Romans crossed here by boat to check that the unruly blue-painted Welsh were behaving themselves. Offa's famous dyke ends in Chepstow, so it's likely that the Anglo-Saxon settlers would also have used this part of the river to cross. I've already told you about St Augustine in 603 and Edward I in 1300, so we know that there have been people crossing the Severn here for centuries.

The site of the new crossing is at what is known as New Passage, although new is a relative term since it has almost certainly been in use as a crossing point for a very long time. In 1876 Great Western Railways opened the first tunnel under the Severn, taking the train from Bristol to Newport and on to Cardiff. When it was built, it was the largest underwater tunnel in the world and also one of the wettest, with 20 million gallons of water having to be pumped out of it every day.

I liked this information centre. It's only a small demountable shack, really, but it was about to be shut down because the local council planners were unhappy with its visual appeal or rather lack of it, in their eyes. These presumably are the same council planners who have given permission for a particularly ugly caravan site to be opened right next to it. I bought a cup of coffee and a biscuit, then signed a petition to keep the centre open. Then I signed it again, using a different name.

That should baffle the buggers!

This was it. I was now on the Binn Wall, which is the sea wall on the escarpment above the Severn estuary. I was taking my final limping strides, accompanied by the buzz of a motorised lawnmower being driven by a council workman around the gardens next to the Binn Wall and the sight of a lone heron sailing majestically along the shoreline. I was at Severn Beach where the Severn Way footpath officially ends. Three weeks and 200 miles previously I had left that peaty bog on the top of Plynlimon and now here I was, my Dance with Sabrina complete.

There is no sign that announces the end of the footpath. There was no band waiting to welcome me. Instead, there were three ponytailed layabouts of uncertain age who sprawled on the concrete footpath of the Binn Wall, each clutching a can of strong White Lightning cider. They were not the welcoming committee I had expected. I had arranged to meet a friend at the railway station whence I would be transported back home, so I asked the cider-drinkers to direct me to the station.

In truth, it's not much of a station. It's just the end of the railway line really with a platform attached to it but I found it and hoped my friend would find it as easily. I had an hour to wait and had been planning in my mind how I would fill that hour by celebrating the completion of my adventure with a pint of beer and a sandwich in one of the Severn Beach pubs referred to in the walkers' guide. So I walked around looking for a pub. The Ordnance Survey map indicates where it is to be found but I could not see it. Was this another example of my crap map-reading skills?

I stood at a crossroads where the pub was meant to be and looked around for someone to ask. The only person within sight was driving a large forklift truck on a building site behind a tall wire fence. He could not hear me because of the noise his machine was making but he saw me gesticulating and switched the engine off.

'I'm looking for a pub,' I began, waving my map at him as

if somehow he could see from 10 yards away through a wire mesh fence the symbol PH that had so beguiled me. 'I think it's round here somewhere.'

'No, it isn't,' he shouted back.

'Do you know where it is?' I asked.

'There isn't a pub round here,' he replied, shaking his head and giving me a resigned look.

'The map and the guidebook both say there is one,' I protested.

'There used to be one,' he volunteered.

'Where?' I asked.

'It used to be here,' he grinned, sweeping his arm around him.

And that's when it finally clicked. It wasn't a building site. It was a demolition site. The piles of bricks I had seen were actually the remains of what had been, until two weeks previously he told me, the Severn Salmon public house. The nearest other pub was about a mile and a half away on the road to Bristol.

I was certainly *not* walking a further mile and a half. So I found a small supermarket in Severn Beach that sold provisions and I bought myself a tuna sandwich and a can of Strongbow cider. Then I made my way back to the Binn Wall, where the other cider-drinkers had been but who had now disappeared. I found a wooden bench and sat down.

And there, as the sunlight sparkled on the waters below and beyond me, I drank a silent toast with warm cider to Sabrina, the goddess of the river.

It was time to say farewell to the kings and castles, the clerics and churches, the poets and potters, the ironmakers and weavers.

My dance was over.

Useful Reading

Andrews, R., Brown, J., Lee, P. and Humphreys, R. (2000), *England – The Rough Guide*, London: Rough Guides.

Anon. (1995), *Coalport China Museum*, Norwich: Jarrold Publishing.

Anon. (1995), *Jackfield Tile Museum*, Norwich: Jarrold Publishing.

Anon. (1996), *Coalbrookdale and the Museum of Iron*, Norwich: Jarrold Publishing.

Anon. (2000), *The Iron Bridge and Town*, Norwich: Jarrold Publishing.

Borrow, G. (1923), *Wild Wales*, London: John Murray.

Bradley, A.G. (1920), *A Book of The Severn*, London: Methuen & Co.

Byford-Jones, W. (1967), *Severn Valley Stories*, Telford: Shropshire Star & Journal Ltd.

Chandler, J. (1993), *John Leland's Itinerary – Travels in Tudor England*, Stroud: Sutton Publishing.

Cobbett, W. (1967), *Rural Rides*, London: Penguin Books.

Darwin, C. (1998), *The Origin of Species*, Oxford: Oxford University Press.

Davies, L. (1990), *Mary Webb Country*, Ludlow: Palmers Press.

Defoe, D. (1971), *A Tour Through the Whole Island of Great Britain*, London: Penguin Books.

Downing, T. and Millman, M. (1998), *Civil War*, London: Collins & Brown.

Fielding, H. (1994), *The History of Tom Jones*, London: Penguin Books.

Fletcher, F.D. (1975), *Lifelines 34: Darwin*, Aylesbury: Shire Publications.

Gillingham, J. and Griffiths, R.A. (1984), *Medieval Britain*, Oxford:

Oxford University Press.
Gough, R. (1979), *The History of Myddle*, London: Macdonald Futura.
Grundy, M. (1988), *Elgar's 'Beloved Country'*, Worcester: Worcester City Council.
Gwilt, C.F. (n.d.), *The Port of Bridgnorth*, Bridgnorth: Bridgnorth Publications.
Gwilt, C.F. (2001), *Bishop Percy's House*, Bridgnorth: Bridgnorth Publications.
Huxley, E., (1993), *Peter Scott: Painter and Naturalist*, London: Faber & Faber.
Jeremiah, J. (1998), *The River Severn – A Pictorial History*, Chichester: Phillimore.
Jervis, E. (n.d.), *Llanidloes Parish Church*, Llanidloes: St Idloes Press.
Kissack, K. (1982), *The River Severn*, Sudbury: Terence Dalton.
Lanchester, M. (1915), *The River Severn – from Source to Mouth*, London: Thomas Murby.
Linnell, B. (1971), *The Battle of Tewkesbury*, Tewkesbury: The Theoc. Press.
Marples, M. (1959), *Shanks's Pony*, London: J.M. Dent.
Marsh, T. and Meech, J. (1999), *Severn Way Official Walkers' Guide*, Shrewsbury: Severn Way Partnership.
Marshall, J. (1989), *The Severn Valley Railway*, Newton Abbot: David St John Thomas Publisher.
Matless, D. (1998), *Landscape and Englishness*, London: Reaktion Books.
Meech, J. (2000), *Shropshire Towns & Villages*, Wilmslow: Sigma Press.
Morris, C. (ed.) (1947), *The Journeys of Celia Fiennes*, London: The Cresset Press.
Owen, W. (1994), *The Works of Wilfred Owen*, Warw: Wordsworth.
Pargeter, E. (1989), *A Bloody Field by Shrewsbury*, London: Headline.
Parker, M. and Whitfield, P. (1995), *Wales – the Rough Guide*, London: Rough Guides.
Peel, J.H.B. (1968), *Portrait of the Severn*, London: Robert Hale.

Peters, E. (1999), *Brother Cadfael Omnibus*, London: Little, Brown.

Porter, A. (1996), *The Priory Church of St Mary at Deerhurst*, Much Wenlock: RJL Smith & Associates.

Priestley, E.J. (1979), *The Battle of Shrewsbury 1403*, Shrewsbury: Shrewsbury and Atcham Borough Council.

Rees, H. (1994), *The Famous in Shrewsbury*, Shrewsbury: MU Publishers.

Rowbotham, F. (1983), *The Severn Bore*, Newton Abbot: David & Charles.

Strawford, G.F. (1992), *A Walk Around and About Tewkesbury Abbey*, Tewkesbury: Tewkesbury Abbey/Tewkesbury Civic Society.

Trinder, Barrie (n.d.), *Bridgnorth – a Town Trail & Brief History*, Bridgnorth: Shropshire Books.

Warren, J. (1995), *The Wars of the Roses and the Yorkist Kings*, London: Hodder & Stoughton.

Waters, B. (1947), *Severn Tide*, London: J.M. Dent.

Waters, B. (1949), *Severn Stream*, London: J.M. Dent.

Webb, M. (1926), *Precious Bane*, London: Jonathan Cape.

Weir, A. (1998), *Lancaster and York – the Wars of the Roses*, London: Pimlico.

Westwood, D. (1999), *Severn Vista: A Pictorial Journey down the River Severn*, Stourbridge: Tortoise Shell Press.

White, R. (1999), *Wroxeter: Life and Death of a Roman City*, Stroud: Tempus.

Williams-Ellis, A. (n.d.), *Robert Owen: Social Reformer & Master Manufacturer 1771–1858*, Newtown: Robert Owen Memorial Museum.

Wilshire, L. (1954), *The Vale of Berkeley*, London: Robert Hale.

Witts, C. (1998), *Along the Severn from Source to Sea*, Cheltenham: Reardon Publishing.